ALPHA BRAVO DELTA GUIDE TO

THE U.S. ARMY

ROBERT F. DORR

SERIES EDITOR

WALTER J. BOYNE, USAF (RET.)

ALPHA

A member of Penguin Group (USA) Inc.

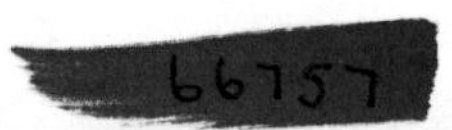

This book is dedicated to Korean War infantryman
1st Lt. Andrew F. Antippas.

International Standard Book Number: 0-02-864495-6

Library of Congress Catalog Card Number: 2003102292

05 04 03 8 7 6 5 4 3 2 1

Interpretation of the printing code: The rightmost number of the first series of numbers is the year of the book's printing; the rightmost number of the second series of numbers is the number of the book's printing. For example, a printing code of 03-1 shows that the first printing occurred in 2003.

Printed in the United States of America

CONTENTS

FOREWORD

War is an ugly thing. War is not kind, nice, or glorious. Gen. William Tecumseh Sherman, one of America's greatest generals, probably said it best: "I am tired and sick of war, its glory is all moonshine … war is hell."

In spite of the horrific consequences of war, we must never forget that there are worse things. Imagine what the world would be like today if our fathers and grandfathers had not stood up to the evil of Hitler's Nazism, Japanese militarism, communism, or any of the other *isms* that challenged the survival of liberty in the twentieth century. As hard as it is to understand, war is not evil. *Evil* is evil, and sometimes you must fight evil if you want freedom. History shows that any people who desire freedom must have the courage to stand and fight for it. It is vital that the citizens of a free nation understand this.

That is why this unique book is important for you to read.

The American Army is as old as America's freedom and has been its guardian for more than two centuries. In 1775, the subjects of the 13 British colonies started a battle against the despotism of a European monarchy that changed the world. As George Washington wrote just before the Battle of West Point in 1781, those Americans "began a contest for liberty ill-provided with the means for the war, relying on our patriotism to supply the deficiency." In the crucible of this long and difficult conflict, these citizen-soldiers transformed into a professional army. They struggled against impossible odds to create something new on this Earth—a government of the people. The ragtag solders who suffered in the bloody snow at Valley Forge eventually became the veteran Army that defeated the superbly trained and splendidly equipped British army at Yorktown. These American soldiers risked their lives, liberty, and futures for a dream—a dream that Americans have the opportunity to live today.

In the chapters of this book, you will learn how the American Army is inextricably linked to the nation that we live in today. This Army—from the War for Independence that gave America its birth of freedom, to the Civil War that was a vital step in establishing the rights of all Americans, to the terrible World Wars that secured the survival of democracy, to the difficult wars fought during the Cold War that kept the world from nuclear annihilation, to today's tough battles against the evils of terrorism in far-off places like Afghanistan—has risked, fought, bled, and died on behalf of the Republic. As our great World War II commander in chief, Franklin D. Roosevelt, once said, "Those who have long enjoyed such privileges as we enjoy forget in time that men have died to win them."

I have proudly served in the U.S. Army for 30 years. In that time, I have met some of the most remarkable people on Earth: soldiers who serve goals larger than self, and people who live by the concepts of duty, honor, and country. These soldiers seldom express their service in these words, but by their actions they live them every day.

This guide is about those remarkable soldiers, their leaders, and the battles that they fought to forge the America we know today. It is about America's Army and the inspiring story of the people in blue, khaki, olive drab, or camouflage uniforms who have fought America's wars and conflicts.

As long as there is an Army, there will be an America.

John Antal
Colonel, U.S. Army (Ret.)
Author of *Proud Legions* and *Infantry Combat: The Rifle Platoon*

INTRODUCTION

> "… Today, Soldiers build upon the 227-year legacy established by veterans who have gone before. From the first battle of the American Revolution to our ongoing war against terrorism, in conflicts around the globe and in humanitarian missions at home and abroad that have saved countless lives, Soldiers have provided the sword and shield that protects our Nation. And they are doing so today—over 190,000 Soldiers deployed and forward stationed in 120 countries around the world …"
>
> —Gen. Eric K. Shinseki
> Army Chief of Staff
> November 2002

The American soldier has never let his country down. In moments bright and bleak, in good times and in times of trial, in victory and in defeat, the American soldier has always been a special breed and the United States Army has always had qualities that no other army could muster.

A band of ragtag troops led by seasoned military commander George Washington transformed an incipient rebellion into the American Revolution and brought into the world a nation with new ideas and new values. A collection of citizens in uniform fought on Guadalcanal and landed at Normandy to save not only their own maturing nation but, in truth, nothing less than the entire world. Possibly the most professional military force ever assembled steamrolled over a vaunted foe in the Persian Gulf in 1991 and—as the Army has always done—completed the job assigned.

In the twentieth century, it was the American officer corps (not that of Germany, or any other country with a rooted military tradition) that was the envy of the world and the focus of the future. From Lexington and Concord to the Ia Drang Valley and the Persian Gulf, it was the American soldier—in most wars, a citizen-soldier, in some a professional—who showed the way.

Americans have known defeat. During the revolt against the Crown, a terrible winter at Valley Forge almost wiped out the Colonial Army before the nation could even be founded. In the Philippines in 1942, American soldiers were outnumbered, outfought, beaten, captured, and tormented.

In the American army of the post-Vietnam era, we often seemed to be creating our own problems with racial strife and drug problems. The United States Army was not always the best equipped, the best trained, or the best led. The nation did not always know its soldiers, or understand them, or even support them. As we begin the twenty-first century in a U.S.A. where the average adult is 30 years of age and has living memory only of an Army that always seems to overwhelm its adversaries, we would do well to remember that history is cyclic, failure has been the marching companion of success, and even the easiest victory was been won at a price.

The U.S. Army has gone from the musket to the microchip, from the horse to the helicopter. It is easy to forget, sometimes, that the basic facts about the American army have never changed: It is the only army ever fielded in which soldiers receive orders from elected officials, the commander in chief is accountable to the people, and the will of the nation determines not only when and how we fight but, almost always, whether we succeed. The towering record of successes in the Army's history and our optimism today, in the face of dark challenges, are possible because what has never changed, not since those early days in 1775, is the American soldier.

Ultimately, the Army is not one organization, or society, or culture, but many—a diverse and rich collection of individual human beings who have won the right to call themselves American soldiers.

Whether pounding a keyboard or loading a howitzer, wearing chevrons or bars, serving as chief of staff or graduating from basic training, the American soldier is the heart of the Army's tale and the reason for the Army's triumph.

The current recruiting slogan extols "an Army of one," but the Army itself is a team, and a testament that thousands of men and women can come together to become a thing that is greater than the sum of its parts.

On the pages ahead, the reader will take a glimpse at weapons, tactics, battles, often bloodshed, and sometimes sacrifice that makes us wonder how we could possibly deserve such heroes. This is the story of the United States Army, but apart from the equipment, the strategy, and even the familiar names of battlegrounds, it is the saga of every American soldier. The men and women of the Army are what makes the Army. This is what they have done. This is what they are doing today.

CHAPTER 1

MEET THE U.S. ARMY TODAY

The United States Army is the most powerful ground fighting force in the world today. It's the best trained. It's the farthest-reaching. It's all volunteer. It's high-tech. And it's highly mobile, and soon to be far more so as a fresh generation of leaders brings about "transformation," readjusting the size and shape of the service to make it capable of deploying anywhere on short notice. The official goal is to make the Army lighter, more survivable, and more lethal.

The Army is about weapons, like "the Beast," the surprisingly nimble but very large M1A1 Abrams main battle tank with its 60-ton chassis, 120-mm gun, and ability to turn on a dime and advance at 46 miles per hour, so that today's soldiers can speed into battle much like mounted cavalrymen of old and overwhelm an enemy with speed, surprise, and force.

The Army is about things, like the Navstar Global Positioning System unit that can be carried in a rucksack or backpack, which connects an individual soldier to a satellite in orbit overhead and pinpoints geographic location down to within feet, so that every ground-pounder in Army green now knows his exact location on the Earth every minute.

The Army is about aircraft, like the AH-64D Longbow Apache attack helicopter, with its two-crew tandem cockpit, twin gas turbine engines, 30-mm Chain Gun rotary cannon, and air-launched AGM-114 Hellfire missiles, able to knock out a tank at a distance of 5 miles, so that the infantryman always has his own close air support and the commander always has the means to reach out and touch the foe.

The Army is even about ships. Yes, the Army has large ocean-going tugs displacing 1,057 tons and Logistical Support Vessels (LSVs) displacing 4,199 tons, capable of operating on the high seas to support military operations.

But weapons, things, and aircraft—even ships—do not make an army.

Organization charts, PowerPoint briefings, and acquisition strategies do not make an army.

Only soldiers do.

They may love freedom and abhor killing, but Americans achieve a unique excellence at fielding soldiers in wartime who are remarkably good at what they do.

They are also different. No other nation has soldiers like them.

In the American Army, unlike any other, it is the everyday soldier who shines—not just a Douglas MacArthur or a Colin Powell, but the everyday working stiff like Corp. Alvin York in the Meusse-Argonne or Pvt. Rodger Young in a South Pacific stinkhole called New Georgia. America has always fielded everyday soldiers who rose to greatness when their moment came.

No other Army places so much trust in soldiers who are so junior. In other armies, a sergeant may be a disciplinary figure but is not likely to be a decision maker. In other armies, a lieutenant may issue orders but is not likely to seize the initiative and change them to fit new circumstances. In the U.S. Army, when everything goes wrong at a place like Omaha Beach during World War II, a handful of sergeants and lieutenants seize the moment, innovate, and turn the tide. No other Army vests so much authority at its lowest levels.

United States Army, Robert F. Dorr

Camouflaged U.S. Army soldiers plan their mission.

FIGHTING FORCE

At the start of the twenty-first century, the Army is crucial to homeland defense and the fight against terrorism, and is caught up in brushfire wars around the world. Yet the Army also remains ready for the unspeakable: nuclear war. Although it is smaller than at any juncture in its recent history, and smaller than many armies around the world, the U.S. Army is the standard by which every other is measured.

The chain of command runs from the president, who is commander in chief, to the secretary of defense, to combatant commanders in the field.

The combatant commanders, known until recently as commanders in chief, or CINCs (pronounced sinks), are responsible for geographic areas or for specific parts of the nation's arsenal. U.S. Central Command, for example, is responsible for most of the Asian continent, including Afghanistan, while U.S. Strategic Command is responsible in wartime for the nation's intercontinental ballistic missile forces. Each combatant commander (the new term for a CINC) is responsible for all the forces, from all service branches, in his area. Among them, they have the world carved into areas of responsibility, or AORs. An order to fight in Europe (or, in jargon, the European AOR) would go from the president to the secretary of defense to the combatant commander.

Not included in this scheme for fighting wars is the brass in the Pentagon. The generals in Washington are readily familiar to the American public. But they have no tanks, no navigation devices, no Apache Longbow helicopters. The secretary of the Army and the Army chief of staff command no one except the members of their staffs. They don't decide how to deploy forces in an emergency, how to conduct a battle, or how to run a peacekeeping force. The big brass in the Pentagon command no troops. They have no divisions, no platoon leaders, and no first sergeants.

But even though they're not part of the organization chart when bullets fly, the Army's leaders in Washington do more than anyone else to determine the size, shape, and appearance of the Army. They, together with Congress, industry, the press, and the public, decide what kinds of weapons will be placed in the hands of America's soldiers.

PENTAGON BRASS

Each service branch has two leaders, a situation that can often be confusing. How much clout each wields is a function of the personalities in place at any given time. Nominally, the secretary of the Army, a civilian, is the boss, but in recent years many of the secretary's duties have been more ceremonial than substantial.

Beginning in 1947 (when the secretaries of War and of the Navy were replaced by a secretary of defense, and jobs were created for secretaries of the Army, Navy, and Air Force), the service's top civilian enjoyed a tremendous amount of influence on all aspects of military procurement, operations, and war fighting. That ended with the passage of the Goldwater-Nichols Act of 1986, which reformed and reorganized the military. Goldwater-Nichols (Public Law 99-433) put new emphasis on cooperation and joint operations by all the service branches. The law removed the service secretaries and the service chiefs from the war-fighting chain of command, while greatly strengthening the role of the chairman of the Joint Chiefs of Staff and of America's field commanders, now called combatant commanders. Some worried that a more powerful chairman and a unified joint staff in the Pentagon would discourage debate within the officer corps and might erode the sacred American principle of civilian control of the military. Those critics would have preferred the secretary of the Army (and the chief of staff) to be more directly a part of military operations than they are now. They argue that shifting power from the service branches to the Joint Staff may narrow the focus of the nation's leadership, creating too much reliance on a single doctrine, weapon, service branch, or geographic region.

Today the secretary of the Army is more likely to be talking to troops about pay and benefits, or testifying to Congress about acquisition than helping anyone prepare to fight a battle. Some critics say that the secretary of the Army has been reduced to little more than a ribbon-cutter. They argue that because the job is now largely ceremonial, the American taxpayer could easily get along quite well without a secretary of the Army at all.

Maybe. Maybe not. At the end of 2002, the Pentagon's own description of the secretary of the Army's job (taken from the U.S. Army website) went like this:

> [The] Secretary of the Army ... has statutory responsibility for all matters relating to Army manpower, personnel, reserve affairs, installations, environmental issues, weapons systems and equipment acquisition, communications, and financial management. [The secretary] is responsible for the department's annual budget of nearly $82 billion. The secretary leads a team of just over one million active duty, National Guard, and Army Reserve soldiers and 220,000 civilian employees, and has stewardship over 15 million acres of land.

When these words went to print, the job was held by Thomas E. White, who became the eighteenth secretary of the Army on May 31, 2001, after nomination by President George W. Bush and the advice and consent of the Senate. The latter is required for all top civilian jobs and all general officer promotions. White is a retired brigadier general and former Enron Corp. executive who has been given temporary responsibilities for the Pentagon's homeland defense effort, seemingly in violation of Goldwater-Nichols.

On any organization chart, the secretary is at the top, but the person who really runs the Army is the chief of staff. The job was created in 1902, replacing that of commanding general of the Army. In 1986, with the passage of Goldwater-Nichols, the idea of a general staff disappeared (now wars are directed by combatant commanders, not Pentagon bigwigs), but the chief of staff remains a crucial figure—and is his service's member of the Joint Chiefs of Staff, which advises the secretary of defense and the president.

Gen. Eric K. Shinseki, who became the thirty-fourth chief of staff on June 22, 1999, is important for both real and symbolic reasons, not least because he is the nation's top soldier. Whoever occupies the chief of staff's slot must explain the Army on Capitol Hill (where Congress holds the purse strings for military programs and equipment) and must set the trend for every soldier in the ranks. The chief of staff (whose position is far weaker today than when it was created in 1902) must make basic decisions about how the Army will look, act, and fight. Shinseki made numerous enemies in the ranks over a seemingly symbolic decision—giving every soldier the black beret that had once been the trademark of the elite Rangers—and has been generally praised for his efforts to transform the Army into a lighter, faster, more efficient force. Shinseki was talking about and acting on transformation long before it became a buzzword of the Bush administration.

No one likes to be embarrassed. At the end of Operation Allied Force, with the war over Kosovo in 1999, U.S. and Russian troops were in a race to see which could first reach Pristina Airport in the newly liberated zone. American soldiers, who rely on heavy, tracked vehicles that are often impractical for use on highways, came in second. The Russian army, which makes extensive use of lighter, rubber-tired vehicles, seized the airport, set up shop, and had coffee ready when the Americans arrived. The Army felt an urgent need to be capable of moving more quickly. Some of the changes were visible during Operation Enduring Freedom, the 2001 conflict in Afghanistan. Many have praised the Army for getting smaller, lighter, and more nimble, and for discarding clunky hardware like the Crusader 70-ton self-propelled artillery gun. Critics, however, say that the current vision of transformation is little more than an attempt to change the Army into a version of the Marine Corps.

ENLISTED SOLDIERS

When these words were written (at the end of 2002), the Army had 484,800 soldiers on active duty, or about 1 percent more than Congress's budgeted strength (480,000). This figure included 3,000 in "stop-loss" status—members of the Reserve component being held on active duty during the war on terror. The budgeted total was 75,000 officers (including warrant officers) and 405,000 enlisted soldiers.

United States Army, Robert F. Dorr

A U.S. Army soldier keeps watch.

The Army National Guard (which, together with the Army Reserve, makes up the "reserve component") had 352,000 soldiers, including 29,002 officers, 7,577 warrant officers, 133,568 noncommissioned officers, and 181,682 soldiers in the lower four enlisted ranks.

The Army Reserve had 206,000 soldiers, including 38,118 officers, 2,750 warrant officers, 75,227 noncommissioned officers, and 89,533 soldiers in the lower four enlisted ranks.

The American soldier of today is probably the best trained, best prepared, and most seasoned combat soldier ever to take the field against a foe. Well, almost. Today's soldier is surpassed in some respects only by the soldier of the immediately preceding generation, the one that fought the 1991 Persian Gulf War. Then and now, the average enlisted soldier has college study time under his or her belt, and many have a college degree.

Racial and ethnic minorities make up a somewhat larger proportion of the Army than of the general population, but the significance of this fact is often exaggerated. Race, once a divisive issue in the Army—especially in the 1970s—is no longer an issue in the everyday life of the soldier. In 2002, the Army was 58.4 percent white, 26.4 percent black, 8.3 percent Hispanic, and 6.9 percent "other." In contrast, the Army National Guard was significantly "whiter," being 73.5 percent white, 15.6 percent black, 7.3 percent Hispanic, and 3.6 percent "other," a breakdown that is not far from the American population at large.

The role of women remains controversial, but less so than in the past. In 2002, some 73,282 women were serving in the active-duty Army, including 9,997 officers, 62,491 enlisted soldiers, and 656 West Point cadets.

Still, American soldiers might be forgiven if they argue that too much social experimentation is going on around them. Polls show that most Americans, and most soldiers, disagree with the late Sen. Barry Goldwater (R.-Arizona), who reportedly said, "You don't need to be straight to fight and die for your country. You just need to shoot straight." The decision early in the Clinton administration to embark on a "Don't ask, don't tell" policy toward gay Americans—less than what Clinton promised in his first election campaign, but more than many Americans wanted—has rattled the Pentagon. In a service that still forbids open homosexual behavior, many soldiers are less than enthusiastic about being required to attend lectures aimed at preventing homophobia. The 1991 baseball bat murder of a gay soldier, Pfc. Barry Winchell, at Fort Campbell, Kentucky, has reverberated throughout the Army, prompting scuttlebutt wherever soldiers gather, triggering debate in military chat rooms, and affecting the careers of several officers. In 2001, the Army dismissed 1,273 soldiers for violating the "Don't ask, don't tell" rule.

OFFICERS

The Army officer of the early twenty-first century is educated, able, and motivated. The American tradition of giving officers more authority at lower levels has gifted the nation with a generation of lieutenants who will one day make fine generals. Some argue, however, that today's Army places too much emphasis on education in areas that are not helpful in fighting wars. Some worry that the Goldwater-Nichols Act has encouraged careerism, forcing officers to compete for the joint assignments that lead to promotion rather than learning how to fight.

Others are concerned about the politicization of the officer corps. George C. Marshall believed so strongly that an officer's life should be devoid of politics that he refused to vote. His refusal to embrace political causes made him enormously credible when testifying before Congress. Officers have typically stayed out of politics—until recently. A 1998 poll showed that 64 percent of military officers view themselves as Republicans, and something like 20 percent see themselves as Democrats. A significant number of retired generals, and one or two still on active duty, have begun speaking out during political campaigns, usually supporting conservative issues or candidates.

When they retire, enlisted soldiers and officers are well prepared to seek a second career in civilian life. According to the Army, the average enlisted retiree is a sergeant first class, age 41, with 22 years of service. The average officer retiree is a lieutenant colonel, age 43, with 22 years of service. In October 2001, there were approximately 526,000 living Army retirees.

ARMY RESOURCES

The secretary of the Army and the chief of staff describe their service's duties in an annual "posture statement," regarded by supporters as a useful thumbnail sketch and excoriated by critics as a whiney plea for Congressional dollars. Cluttered with Washington words such as "resourcing," the 2003 United States Army Posture Statement tells us the official view of the Army's job:

> The 2001 Quadrennial Defense Review (QDR) established a new strategic framework for the defense of the Nation that struck a balance between near-term readiness and our ability to transform

ourselves in order to meet current and future conflicts. The report outlined a new operational concept that gives continued priority to homeland defense, promotes deterrence through forward presence, and asks that we have the ability to conduct both smaller-scale contingencies and large-scale, high-intensity combat operations simultaneously.

Our Soldiers can defeat enemy armies, seize and control terrain, and control populations and resources with minimal collateral casualties and damage. They can operate across the spectrum of military operations, whether it is full-scale conventional conflict, fighting terrorists, or setting the conditions for humanitarian assistance. This multifaceted ground capability enables us to assure our allies and friends, dissuade future military competition, deter threats and coercion, and, when necessary, decisively defeat any adversary.

As The Army continues to work with other departments, agencies, and organizations, emerging requirements that are not fully defined in the 2001 QDR may require additional resourcing, whether technological, logistical, or force structure. Despite 10 years of downsizing, The Army has accomplished all assigned missions to a high standard. In short, we are doing more with less, and the strain on the force is real. Our Soldiers continue to give us more in operational readiness than we have resourced.

While we fight and win the global war on terrorism, The Army must prepare itself to handle demanding missions in the future strategic environment. Over two years ago, The Army undertook transforming itself into a force that is more strategically responsive and dominant at every point on the spectrum of military operations.

ARMY BRANCHES

Every officer wears a lapel emblem reflecting the fact that Army careers are categorized into specialized branches, each with its own mission. For officers, being in a branch is a part of their identity; for enlisted soldiers, it is an assignment. Branches are grouped by major functions—*combat arms* (infantry, artillery, armor), *combat support* (intelligence, signal corps, military police), and *combat service support* (adjutant general, chaplains' corps, finance).

Within the combat arms, the *infantry* slugs it out on the ground, often in new ways that reduce the number of miles a soldier must rely on shoe leather; the *field artillery*, the "King of Battle," neutralizes or suppresses the enemy with cannon, rocket, or missile fire. *Air defense artillery* units operate the Patriot, Hawk, and pedestal-mounted Stinger surface-to-air missiles and Chaparral or Vulcan guns. *Armor* units (including Armored Cavalry and Infantry) operate tanks and infantry fighting vehicles. *Aviation* flies helicopters like the UH-60M Blackhawk and AH-64D Longbow Apache, as well as fixed-wing airplanes like the C-23 Sherpa. Combat missions for the *corps of engineers* include building or (when necessary) destroying bridges, general construction and destruction of emplacements, defenses, or buildings, and laying or breaching minefields.

Special forces, the Army's Green Berets—pivotal in Afghanistan—are the service's experts on unconventional warfare, direct action, and counterterrorism.

The combat support branches include the *chemical corps* (the Army's experts in nuclear, biological, chemical, and flame operations), *military intelligence* (which determines an enemy's plans, intentions, and capabilities and, with 30,000 members, is the largest branch in the Army), the *signal corps* (whose crossed semaphores represent the Army's ability to communicate), and the *military police* (cops, of course, but also defenders of facilities and installations).

Combat service support branches include the Adjutant General's Corps, which handles personnel issues from accession of new soldiers to discharge and retirement. Other branches (each part of a corps bearing the branch's name) include medical specialists, dentists, nurses, chaplains, finance experts, Judge Advocate General lawyers, medical service people, ordnance, quartermasters, transportation specialists, and Army veterinarians.

STATESIDE DUTY

For most soldiers today, life bears little or no resemblance to life in their grandfathers' Army. The officers' and enlisted members' clubs, once the social center at any post, are now all but abandoned now that most soldiers are married—some to each other—and go home after work. The hard-drinking soldiers of yesterday would be surprised at the number of teetotalers in an Army; a single drunk-driving charge can wreck a career.

Those who remember racial strife and iron discipline, with every other word a "sir," will be surprised at the diversity and harmony within the Army and at the somewhat relaxed attitude toward military spit and polish, a measure of the confidence officers and enlisted troops have in each other. Supporters point out that the Army consistently ranks higher than corporations or state, local, and federal governments in winning the approval and confidence of the public. Critics say the Army is itself becoming too much like a corporation, with an inner circle, a glass ceiling, banker's hours, and too much time spent in the office and not enough on the firing range.

As recently as the Vietnam War era, no one would have imagined an Army with day-care centers on post. In basic training today, a drill sergeant is not allowed to touch a recruit without asking permission first. No one swears anymore. When a "sir" does escape the mouth of a soldier, about 18 percent of the time it is likely to be addressed to a "ma'am"!

THE ARMY AT HOME

The Army has 13 major commands on U.S. soil, including highly specialized commands like U.S. Army Special Operations Command at Fort Bragg, North Carolina; the Criminal Investigation Command at Fort Belvoir, Virginia; and Intelligence and Security Command, also at Belvoir. Other major components have obviously specialized purposes, such as Space and Missile Defense Command in Arlington, Virginia; Army Medical Command at Fort Sam Houston, Texas; and the corps of engineers in Washington, D.C. Also in the region surrounding the nation's capital are the Military District of Washington, Army Materiel Command, and Army Military Traffic Management Command. U.S. Army Pacific is located at Fort Shafter, Hawaii, while U.S. Army, South is located at Fort Buchanan, Puerto Rico. Most important among these diverse organizations is Army Forces Command (Forscom, in jargon) at Fort McPherson, Georgia, which, as the Army puts it, "trains, mobilizes, deploys, and sustains active and reserve component forces."

With its "Army of One" recruiting campaign aimed at Generation Y, the Army repeatedly emphasizes that the building block of all Army organizations is the individual soldier. A small group of soldiers organized to maneuver and fire is called a squad, a term that hasn't changed in about a century. Here is how the Army describes each of its units:

- A *squad* has 9 to 10 soldiers, is typically commanded by a sergeant or staff sergeant, and is the smallest element in the Army structure, although its exact size varies according to mission.
- A *platoon* makes up 16 to 44 soldiers. A lieutenant leads a platoon with a noncommissioned officer as a second-in-command. A platoon is made up of two to four squads or sections.
- A *company* has 62 to 190 soldiers. Three to five platoons form a company, which is commanded by a captain with a first sergeant as the commander's principal noncommissioned assistant. An artillery unit of equivalent size is called a battery, and a comparable armored or air cavalry unit is called a troop.
- A *battalion* consists of 300 to 1,000 soldiers. Four to six companies make up a battalion, which is normally commanded by a lieutenant colonel with a command sergeant major as the principal noncommissioned assistant. A battalion is capable of independent operations of limited duration and scope. An armored or air cavalry unit of equivalent size is called a squadron.
- A *brigade* is made up of 3,000 to 5,000 soldiers. A brigade headquarters commands the tactical operations of two to five organic or attached combat battalions. Normally commanded by a colonel with a command sergeant major as the senior noncommissioned officer, a brigade is employed on independent or semi-independent operations. Armored cavalry, Ranger, and Special Forces units this size are categorized as regiments or groups.
- A *division* consists of 10,000 to 15,000 soldiers. Usually consisting of three brigade-size elements and commanded by a major general, divisions are numbered and assigned missions based on their structures. The division performs major tactical operations for the corps and can conduct sustained battles and engagements.
- A *corps* is made up of 20,000 to 45,000 soldiers. Two to five divisions constitute a corps, which is typically commanded by a lieutenant general. As the deployable level of command required to bring

together and sustain combat operations, the corps provides the framework for multinational operations.

- An *army* is made up of 50,000 or more soldiers (though the Eighth Army in Korea has about 30,000). Typically commanded by a lieutenant general or higher, an army combines two or more corps. A theater army is the ranking Army component in a unified command, and it has operational and support responsibilities that are assigned to the theater combatant commander (until recently called the theater commander-in-chief, or CINC). The combatant commander and theater army commander may order formation of a field army to direct operations of assigned corps and divisions.
- An *army group* plans and directs campaigns in a theater and is composed of two or more field armies under a designated commander. Today the concept of an army group is purely theoretical: The Army has employed none since World War II.

THE ARMY OVERSEAS

The Army, which seemed to be everywhere on the globe during the Cold War, now has only two major commands permanently located overseas. In Germany, the Army's European command is headquartered at Heidelberg. In South Korea, the Eighth Army, which is part of the United Nations Command and of the U.S.–Korean Combined Forces Command, is headquartered on the Yongsan post in the city of Seoul.

In a typical day, about 160,000 American soldiers are "forward stationed," or deployed around the world, in Korea, in Kosovo, in Afghanistan, and in Germany. The Army has been in Afghanistan since 2001, in Kosovo since 1999, in Bosnia since 1994, in Korea since 1950, and in Germany since 1945.

Some of the stomping grounds of American soldiers are new; others familiar to generation after generation. Older soldiers of today remember Army careers that moved them around, like pieces in a shell game, among three countries—the U.S., Germany, and Korea.

Soldiers have lived, trained, and readied themselves in Germany (in earlier years, West Germany) since 1945. Almost any career sergeant or officer can say a few words in the language, fancy a plate of schnitzel, or reminisce about Oktoberfest. The Army's Combat Maneuver Training Center in Hohenfels—once used by "Desert Fox" Erwin Rommel to train his Afrika Corps for World War II, and operated by the Army's Seventh Training Command since the 1980s—offers one of the best training sites in the world, and it is not unusual to see M1A1 Abrams tanks rumbling across Hohenfels' rugged terrain, carrying out a computer-monitored war exercise aimed at defending ground or killing T-80 tanks.

American soldiers also have a longstanding acquaintance with Korea, dating to 1945 when U.S. forces accepted the surrender of Japanese troops there. The 1953 Korean armistice was a cease-fire rather than a peace agreement, and the U.S. still maintains an infantry division and 38,000 troops close to the Korean demilitarized zone. Many American soldiers can utter a few phrases in Korean, order up a meal of barbecued pulkogi, or sing verses to the mournful ballad *Arirang*. Today, as in the past, the huge mass of armor and manpower north of the DMZ remains a threat that U.S. soldiers take very seriously.

Just as Americans could not have predicted a war against Iraq in 1991, most had no idea that large numbers of American soldiers would be in Afghanistan in 2001 and 2002. Operation Enduring Freedom, the war in Afghanistan, has tested the fighting mettle of troops and the worth of new techniques, such as target spotting for satellite-guided munitions. But Afghanistan has also challenged traditional skills, developed in the Army over centuries: road building, mine clearance, and psychological operations. Afghanistan has proven a remarkable challenge to Special Forces troops, who have done everything from undergoing cave fighting to guarding the chief of state. American soldiers have many and diverse duties—but that is nothing new. The Army began with challenges.

CHAPTER 2

THE WAR FOR INDEPENDENCE (1775–1783)

The United States Army considers its birthday to be June 14, 1775, the date the Second Continental Congress authorized enlistment of riflemen—those impertinent colonial Americans who took up arms against the British Crown and caused a Revolution. That date is three days before the Congress tapped seasoned warrior George Washington (1732–1799) to form the fledgling Continental Army.

The Revolutionary War, or the War for Independence, began on April 19, 1775, when British soldiers clashed with the Massachusetts militia on Lexington Green. The fighting essentially ended with the capitulation of Lord Charles Cornwallis (1738–1805) at Yorktown, Virginia, on October 8, 1781. The formal end came on September 3, 1783, when the Paris Peace Treaty became final.

It was a war of opposites. The Americans (the Colonials, the Rebels) fought in unconventional ways, often not because of genius, but because they were unfettered by military practices and traditions. The British (the Redcoats, the Royals, the Crown) put a completely orthodox army on the field and usually fought in very predictable ways. The Americans often came close to giving up, but never did. The British several times came close to winning the war, but never gave it as much effort as they could have. When it was over, Americans had the beginnings of a nation, and the nation for the first time possessed an army.

But the Army's story—birthday or no birthday—goes back farther than the upstart rebellion against King George III. The earliest predecessor of today's Army is probably the St. Augustine City Guard, formed in the Florida city in the mid-1500s. The Army also traces its origins to rugged militiamen who took up arms to fight Indian tribes and later to wage the French and Indian War, long before the Revolution. Those citizen soldiers of the militia became part of the fight for independence. The experience of the French and Indian War created military traditions that continued during the Revolutionary War and have not been interrupted since.

Long before the War for Independence, the American colonies had men who were trained for warfare. All colonies except Pennsylvania had militia, consisting of able-bodied men who were required to own weapons, undergo periodic training, and defend their homes. The militia were created to guard against Indian attack, but they fought throughout the Revolution without ever being part of the Continental Army.

In the aftermath of upheaval in Boston in 1774, Minutemen were born. Minutemen were members of a kind of super militia, open to the notion of independence and free of loyalties to the Crown, and they trained more rigorously than other militia units. Their name derived from their high state of readiness, which made them able to turn out at a minute's notice.

The Continental Army was formed by Congress under George Washington and initially consisted of diverse troops, many of whom were poorly prepared. Washington gave them a military structure, ranks, emblems, and training, and provided the leadership that ultimately enabled colonial soldiers to prevail.

THE ROAD TO WAR

The formation of an army by the Colonials was the inevitable result of years of growing tensions between the 13 colonies and the Royalist British government.

Focal point of the tensions was Boston. A handful of figures in Massachusetts were key to setting in motion the events of 1775. Joseph Warren

(1741–1775), John Hancock (1737–1793), Paul Revere (1734–1818), Samuel Adams (1722–1803), and his lesser-known cousin John Adams (1735–1826) were among those who resented rule by England. British occupying forces in Boston were meant to police an unruly colony but actually served to exacerbate a tense situation. Conflicts arose—the British fired on protesters in March 1770 and the Colonials dumped a shipment of tea into Boston Harbor in November 1773. Committees of correspondence were created, and arms and weapons began to be gathered in secret. By then, the British had as many as 4,000 troops in Boston, a city with a population of just 16,000, and the pressures on the Colonials became enormous.

On September 5, 1774, the upstart Colonials convened the Continental Congress (later called the First Continental Congress) in Philadelphia as an executive body to coordinate the efforts of the very different colonies and to provide resources and forces. Two months of meetings in September and October often seemed to be dominated by conservatives, who wanted to smooth out relations with the Crown, but others began to believe it was too late for reconciliation. George Washington, Patrick Henry (1736–1799), John Jay (1745–1829), and the cousins Samuel Adams and John Adams were among the leaders who put on paper a list of complaints to send to King George III and a declaration of basic rights. Many of those in attendance felt that war could be avoided with concessions from the Crown. Most did not. After they adjourned on October 26, King George recognized, "The die is now cast. The colonies must either submit or triumph."

At conventions in Virginia in 1775, Washington, Thomas Jefferson (1743–1826), Patrick Henry, and others gathered in defiance of Lord Dunmore (John Murray, the Earl of Dunmore), Virginia's colonial governor. On March 23, 1775, at a church in Richmond, Virginia, Henry uttered his poignant demand: "Give me liberty or give me death!"

Defiance was in the air throughout the colonies. King George said the colonies were in a state of open rebellion. On April 19, 1775, came the battles of Lexington and Concord. Gen. Thomas Gage (1721–1787), the British commander in Boston, sent 700 troops to confiscate guns and powder held by militiamen ready to pick up their muskets and fight on a minute's notice, the "Minutemen." At the Lexington, Massachusetts, village green, an unplanned action that began with a single shot—the "shot heard 'round the world"—left eight Minutemen dead.

The British brushed aside the Minutemen at Lexington and Concord, and finished their mission of seizing the stores at Concord successfully. But things changed for them as they began their return to Boston. The gathering storm of Minutemen, using hit-and-run Indian tactics, shot up the Redcoat column as it was returning. The British sustained unprecedented casualties: 73 dead and 174 wounded. The loss caused Gage to be replaced by his deputy, Gen. Sir William Howe (1729–1814), as British commander in the colonies. Once the militiamen fought the Redcoats at Lexington and Concord, and Washington was chosen to command the new Continental Army, the stage was inevitably set for revolution.

May 9, 1775, brought the capture of the British Fort Ticonderoga in upper New York by Ethan Allen (1738–1789) and his Vermont irregulars, the "Green Mountain Boys," accompanied by Col. (later Maj. Gen.) Benedict Arnold (1741–1801), who tried to assume command. Separately, rebel militia seized the British garrison at Crown Point on Lake Champlain.

The Second Continental Congress met at Philadelphia in 1775 with the scent of war in the air and any thought of settling for concessions from the Crown gone from the table. Virginia's Thomas Jefferson, who had not been chosen for the First Continental Congress, was now in attendance. The patriots authorized the formation of an army and gave it a name that was not associated to any single colonel: the Continental Army. As commander of the Continental Army, they chose George Washington, a 43-year-old delegate from Virginia, a planter and a ranking militia officer in the French and Indian Wars. The four New England colonies had raised their own armies in the aftermath of Lexington, and New York followed suit with encouragement from the Continental Congress. The choice of Washington, also a Virginian, helped ensure that the South would join the movement.

Washington arrived at Cambridge, Massachusetts, on July 3, 1775, to take command of the Continental Army.

His appointment took place June 17, 1775, the same day as the Battle of Breed's Hill, better but incorrectly known as the Battle of Bunker Hill. Seeking to dislodge British troops from heights overlooking Boston Harbor, militiamen were given the famous order, "Don't fire until you see the whites of their eyes." A newly minted Colonial brigadier general, Seth Pomeroy, already quite aged, fought at Bunker Hill as a volunteer and retreated only when the Americans ran out of ammunition. He reportedly backed down the hill in the face of the British with his musket serving as a club.

William Prescott (1726–1795) commanded Colonial forces at Breed's Hill. The battle claimed the life of Joseph Warren, who commanded at Bunker Hill and was killed by bayonet when the militia ran out of ammunition. Though the loss of Warren was painful, by inflicting casualties on the much-respected British army in a costly battle, the Colonials showed that rebellion had a chance and fired up a spirit of national pride. Col. (later Maj. Gen.) Nathanael Greene (1742–1786), one of the rebel leaders, later said, "I wish we could sell them another hill at the same price."

WHY A REVOLUTION?

The American Revolution happened because the English-speaking communities on the far side of the Atlantic had matured to the point that their interests and goals were distinct from those of the ruling classes in the mother country. British statesmen failed to understand or adjust to the situation. Ironically enough, Britain's victory over France in the French and Indian War set the stage for the revolt, for it freed the colonists from the need for British protection against a French threat on their frontiers and gave free play to the forces working for separation.

Historians say that economics and class conflict prompted the rebellion in the Colonies. In fact, the Revolution was rooted in irreconcilable differences about how the American colonies should be governed. By 1776, the British were committed to the view that Parliament must exercise unchallenged authority in all parts of the empire, including the power to tax Americans without their consent. Taxes were no less demanding in the colonies than in England itself, but their heavy-handed implementation, especially with the Sugar Act of 1764 and the Stamp Act of 1765, encouraged defiance. The Colonials believed that they were entitled to fundamental rights, the "rights of Englishmen," which put certain activities beyond the reach of any government. "Taxation without representation" was the banner cry for those who resented paying tribute to the Crown in any form. Although the move toward rebellion began as a quest for concessions rather than independence, it quickly became evident that between the two sides, there was little leeway for compromise. After the first battles had begun, in January 1776, Thomas Paine (1737–1809) published his pamphlet

"Common Sense," a litany of complaints against King George III that stirred passions in a public increasingly ready for change.

As the Colonials became more defiant and a fight for national independence became inevitable, the American leaders understood that there was an important player behind the stage: France. The rebels held no illusions. No one in Paris, they realized, was a champion of American freedom, independence, or sovereignty. To the contrary, France's youthful, shrewd, and self-centered monarchs, Louis XVI (1754–1793) and his wife, Marie Antoinette (1755–1793), were obviously believers in royalty and, under most circumstances, were reluctant to support any uprising that would undermine another monarch. Still, the French ruler would have supported anybody or anything if it offered him a chance to undercut his arch foes, the British, and especially if it left portions of the North American continent open to his own adventures. The Americans were embarking on a course that would change the world forever, most of them well aware that France would probably come to their aid—secretly, at first. They could not have known that without French help, their revolution was surely doomed. They also could not know that their historic struggle for freedom would inspire Louis XVI's own subjects in just a few short years. For helping the Americans for purely selfish reasons, the French king's head eventually would roll.

MAJOR PLAYERS

The Revolutionary War was a match between colonial upstarts, in a rebel army that often seemed ragged and ill equipped, and British officers and troops who were usually better trained and better disciplined, but who frequently failed to act decisively when they had the chance. George Washington, a towering figure not just in legend but also in physical size, had been repeatedly tested on the battlefield. Washington was the dominant leader in a war that also included Benedict Arnold, Washington's best combat commander, a talented innovator, an inspiration to his men, and ultimately a traitor; and "Mad" Anthony Wayne, a fearsome and aggressive fighter who became pivotal at Yorktown.

On the British side, no single figure loomed as Washington did. Cornwallis was a lifelong soldier and servant of the Crown who won early victories but seemed to have no grand strategy to defeat the rebellion; he was ultimately overwhelmed at Yorktown. Sir Thomas Gage occupied Boston and fought the initial battles in New England. The brave but sometimes hasty John "Gentleman Johnny" Burgoyne (1722–1792) won a few skirmishes, lost badly at Bennington and Saratoga, and returned to his preferred life as a playwright. Gen. Sir William Howe, once a daring young colonel 20 years earlier in the battle for Quebec, replaced Gage and occupied Philadelphia. And Lt. Gen. Sir Henry Clinton (1738–1795) replaced Howe but proved himself more adept at planning than execution.

The American army consisted of the Continental Army—nationally organized troops commanded by Washington—and state militias. At least 230,000 soldiers served in the Continental Army and 165,000 served in the state militias, but only about 20,000 were on the battlefield at any moment. There was rivalry between Colonials and militias, but neither group was steeped in military tradition, and both had soldiers who balked at discipline, were often poorly supplied and equipped, and were uncomfortable being away from their homes and farms for extended periods. Most fighting took place during the summer, partly because troops were poorly provisioned for the harsher winter months and partly because they needed to return home to harvest crops. Crucial to morale and to success in battle was the simple truth that Colonial soldiers were fighting on their home turf, in a conflict that enjoyed public support.

From its inception, the American officer corps believed that elected civilians should give the orders. The Continental Congress instructed George Washington. When the fighting ended, Washington could have held any title he asked for—generalissimo, even king—but chose to doff his uniform and become a civilian president. The founders believed service should be temporary.

So, too, did the General Society of the Cincinnati, created in May 1783 at Fishkill, New York, by Continental Army officers. Maj. Gen. Baron Wilhelm von Steuben chaired the first meetings. About 2,150 officers (of 5,500 eligible) joined. Washington became the Society's first head, succeeded after his death by Alexander Hamilton.

Cincinnatus was a Roman senator of the fifth century B.C.E. When the Roman Senate established the position of dictator to resolve a crisis, it sent delegates to Cincinnatus's farm. They found him behind his plow and told him he had to serve as dictator. He took command of a consular army, achieved a victory, and returned to Rome, like Washington, as a triumphant military figure—only to shed his power and return to plowing his fields.

Except in lore (such as *Seven Days in May,* a 1964 film with Burt Lancaster, Kirk Douglas, and Ava Gardner), the American officer corps has never tried to take over the country. Even when they disliked the commander in chief, officers followed orders and returned to civilian life when their work was finished. It should be noted that the hero in *Seven Days in May* (Kirk Douglas) was a military man who refused to go along with plotters because he understood that the Constitution put civilians in charge of the armed forces.

The British army comprised 42,000 professional soldiers. Although many of these men were hastily enlisted, they received excellent training and were subjected to extreme discipline. The British military had a strong organizational structure that the colonial army lacked. To supplement their ranks, the British government purchased the services of 30,000 troops from German princes.

The British infantry was the best trained in the world at the time and remained so until the late nineteenth century. Its forte was the bayonet charge and the British Square (a formation of bayonet-wielding men to break a cavalry charge), the latter never broken. It was a tactical advantage of the day to let the foe shoot first and then to fire second and charge with the bayonet. British commanders trained relentlessly for this eventuality, and the sight of a Briton charging with his blade could evoke sheer terror. The Americans frequently did not have bayonets, nor were they well trained to use them—but they had learned much from the Indians about hunkering down, hiding behind trees, and moving in loose, fluid formations. To put it plainly, the impertinent Americans cheated. At times they defeated the best army in the world through sheer ignorance about what the other side expected them to do.

NEW ARMY

To Washington fell the unenviable task of trying to whip up enthusiasm for re-enlistment among the New England troops whose terms of service expired at the close of the year, to look to colonies outside New England to fill their promised quotes of troops, and to win the trust of soldiers who were leery of signing up for more than a year at a time.

Washington recognized the need to make the Colonial Army a national army. The Patriots thought of themselves as men of Massachusetts, or Connecticut, or New York: The idea that they belonged to a "United States" or were "Americans" lay in the future. Washington worked hard to improve the structure and operations of the army, to create battalions that brought together men from different colonies, and to improve morale for expected military campaigns in 1776. Neither sentiment nor the Continental Congress would allow the commanding general to mix officers from different colonies in the same unit, and at the beginning, at least, all of the colonies were deficient in supplying the numbers of troops promised. Washington had to warn the Congress of the danger if he were forced "within musket shot of the enemy" to "disband one army and recruit another." It was not immediately obvious, even to Washington himself, that recruitment would be a constant challenge and that the war would be long and grueling.

Washington initially envisaged an army of 20,000 men organized into 26 battalions of 728 men each, plus artillery units, rifle companies, engineers, and support troops. The British army was his model, but his army would be more robust, with each battalion having 640 musketmen instead of 448 as in the British example. On November 4, 1775, Congress approved this reorganization. As reported in the Army's own official history, *The Continental Army*, by Robert K. Wright Jr. …

> Congress ordered that uniforms were to include brown coats with different colored facings (collar, lapels, cuffs, and inside lining of the coattails) to distinguish the regiments, a system borrowed from the red-coated British Army. Each regiment contained 3 field officers (who could not be generals or captains), a small staff, and 8 companies. Each company had 4 officers and 2 musicians, plus 8 noncommissioned officers and 76 privates evenly divided into 4 squads. At full strength the regiment deployed 640 privates and corporals—the soldiers who stood in the ranks with muskets—or 88 percent of its total of 728. The 32 officers and 32 sergeants provided a favorable ratio of 1 supervisor to 10 rank and file for maintaining company-level control.

Washington's troops adopted ranks drawn from European usage in the Middle Ages. The terminology came from the feudal era, when sovereigns fielded armies. The Continental Army had four types of enlisted grades—privates, musicians, corporals, and sergeants. Musicians, of course, were not for entertainment, but for signaling: The roll of a drum could transmit an order to an entire front line of soldiers.

From May 1778 on, the Continental regiments had a sergeant major, a quartermaster sergeant, a drum major, and a fife major on the regimental staff. The officer ranks included lieutenants, captains, colonels, generals, and several now-obsolete ranks, including coronets (usually, the cavalry equivalent of a lieutenant), subalterns, and ensigns (a standard bearer, from the Latin word *insignia,* for an emblem or banner), with some ranks being unique to cavalry units. The ranks included …

- **Private:** A common soldier without title of rank; a private soldier.
- **Corporal:** Influenced by "corps"; head, chief.
- **Sergeant:** Servant; attendant upon a knight in the field.
- **Lieutenant:** An officer representing and exercising powers on behalf of his lord or sovereign.
- **Captain:** The word in Latin means "head" of a body, and the captain was the term for the leader of a body of troops.
- **Colonel:** An officer commanding a "column" (*columna,* in Latin) of soldiers; an officer entrusted with a command or fort under a sovereign or general. Pronounced "kernal" because the British adopted the French spelling "colonel" but the Spanish pronunciation "coronel," and then corrupted the pronunciation.
- **General:** originally meant to be of similar "birth" or "class" with the sovereign; the more recent interpretation is an officer too high to remain a specialist—that is, a "general" officer.

Clothing was anything but "uniform" for the typical Colonial Army soldier (the word derives from the Latin *unus,* for "one," and *forma,* for "form," and refers to the style of dress adopted by the military). There were to be times when Colonial Army soldiers did not have sufficient clothing, let alone uniform clothing, especially during the winter at Valley Forge. There were prolonged periods, both while campaigning and in garrison, when a pair of shoes of any variety was a rarity.

Still, soldiers adapted. Many prized the "cocked hat" that set them apart from civilians, although hats were difficult to obtain and few in number. A quartermaster report described the importance of headwear:

> Those who could get it, cocked it and decorated it, according to the regimental design. Officers and soldiers wanted to appear 'swank' and were very fond of strutting around in their full regalia, when they were fortunate enough to own such. This was only natural, since history relates that in the older countries of Europe, they strutted about and vainly displayed themselves. In this new country, just because they were fighting for freedom, men's vanity had not changed. Field officers were ordered to wear red- or pink-colored cockades in their hats, the Captains yellow or buff, and the Subalterns green. The 1st Virginia Infantry wore white binding on their hats, while Massachusetts troops wore a cocked hat with a silver button loop and a small button with the number of the regiment thereon. Large numbers of the soldiers wore leather hats and caps, while others wore those of fur skin.

STRATEGY FOR WAR

From the beginning, Washington understood that his goal was not so much to win in a struggle against the better-trained, better-equipped British army, but to avoid losing. His troops were more enthusiastic than able: Even the officers who came to him from the militias often struck Washington as ill prepared. His policy during the eight-year Revolutionary War was to keep his army intact and in the field, knowing that the British had mixed feelings about the war and were far from eager to maintain a large army on the far side of a vast ocean. The goal was to be credible even when, as happened frequently, losing a battle. If the Colonial Army could acquit itself in action, the tide of public opinion in the colonies would be overwhelming. Moreover, France, always important in the thinking of the rebels, might be persuaded to support the revolution if it appeared to have a chance of success.

After the Battle of Breed's Hill, British troops occupied Boston and Washington's troops besieged the city from high ground behind it. The city was stricken with a smallpox epidemic—one of several outbreaks in the colonies during the era. British troops, who were likely to have been exposed to the disease as children, were not typically vulnerable. Also immune was Washington himself, who had been afflicted as a youth. But the Colonial Army was made up of men who had never experienced the highly contagious disease. Later in the war, Washington made the painful decision to inoculate the Continental Army—not to be confused with vaccination, which was invented later, the procedure involved infecting troops with small doses—a decision that may have helped in the fighting as much as the cannon or the musket.

In any event, Washington besieged Boston and gave some thought to an attack that might overwhelm and decisively defeat the British. The final attack never took place because the British withdrew before it could happen. In May 1776, shortly after rebel forces captured Dorchester Heights overlooking Boston harbor and forced a British evacuation of Boston, King Louis XVI of France secretly authorized arms and munitions to assist the Americans—though he held short of offering help from his navy or sending troops.

Booted from Boston, British forces were taken to Halifax and then brought to Staten Island, New York, in the summer of 1776. Sir William's elder bother, Adm. Lord Richard Howe (1726–1799), brought in British and German mercenary reinforcements for a total of 32,000 troops. The decision to use the Germans, known as Hessians after the region of Hesse-Cassel from which many came, bolstered the Crown's forces considerably—they ultimately made up as much as a third of the troops in action on the British side—but it undoubtedly swayed many in the colonies who had not yet made up their minds. Throughout the long Revolutionary War, with its sharp battles punctuated by long periods of idleness and preparation, public opinion was as important as cannons and muskets. Ultimately, those in the colonies who remained loyal to the Crown, at least a third of the population at the beginning, were reduced to an impotent minority.

In the South, so vital to an integrated effort against the British, on June 28, 1776, Gen. Charles Lee (1731–1782) fended off a British attack in Charleston, South Carolina, and inflicted damage on the British fleet. The British would not return to the South for two years. The diminutive, slovenly Lee (at 5 feet, 8 inches, fully 7 inches shorter than the tall, neat Washington) joined Washington in New York. He was later briefly captured by the British and released. He commanded at the battle of Monmouth, New Jersey, in 1778, where his failure caused him to be court-martialed and cashiered.

In the North, where so much of the war was to be fought in a confined area, including within the new city of New York (population 20,000), Britain's Howe uprooted his army from Halifax, Canada, where his troops had loitered since his withdrawal from Boston. Howe planned to swarm down on New York and split the rebellious North from the southern colonies. The British believed that sentiment in support of the Crown was stronger in the South and that by driving a wedge between the two very different halves of the would-be nation, they could reduce their military problem to manageable size. This belief was something of a miscalculation, as the Redcoats would learn upon shifting the conflict to the South much later.

On August 27, 1776, came the Battle of Long Island, or Brooklyn Heights. Howe defeated Washington, but about half of the Continental Army troops escaped to Manhattan two nights later. The British lost 400 troops; the Americans lost more. Washington evacuated New York the following month. Meanwhile, Howe lost a shining opportunity to pursue and destroy. Deterred in part by memories of Bunker Hill, where the upstarts had fought tenaciously when on the defensive, Howe chose not to press on against his opponents, even though he might have been able to win the war by doing so.

Instead, the two armies backed away from each other near what is now Central Park. Washington bivouacked along a line at Harlem Heights, and for three weeks the two sides remained encamped within eyesight and did nothing. Now it was Washington who missed an opportunity. For a brief moment, he might have been able to bottle up the larger British force and hack away at it. He knew that both size and momentum would favor Howe as soon as the British went on the move again, but he failed to use the knowledge.

Finally, the British moved again and the Americans fell back in a defensive mode from which they would not easily budge. The year seemed destined to end on a note of defeat for the Colonials after they sustained defeats at White Plains, New York; Fort Washington on Upper Manhattan; and Fort Lee, New Jersey, in October and November. But in a surprise attack on Christmas night of 1776, Washington led 2,400 troops across the Delaware River, which was partially covered with ice, and raided British forces at Trenton, New Jersey. His main attack struck a garrison of Hessian troops who were still drunk or hung over from a holiday celebration. The Americans took 900 to 1,000 prisoners, marched on to Princeton, and again prevailed over the British. In the latter battle, on January 3, 1777, the British lost 100 killed and 300 captured; Colonial casualties were light but included an American commander named Hugh Mercer, who was bayoneted.

Militarily, Trenton was a small victory and Princeton even smaller. But they were what the public needed to keep the fires of rebellion alive. For the struggling Colonial Army, success at Trenton prompted re-enlistments by many Colonial soldiers whose enlistments were about to expire.

After the battle of Princeton in January 1777, Washington decided to try to make a run for New Brunswick, New Jersey, where the British had their stores. After starting, he changed his mind. His troops were exhausted and nearly all barefoot. Washington changed direction and went to Morristown, New Jersey. Howe was faked out and went to New Brunswick to fortify the town, expecting to defend it. The Rebels spent the winter in Morristown.

WAR IN 1777

An action on April 26, 1777, highlighted the Colonial Army's Brig. Gen. Benedict Arnold, who was not yet a traitor but, despite his brilliant combat record, had been without assignment since January. Arnold moved his troops to Ridgefield, New Jersey, in April 1777 to combat British and Hessians who had landed at Compo Beach on the shore of Long Island Sound, the body of water that separated British encampments on Long Island from American logistical bases in Connecticut. The British had marched north to Danbury, Connecticut, and torched homes and community buildings. Waiting for them at Ridgefield, Arnold orchestrated what became Connecticut's only inland battle in the eight-year War for Independence. His adversary was Brig. Gen. William Tryon (1729–1799), the Crown's temporarily deposed governor of New York and former governor of North Carolina. At the outbreak of the Revolution, Tryon had been forced to remain on a British ship in the harbor, only to return to power when William Howe took the city in 1776.

As the Battle of Ridgefield unfolded, Arnold narrowly escaped death when his horse was shot out from under him. On the ground, he pulled a hidden pistol from his boot and shot a British soldier who was about to decapitate him.

The two sides in the war remained locked in a delicate balance: Howe was secure in New York, Washington was able to maneuver behind the shield of the Delaware River. This meant that, throughout 1777 and 1778, the opposing armies fought largely in a Middle Atlantic corridor about 100 miles long and 50 miles wide between Philadelphia (which was essentially undefended and vulnerable) and New York. Other fighting took place in upper New York, with the rebels responding to the implicit British plan to use the Hudson River to bisect the Colonies.

In July 1777, the British retook Fort Ticonderoga, and a 20-year-old French nobleman, the Marquis de Lafayette (1757–1834), arrived in the Colonies to offer his services to the revolution. He and Washington hit it off immediately.

That month, General Burgoyne took the first steps for an invasion of New York. "Gentleman Johnny" had returned to England briefly and given the British ministry his personal plan to win the war in the campaign of 1777. He was aware that the longer the fighting dragged out, the more likely the Colonials were to prevail. His plan was to capture Albany and join with other British forces under Sir Henry Clinton advancing from New York City and the Mohawk Valley. The British strategy, if successful, would cut off New England from the South (where virtually no fighting was taking place at the time), sealing off the Colonial forces in the North and leaving them little maneuver room. The idea was flawless, but Burgoyne worked for the British commander in Canada while Howe commanded in the Colonies. Each reported separately to London, making coordination difficult. In days to come, a shortage of food would greatly hamper Burgoyne, who was far from home even though he had Lakes Champlain and George as potential supply routes.

Howe endorsed Burgoyne's ideas and, soon afterward, also thinking of splitting the Colonies, asked for 15,000 more British soldiers—which might have been just enough to make the difference. But Parliament balked. Howe's plan for attacking Pennsylvania by sea was approved, but no arrangement was made for coordination with Burgoyne. Howe wrote to Sir Guy Carlton, the British commander in Canada, that he probably could not spare troops to meet Burgoyne's forces in New York.

Howe boarded his army on 260 Royal Navy vessels at Sandy Hook, New Jersey, on the lower side of New York Bay. Washington mistakenly believed that Howe intended to advance up the Hudson to meet up with Burgoyne and split the colonies in half, so he positioned Colonial troops all over New Jersey for possible moves north or south. But Howe's intention was to move up the Delaware River to attack Philadelphia.

The British fleet went south and landed the British near New Castle, Delaware, on August 14, 1777. Two days later, Colonial troops fought the Battle of Bennington (Vermont), which actually took place in Walloomsac, New York. They defeated a formation of Burgoyne's troops.

The Battle of Bennington is considered by historians to have been the turning point in the American Revolution. It marked the moment when the Colonials knew they would not lose, if only they could survive and hold out against their formidable foe.

Burgoyne sent 600 British troops and Canadian Brunswickers (like all mercenaries, called Hessians by the Americans), accompanied by 150 Indians, down the New York side of the Champlain Valley to seize colonial provisions and weapons stored at Bennington.

BENNINGTON BATTLE

Burgoyne's drive to the south had taken longer than anticipated, with each day and the unexpected engagements en route consuming his munitions and provisions. The supplies, much needed by Burgoyne, were reported to be in Bennington, which led him to halt and send out a force to seize them. But the rebels were forewarned. In Walloomsac, 5 miles west of Bennington, a ragged force of ill-equipped and often barefoot New Hampshire rebels led by Gen. John Stark (1728–1822), plus a smaller force of Vermonters under Seth Warner, met the British advance head-on at positions that were hastily prepared and occupied on August 15. Stark supposedly proclaimed, "There are the Redcoats and they are ours, or this night Molly Stark sleeps a widow." In a battle for a small hilltop, many of the British Canadians and Indians lost their will to fight, but a band of dismounted cavalrymen stood fast, their swords flashing. In a two-day battle that Stark later called "one continuous clap of thunder," the on-scene British commander Lt. Col. Friedrich Baum was overwhelmed and killed, and the British were soundly defeated. The British force lost 207 soldiers and had 600 taken prisoner. Additionally, irreplaceable cannon, muskets, shot, powder, and horses were forfeited. The Americans lost 40 men and had 30 wounded.

Burgoyne lost valuable time and momentum in his disastrous attack on Bennington. Having failed to obtain supplies, and finding his progress halted by the entrenchments of Maj. Gen. Horatio Gates (1728–1806) at Bemus's heights, nine miles south of Saratoga (Schuylerville), he endeavored to extricate himself by fighting. The first battle, on September 19, was inconclusive, but another lay ahead.

Also ahead stretched a long road for the Colonial Army and the militiamen. Everybody knew Burgoyne was coming down from Lake Champlain with the intention of taking Albany and cutting off the Colonies at the Hudson River while also marrying up with the British forces advancing on Albany from the west. When Howe loaded his forces on ships and sailed south, Washington expected him to land at the Hudson and turn northwest to link up with Burgoyne, cutting the Colonies in half. Unaware that the fort at West Point was not yet finished and the Hudson was not well defended, Howe instead landed farther south in Delaware to attack Philadelphia rather than join up with Burgoyne. On September 11, 1777, in the Battle of Brandywine Creek, Pennsylvania, Washington fought Howe's troops but could not save the city. Washington himself came under the aim of a British sniper who had musket and ball ready but was so respectful of the Colonial Army general that he declined to shoot him—missing a chance to alter the world forever.

The flintlock musket carried by the Colonial and British infantryman was essentially a large smoothbore shotgun. The soldier loaded the muzzle with black powder and a round lead bullet (ball) from a cylindrical, paper-wrapped cartridge. He fired with the flintlock action above the trigger. The flint ignited priming powder in a projecting flashpan, sending flame through the barrel's touchhole to reach the main charge. Battles were often cancelled because a musket would not fire in the rain. Nor could it function without a sharp flint. This made it essential to have a bayonet—but Colonial rifles usually didn't.

The musket was accurate only to about 50 yards. There was no rear sight, so the soldier aimed using only a front-mounted sight (a "bead"). Troops fired volleys in unison. A capable soldier could load and fire three shots a minute, standing to expose himself each time. The musket was heavy and difficult to use, but when a round hit a foe, he went down and stayed down. Colonial troops preferred to scavenge the British musket, called the Brown Bess, which came in four main models and was more reliable than American flintlocks. The British called their best weapon the "Tower" musket because it was made in the Tower of London arsenal. Colonial soldiers liked the British musket because it always came with a bayonet.

A few troops were armed with rifles—longer weapons, with grooving in the barrel, accurate to 300 yards. Virginia riflemen led by Col. Daniel Morgan (c. 1732–1803) used their precision sharpshooting weapons with great effect. Morgan reportedly ordered his men not to "waste your shot on those who fight for sixpence a day. Save your shot for the epaulet men." Shooting officers was a new practice and devastated British morale. Musket-armed infantry usually accompanied riflemen because the rifles of the era could not accommodate a bayonet—still viewed as the soldier's primary weapon.

The Americans sustained a defeat and Congress withdrew from the city to safety in York, Pennsylvania, but Howe—despite being on the attack, called "lethargic" by one critic—failed to follow up on his success. On the rebels' side, Gen. Anthony Wayne's forces fought well. One participant was the young French volunteer, Lafayette, who sustained a leg wound that lent him military credibility. A young captain, James Monroe (1758–1831), a future president, tended the French soldier's wound.

Howe occupied Philadelphia on September 26. On October 4–5, the two sides fought the Battle of Germantown, Pennsylvania. The Colonials suffered a defeat, but again, Howe failed to follow up and was unable to finish off Washington.

In the Second Battle of Saratoga on October 7, 1777, fought on virtually the same ground as the first, the Colonials defeated and routed Burgoyne's forces. In fact, Burgoyne had to abandon his sick and wounded to the mercies of Horatio Gates. Burgoyne retreated to Saratoga and, with provisions having given out and Stark advancing on his rear, saw no outlet. He capitulated with his entire army on October 17, 1777.

The American success at Saratoga, building upon the Bennington victory, more than offset the loss of Philadelphia and raised Colonial spirits to new heights. The victory had been possible in part because the Colonials had received 23,000 Charleville muskets from the French the previous summer.

On October 22, Howe resigned; Sir Henry Clinton soon replaced him. If Bennington was not the turning point of the Revolution, Second Saratoga surely was. It gave the upstarts a credibility that allowed France to intervene on their side. And it hastened Burgoyne's second career: play writing.

The British should have won the campaigns of 1776–1777, according to scholar John Keegan. In *Fields of Battle*, Keegan pointed out that the British enjoyed the strategic advantages of control of the St. Lawrence River and the Great Lakes, and the military advantages of "a large regular force onshore and an unchallengeable fleet offshore, supported by a string of excellent bases at Newport, New York, and Philadelphia." The British also enjoyed the support of a large proportion of the population among which their army operated. If the loss of Massachusetts were accepted as a given, the theater of operations was reduced to a manageable size. Had the British not lacked the stomach for winter warfare, in Keegan's interpretation, they could easily have overwhelmed Washington in his winter quarters. None of this happened. On the rebel side the challenge remained the same as always: to survive, in the hope British resolve would wear down.

In a portent of the role of his countrymen to follow, at the end of 1777, Lafayette took command of the Virginia division of the Continental Army. With these troops, he joined Washington for a difficult winter ahead at Valley Forge, Pennsylvania, just outside Philadelphia.

Valley Forge might be viewed as a test of the mettle of an army, but it was really a time of misery and suffering. There was no holiday festivity at the encampment. The soldiers were reduced to eating "fire cake"—flour and water batter fried on a griddle—and suffered from cold, malnutrition, and disease.

When the army arrived at Valley Forge on December 19, 1777, it had 12,000 soldiers, plus wives, children, and camp followers, making it the third-largest settlement in the Colonies. Washington oversaw the building of huts for protection from the elements, including the snow that began the day after Christmas, but the structures meant for 12 men each were drafty, damp, and smoky. Even then, clothing and feeding the Colonials proved an almost impossible task. Washington lacked wagons for transport. His money (the much-maligned "continental") was valueless for purchases from farmers nearby. He was shackled with a lackluster quartermaster and neglected by Congress, which must be blamed for neglecting troops who were cold, hungry, and shoeless. As the winter wore on, the size of the encampment fell because of death from typhus, typhoid, dysentery, and pneumonia; from desertions; or from leave granted to those who lived nearby. Living conditions did not begin to improve until the advent of warmer weather in the spring, coupled with a new quartermaster in the person of Bunker Hill veteran Nathanael Greene. To Greene, the job of clothing, housing, and feeding troops was thankless, but he attacked it with fervor. He remained Washington's quartermaster until 1780.

A NEW ALLY

In February 1778, France came out in open support of the Colonials—in reaction to their success at Second Saratoga—and the two parties inked treaties of alliance and commerce in Paris. The French were in a position to demand anything they wanted from the struggling Colonists, but they settled for straightforward agreements on trade and mutual support.

Baron Friedrich Wilhelm von Steuben (1730–1794), a Prussian count, reached Valley Forge in February 1778, arriving with an introduction from the French war minister. Steuben introduced European-style military discipline and training to Washington's troops. This began with a "model company" of 100 men and soon expanded to the entire army. Steuben introduced a system of progressive training that sharpened each soldier's skills, taught close-order drill and tactics (such as they were, in an age when men stood in lines, faced each other, and fired in volleys), and also assisted with sanitation. Relying on a Colonial officer to curse the troops for him when his French and German proved inadequate, he prodded and drove Washington's men, and is credited with transforming them into a disciplined military force. He wrote a manual for the military training of soldiers called *Regulations for the Order and Discipline of the Troops of the United States*, the first time the new Army had a rulebook.

The Revolution was producing an Army, and it was also producing a nation. In 1778, the Congress began work on and signed the Articles of Confederation, the first document to spell out the creation of a new country to be called the "United States of America." The country still existed more on paper than in reality, but its military force was one step closer to becoming the United States Army. The Articles of Confederation contained significant weaknesses later addressed by the new Constitution in 1787. A number of these impeded the effort to coordinate the prosecution of the war:

1. Power was largely left in the hands of the states, which often were slow to meet the needs of the army and their own militias;
2. Internal trade relied on agreements between states, which impeded the growth of commerce necessary to sustain a war;
3. States did not necessarily honor laws of their neighbors;
4. Congress had to rely on the states to raise and equip armed forces;
5. The ability of Congress to impose taxes and thus raise revenue for support of the Army was restricted.

The States remained concerned about giving too much power to the central government after they had begun a revolution against the British Crown and its absentee power. Yet despite these limitations of the new government, the Colonial army persevered.

Britain might yet have squashed the Colonials' ambitions, had it been willing to commit the troops necessary, especially British troops rather than Hessians. But the Crown was pursuing the war with something less than its best and brightest. Sir Henry Clinton became the British commander in the Colonies on May 8, 1778. His appointment initially was not much help. Additionally, many British had some level of sympathy for the cause of independence being waged by the Colonials. The support of such men as Edmund Burke (1729–1795), a Whig member of Parliament, for more conciliatory treatment of the Colonials had a negative impact on British enthusiasm for the fight being waged far from home soil.

As Clinton prepared to evacuate Philadelphia after being ordered to do so, a French naval squadron of 11 warships, along with transports carrying 4,000 French troops, sailed from France in May 1778 and headed to America. Clinton moved out by land rather than by sea, as ordered, partly because he lacked the vessels to move his 3,000 horses over sea. Clinton set out from Philadelphia with his 10,000 men, including local residents loyal to the Crown known as Tories. On June 18, Washington and his growing army of 12,000 men occupied Philadelphia and began pursuit of Clinton.

Undecided whether to risk attack on the British column while it was on the march, Washington convened his staff and found it divided. Anthony Wayne, the boldest of the staff, and Lafayette, the youngest, urged an attack on the British troops while they were strung out on the road. Others preached caution. On June 26, 1778, Washington sided with a bold approach but failed to make his intention clear to his subordinates.

Gen. Charles Lee, who had been opposed to an all-out engagement with the British, was drawn into battle by British forces at Monmouth, New Jersey. Amid chaotic fighting, Lee directed his troops to retreat. This infuriated Washington, who ordered Lee and "Mad" Anthony Wayne to fight a delaying action while he organized Continental troops in a defensive position. For the rest of the day, the two armies clashed in terrible heat, withdrawing only after 5:00 P.M., exhausted. Washington intended to resume the sizzling slugfest the next day, but Clinton and his men slipped away. Neither side emerged a clear winner of the battle, but the American forces had proved themselves as a professional fighting force.

A legendary figure at the Battle of Monmouth was Molly Hays (1754–1832), known today as Molly Pitcher, who spent that miserably hot day bringing water to her husband and his fellow gunners as they fired their cannon. When she returned from fetching water, she discovered that her husband had fallen in battle. She took his place, serving as a gunner for the remainder of the battle.

On July 8, Washington established Continental Army headquarters at West Point, New York, that prominent piece of high ground along the Hudson where, in decades and centuries to come, many of the nation's best officers would learn their profession. Washington considered the site of West Point to be so strategic that he called it the key to the continent. He also feared that if the British ever commanded the forts at West Point, they would have a stranglehold on the colonies—a fear soon to be exacerbated by the perfidy of his first commander there, Benedict Arnold.

SAVANNAH

With a French fleet now operating off the coast, the British began their campaign in the South. On December 29, 1778, some 3,500 troops under Britain's Lt. Col. Archibald Campbell, among them two battalions of

Hessians, made an early-morning landing at Brewton Hill, 2 miles below Savannah, Georgia. The American commander, Brig. Gen. Robert Howe of North Carolina (no relation to the British general and admiral named Howe), with only 700 men, made an attempt to defend the city but lacked the means. Therefore, with troops at the Americans' front and rear, Campbell was able to take Savannah with little resistance. The Americans lost 550 men and all of their artillery. Howe was forced to retire into South Carolina.

While the rebels were fighting for Savannah, Britain's Brig. Gen. Augustine Prevost and 2,000 men marched north from Florida. Prevost's path toward embattled Savannah from Florida took him through Augusta, Georgia. On January 29, 1779, they took control of that city. Augusta sits astride the Savannah River and marked an important victory for the British because it gave them control of the river, enabling them to readily transport their supplies, personnel, and equipment.

In the winter of 1778–1779, Washington reviewed the situation. He now had 15,000 Continental troops in the field, an inadequate number even though all had now been trained by Baron von Steuben. Washington knew that the Americans' militia forces were undependable. The British were installed in force in Manhattan and Newport, Rhode Island, while the Americans were secure at West Point and the Hudson Highlands. Britain, preoccupied with its war with France, seemed unwilling to spare additional resources for the fatal blow that would dash the Americans' hopes forever. French assistance was coming. Time was on the side of the Americans, Washington concluded. Even a deadlock, which was an apt description for the situation, worked to the eventual advantage of the Americans. However, Washington also had to keep in mind that on the western New York and Pennsylvania frontiers, hostile Indians allied with Tory forces were harassing frontier communities. The New Year would have to take the Indians into account.

The U.S. Military Academy at West Point, New York, traces its history to the Revolutionary War, when both the Colonial and the British armies realized the strategic importance of the commanding plateau on the west bank of the Hudson River. Gen. George Washington considered West Point to be the most important strategic position in America. Washington selected Thaddeus Kosciuszko, one of the heroes of Saratoga, to design the fortifications for West Point in 1778, and he transferred his headquarters there in 1779. Continental soldiers built forts, batteries, and redoubts and extended a 150-ton iron chain across the Hudson to control river traffic. The British, despite Benedict Arnold's treason, never captured the fortress West Point. Today it is the oldest continuously occupied military post in America.

FINAL FIGHTING

In January 1779, Washington dispatched Gen. John Sullivan (1740–1795) with a combined force of 5,100 men to the upper New York area to attack and destroy Mohawk Indians and their sources of livelihood, farms and orchards. By June 18, 1779, Sullivan's army started under great difficulty, since the landscape of Northeast Pennsylvania and Southwest New York was covered with impassable forests and mountains. By late August, Sullivan's reduced force of 3,000 had managed to defeat and intimidate the Indian force of about 1,200 at the battle of Newtown in the Finger Lakes area. The expedition completed its counterinsurrection efforts by late September 1779, effectively establishing American presence in the Northwest of New York and placing over a thousand Indian warriors as a burden on the British to feed in Canada.

On February 25, 1779, Americans under George Rogers Clark (1752–1818), a redheaded 26-year-old, arrived at Vincennes in what is now Indiana after a long march that included fording four icy rivers. Clark's troops were hardy frontiersmen from Kentucky, then a County of Virginia. Because Vincennes was atop a small peak, Clark marched his men around the hill to confuse the British and Indians nearby. He then captured six Indians and tomahawked them, and chucked their bodies into the river. By deceiving the foe about the size of his force and brutally killing his captives, Clark bluffed the British into surrendering. He won a minor victory, but one that had little impact on the larger war.

The king's forces struck a lightning blow to the South on May 10, 1779, when Vice Adm. Sir George Collier (1738–1795) entered Chesapeake Bay and sailed into Hampton Roads, Virginia. He delivered troops under Gen. Edward Matthews and quickly captured Fort Nelson and Portsmouth while also destroying the naval stores at Suffolk. During the Collier-Matthews Raid, the British burned Portsmouth and Norfolk, seized over

100 vessels, and departed from the area. It was a dramatic strike but, again, one that was to have little impact on the war. More important—and ominous—to the British cause were Spain's declaration of war on Britain on June 16, 1779 (though the Spanish sought no alliance with the American Colonials) and "Mad" Anthony Wayne's even more dramatic raid on Stony Point, New York, on July 15, 1779.

The Battle of Stony Point was fought during the nocturnal hours of July 15–16, 1779, when 1,500 Continental troops led by Gen. "Mad" Anthony Wayne pulled off a bold and stealthy assault on the British fort along the Hudson River, 25 miles north of Manhattan.

The Colonials were armed only with unloaded muskets and fixed bayonets, to avoid detection and preserve the element of surprise. Secrecy was so vital to the plan devised by Washington and modified by Wayne that the Americans marched south from West Point and staged at a farm, a mile and a half from Stony Point, before soldiers were told of the plan for the attack. As they approached the peninsula from the west, they formed two attack columns and wore pieces of white paper in their hats to avoid confusion in the darkness.

It was a daring plan, but Wayne was an inspiration to his troops. Given the order to plan the attack, he uttered his most famous quote: "Give the order, sir, and I will lay siege to hell."

Wayne's troops rounded up or destroyed all dogs in the region to prevent them from alerting the British. He picked 20 men for the dangerous mission of taking out British sentries.

The actual fight for the fort at Stony Point was an anticlimax. During a 30-minute period just after midnight, the fighting flared—then ended. The Continentals killed 63 British soldiers and captured 543.

A British bullet grazed Wayne's skull during the attack. He ordered his men to carry him over the fort's walls so he could die victorious. He did not expire, however. His victory at Stony Point rallied an American public that had been tiring of seeing the Continental Army defeated time after time.

More important, and more ominous yet, on August 19, 1779, an American leader drove the British from Paulus Hook, a fortification at what is now Jersey City, New Jersey.

Maj. Henry Lee III (1756–1818) was called "Light Horse Harry" because of his adroit horsemanship. A veteran of Anthony's raid at Stony Point, Lee moved aggressively at Paulus Hook. He led a bayonet charge, overwhelmed the Redcoats, and captured 400 British soldiers with the loss of only 1 of his own. He was later known for his spoken epitaph for his idol Washington ("First in war, first in peace, and first in the hearts of his countrymen") and for one other, very important fact: He was the father of Robert E. Lee.

To the north, in another step ahead for the American cause, on August 29, 1779, Gens. John Sullivan and James Clinton defeated combined Loyalist and Indian forces at Newton (Elmira, New York).

From September 3 to October 28, 1779, American and French combined forces suffered a disastrous setback in an attempt to recapture Savannah. The Siege of Savannah occurred in early October 1779. This battle was the second-bloodiest battle of the Revolution; only at Bunker Hill did more men die in battle. The Americans relearned a lesson familiar in warfare throughout the centuries: Infantry assaults on entrenched positions are invariably costly in terms of casualties. Despite the difficulty at Savannah, the Americans sensed they were wearing down Britain's resolve; on September 27, 1779, Congress appointed John Adams to negotiate peace with England.

The war was now largely one of attrition. On October 17, 1779, the Continental Army returned to winter quarters at Jockey Hollow in Morristown, New Jersey, to experience a winter even worse than the one the year before at Valley Forge. Desertions and mutiny were commonplace.

In December 1779, Sir Henry Clinton embarked the bulk of his army for the campaign in the Carolinas. Clinton took Savannah and then proceeded north to besiege Charleston.

COMBAT IN 1780

A new year arrived and the war ground on. On February 1, 1780, a British fleet carrying 8,000 men from New York and Newport reached Charleston. On May 6, 1780, Fort Moultrie fell to the British and, with it, Charleston. In the heaviest single American defeat of the war, 5,400 Americans were captured along with ships, munitions, and food supplies. The city and surrounding country was subjugated by mid-June 1780. Clinton returned to New York, leaving Cornwallis in charge in the South.

The American army was still struggling with the practical difficulties of a prolonged war with no end in sight. Mutiny now became almost as much of a threat to the cause of independence as the British. In early May 1780, some 1,300 Pennsylvania troops in Morristown became disgruntled over their genuinely appalling living conditions, which included frostbite and scurvy, and decided to take their grievances to Princeton. They were en route when Anthony Wayne intercepted them and deflated their uprising with a promise to see their complaints forwarded to the Continental Congress. Apparently, the troops were unaware that Congress had done, and would do, little about the poor quality of their food, clothing, and housing. On May 25, 1780, another mutiny in Morristown was put down, ironically, by Pennsylvania troops. Two leaders of the mutiny were hanged. Congress gave Washington authority to declare martial law.

On June 22, 1780, Washington began sending reinforcements to join Horatio Gates in North Carolina; the focus of the war now seemed certain to remain in the South. The following month, 5,000 French troops under Comte de Rochambeau (1725–1807) arrived at Newport but were trapped by a British blockade. The shift of emphasis to the South did not prevent the famous betrayal by Benedict Arnold at West Point.

Today a statue of a cavalryman's boot marks the Colonial victory at Saratoga. A plaque honors the "most brilliant soldier of the Continental Army"—but does not name him.

Historians say Benedict Arnold's boot is the only honorable part of him. The statue reflects his wound when a bullet shattered Arnold's left leg October 7, 1777.

Arnold fought courageously at Fort Ticonderoga in 1775, the first victory by the Colonists, and at Saratoga two years later. George Washington called him "the bravest of the brave." Yet Benedict Arnold's name means, in plain talk, a traitor.

Footwear also figures in Arnold's betrayal. Arnold sought command of the strategic fort at West Point in 1780. He entered into secret talks with Sir Henry Clinton, commander of British troops based in New York City. Arnold negotiated a deal with British Maj. John Andre to deliver the fort at West Point to Clinton in return for 20,000 English pounds, a fortune. But highwaymen robbed Andre on his way to New York City and found proof of Arnold's plot in Andre's boot. They informed Colonial troops, and Arnold's perfidy became known.

Arnold escaped on a British ship. The Colonials hanged Andre as a spy. In 1781, Arnold led a few raids for the Redcoats, but he never got a major command or a permanent commission in the British Army. Today apologists say that Arnold was a complex man who changed sides only after soul-searching and being swayed by his beautiful wife, Margaret. They want Congress to posthumously reinstate Arnold's citizenship, as it did with Confederate Gen. Robert E. Lee. In reality, Arnold was a loathsome figure who made a personal choice. He lived in England, where he was shunned until his death, a lonely and bitter man, in 1801.

On August 16, 1780, at Camden, South Carolina, Britain's Cornwallis overwhelmingly defeated American forces under Gates. Fifty percent of Cornwallis's army consisted of Loyalist Americans, to say nothing of more than a few deserters from the Continental Army at Valley Forge, reflecting a population still at odds with itself. Gates lost his command.

The seesaw of wins and losses continued to shift two months later on October 7, 1780, in the Battle of Kings Mountain, North Carolina. A frontier militia force defeated a British Tory force of more than 1,000 and killed the British commander. The rebels also captured 1,100 Loyalists and forced Cornwallis to abandon plans for an invasion of North Carolina.

On October 14, 1780, Nathanael Greene, always one of Washington's most trusted and dedicated leaders, replaced Gates as commander of the Colonial Army in the South. Greene began a guerrilla war of harassment against the British.

THE END IN SIGHT

In early January 1781, a British force of 1,600 regulars and Tories from New York led by Benedict Arnold disembarked in lower Chesapeake Bay, raided James River plantations, and occupied Richmond, Virginia. Arnold's forces moved on to Portsmouth, and Washington sent 1,200 men under Lafayette—recently returned from a stay in France—to intercept Arnold and prevent a link-up with Cornwallis in the Carolinas. A French fleet sailing from Newport to seal off Portsmouth was chased by the much larger British fleet, which forced it to return to Newport. Arnold was reinforced with 2,000 troops, and command of Portsmouth was taken over by another British officer.

On January 17, 1781, in the Battle of Cowpens, South Carolina, American forces under Gen. Daniel Morgan (1736–1802) won a decisive victory.

Col. Banastre "Bloody Ban" Tarleton (1754–1833), perhaps the most hated British officer of the war, despite his relative youth, lost 600 of his force, while Morgan lost only 80. Tarleton's "British Legion" of mostly American Loyalists from New York and Pennsylvania wore green jackets to distinguish them as a Tory regiment, but their days of success were ending. Cornwallis attempted to pursue Morgan before he could join forces with Gen. Nathanael Greene, but he was not successful.

On March 15, 1781, despite a victory at the Battle of Guilford Courthouse, North Carolina, Cornwallis suffered heavy losses, abandoned plans to control the Carolinas, and retreated to await reinforcements. He left Wilmington, North Carolina, in April, and arrived at Petersburg, Virginia, a month later.

Anthony Wayne took his troops to Virginia in June 1781 to join Lafayette in the fight against Cornwallis. Meanwhile, Washington learned that French Admiral de Grasse was bringing a fleet (from Haiti) with 3,000 men to Chesapeake Bay. Washington secretly abandoned plans to attack Clinton in New York and moved south instead. De Grasse's troops landed and joined Washington's forces on August 31. Two weeks later, the French fleet was victorious in a naval battle off Yorktown, and additional French troops arrived from Newport. Their presence made it impossible for Cornwallis to retreat. Thus, the stage was being set in the South for the final major battle of the War for Independence. On September 28, 1781, a combined force of Americans and French laid siege to Yorktown. From the French point of view, the battle was crucial in the context of the broader war between the British and the French.

> To honor how he fought—and was wounded—for American independence, an American flag has flown over the grave of the Marquis de Lafayette in France ever since his death in 1834, even when France was occupied by Nazi Germany during World War II.

Cornwallis was receiving confusing and contradictory instructions from his superior, Clinton, in New York, who intended to move his own forces to help but was slow to act. Cornwallis's decision to position his weakened army at Yorktown rather than Portsmouth, hoping for resupply that would not arrive in time, was his undoing. Washington seized the French offer to blockade Chesapeake Bay and moved into position with his 9,500 troops (including 3,000 militia). About 8,800 French troops under Rochambeau (some transported by the French fleet) also took up the siege of Yorktown, giving Cornwallis's adversaries a strength of about 18,300 troops to his 8,000.

Cornwallis worsened his lot by abandoning his initial defensive positions, which Washington had thought very formidable. The Americans, with leadership from skilled siege engineers, laid the groundwork for the French to bring up heavy siege guns. The Americans had not enjoyed such heavy artillery previously, but now, when the actual siege began on October 9, they were in a position to make life miserable for Cornwallis's troops.

On October 14, the Americans and French seized two crucial redoubts, or defensive positions, one of which was taken by 400 troops led by Col. Alexander Hamilton. Two days later, the British counterattacked at the center of the French-American lines and spiked a number of siege guns before being repulsed. Now the British attempted to evacuate their forces across the York River to their fortified position at Gloucester, but they lacked the ships to do the job. With escape through Gloucester cut off and the French fleet still blockading the entrances to the York River and Chesapeake Bay, Cornwallis had no choice but to ask for terms of surrender, which he did on October 17. On October 19, Cornwallis officially surrendered. His troops laid down their weapons in a procession more than a mile long, with the British band rendering a marching tune, "The World Turned Upside Down." Arriving only after this defeat, Clinton reached the area with a powerful fleet and 7,000 troops on October 28—and had no choice but to turn around and retreat to New York in dismay. One of the men who was key to the success at Yorktown, French Admiral de Grasse, never left his ship while in American waters. The fledgling American army, with significant help from the French, had pulled off the impossible. For all practical purposes, fighting in the Revolutionary War was over.

The French kept garrisons in Williamsburg and Yorktown for another year. The Continental Army spent the winter of 1781–1782 in New York. The Treaty of Paris, which officially ended the war and recognized the independence of the United States, was signed on September 3, 1783.

Estimates of the total number of troops in the Colonial Army through the entire war range from 250,000 to 395,000. The Army reached its greatest strength of 35,000 in November 1778. Total battle deaths accounted for in official records were 4,044, with 6,004 wounded, 6,642 taken prisoner, and 2,124 missing in action. No total was recorded for soldiers who died of disease, but the figure had to be in the many thousands. Occurring during the same years as the American Revolution, multiple outbreaks of smallpox killed many times the number of people who lost their lives in warfare. The figures for battle losses are for the Army only and do not include those for the Colonial Navy. The numbers may seem modest when measured against the achievement they represent.

An upstart army of rebels had wrested victory from the empire that ruled much of the earth. Even Washington wondered if future generations would believe that mighty Great Britain "could be baffled ... by numbers infinitely less, composed of men oftentimes half starved, always in rags, without pay, and experiencing, at times, every species of distress which human nature is capable of undergoing." The agrarian Colonies had produced sufficient food to support an army; inadequate transportation had hindered the delivery and distribution of provisions. When the first shots of war rang out in April 1775, the rebelling colonists, divided among themselves on objectives, had neither an army nor a navy. They had lacked a strong centralized government to direct operations and had no stable currency for financing a war. Yet they had raised and kept an army in the field for eight years, and with foreign assistance, they had won.

CHAPTER 3

THE WAR OF 1812 AND THE MEXICAN WAR (1783–1860)

On June 13, 1783, with the struggle for independence won, the bulk of the Continental Army disbanded. A small number of soldiers stayed in service—for a brief period in 1784, the senior officer on duty was a major—and George Washington even came back into uniform to deal with issues near the end of the eighteenth century. But the nation maintained no more than a small frontier Army—in fact, the very smallest it could get away with, made up of just a few thousand troops who often lacked adequate equipment, weapons, and resources. Fully a decade into the nineteenth century, the Army had only 3,000 regulars, and the Navy possessed just 20 frigates and sloops and 150 gunboats for harbor defense. Men who believed it unseemly to maintain a standing army in peacetime topped the list of leaders in the new country. It became the American way to disarm in peacetime and build up again when war loomed; the U.S. never really maintained a large peacetime force until 1940.

The founders gave the new nation a Constitution that stressed civilian rule of military forces. Americans were distrustful of strong central governments, of authoritarian rule, and of a general staff in their capital. They didn't want generals running the country, and they weren't going to make it easy for the Army to carry off a military coup d'état. They established the elected president as the commander in chief of the military. A second civilian was next in the chain of command, a secretary of war (for the Army) and a secretary of the Navy, although these positions were often filled by military men. The power to declare war was vested in Congress.

Section 2 of Article II of the Constitution spells out the president's role as supreme commander: "The president shall be commander-in-chief of the Army and Navy of the United States, and of the militia of the several states, when called into the actual service of the United States."

George Washington, all 6 feet, 3 inches of him, was a genuine hero on the battlefield and was so popular that he easily could have grabbed power after the Revolution. Instead of seeking to become a military ruler (or even a king), Washington happily served as a civilian president for two terms and then retired to his farm.

Washington was president from 1789 to 1797. His successor, John Adams, served a single term, from 1797 to 1801. Thomas Jefferson became the third U.S. president in 1801 after the contentious administration of John Adams and began by undoing the negative effects of the Alien and Sedition Acts imposed by Adams to quell internal dissent. With a Democratic Party majority in Congress, Jefferson repealed a number of obnoxious internal taxes such as one on liquor. To encourage immigration, naturalization was permitted after a period of 5 years of residence rather than 14 years, and a sinking fund was created for the reduction of the national debt. Jefferson oversaw the admission of Ohio to the Union and, in 1803, arranged the Louisiana Purchase.

History's greatest Indian victory over an American military force happened on November 3, 1791. A thousand Native American warriors, mostly Potawatomis allied with the British, attacked the 2,300-man army of Gov. Arthur St. Clair along the Wabash and killed 674 men. Incredibly, history has not given the battle a name.

EXPLORING THE LAND

The new nation was going to expand. This meant that the Army now had more to do than fight Indians. The Army was the only likely source of explorers who could study and chart the untamed lands to the west. One such explorer was Brig. Gen. Zebulon Pike (1779–1813), who, as a lieutenant in 1805, led a party to search for the source of the Mississippi River.

To head an even more ambitious expedition into the vast western region acquired in the Louisiana Purchase, Jefferson chose his young secretary and fellow Virginian, Capt. Meriwether Lewis, who invited his friend Lt. William Clark of Kentucky to share the task. The two seasoned Army veterans led an exploration of the West from 1803 to 1805 that consumed two years, four months, and nine days, and covered 6,000 miles. Lewis and Clark are credited with being the first Americans to chart the vastness of the West, see the Rocky Mountains, and reach the Pacific by land. The great contribution of Lewis and Clark was to show the immense size of the territory acquired in the Louisiana Purchase. It had not been fully appreciated that the claim would go all the way to the Pacific Northwest.

All but one of the soldiers and civilians who accompanied the Lewis and Clark expedition of 1804–1805 survived the trek. Sgt. Charles Floyd, the sole casualty, succumbed to infection after suffering a burst appendix, a medical situation then not understood by doctors.

In 1806 and 1807, Zebulon Pike, still a lieutenant, led an expedition to explore the headwaters of the Arkansas and Red Rivers and to reconnoiter Spanish settlements in distant New Mexico. Pike and his men went up the Arkansas River to Pueblo, Colorado, and discovered a 14,110-foot mountain that he wanted to name the Grand Peak, but it became Pikes Peak. Pike attempted to climb the peak, failed, and predicted that no one ever would (the peak was scaled by a climber in 1820).

The Army was good at this sort of thing, but not well equipped for much else. Jefferson helped a little on an inconsistent basis, but not much. Even after he ordered an attack that defeated Mediterranean pirates that were capturing American ships and had forced the U.S. to pay tribute, Jefferson deliberately downplayed the importance of military forces. He reduced the size of the Army and turned the Navy into a coastal defense unit.

On March 16, 1802, President Jefferson signed legislation that permanently established the corps of engineers; stationed the corps at West Point, New York; and constituted the corps as a military academy. The importance of the act may not have been apparent at the time, but transforming the great fort astride the Hudson into the nation's premier training school for officers created a tradition that would be a crucial part of the Army's story in every war to follow.

BIT PLAYER

In the world leading up to the War of 1812, the new United States of America was a bit player, and its Army—established on a permanent basis only in 1802—was not even large enough for a cameo part. Issues between Britain and its former colony were serious, however, and in much of the country hostility toward Britain was growing.

Atop the list of complaints was impressment. Warships of the powerful Royal Navy were boarding neutral merchant vessels on the high seas and impressing young men into naval service. The Crown claimed that the men were Royal Navy deserters, but many had a claim to U.S. citizenship.

England's "Orders in Council" required the seizure of all ships trading between the Caribbean and Europe, the intention being to cripple Napoleon's economy. In 1807, a British man-of-war patrolling the Chesapeake Bay attacked the American frigate *Chesapeake* departing Norfolk for the Mediterranean and forced the surrender of three Royal Navy deserters on board. France, for its part, issued a decree placing the entire coast of Britain under blockade and punishing nations that traded with England by confiscating ships and cargoes. The United States was infuriated by impressment and the blockade but had no real way to respond because its Army and Navy were weak. Even Danish privateer vessels were seizing American merchantmen in the Baltic Sea. When the ship owners asked for permission to arm their ships, given that there was no navy to protect them, Congress, under control of Jeffersonian Democrats, refused, saying this would be a warlike act.

In what is known today as Indiana and Illinois, but was called the Northwest at the time, Tecumseh, a Shawnee chief, tried to unite all of the tribes between the Great Lakes and Mexico to attack the Americans. In the autumn of 1811, Maj. Gen. William Henry Harrison began operations against Tecumseh's tribes.

In November 1811, Gen. William Henry Harrison (1773–1841), governor of the Indiana territory, led 1,000 troops who came under attack from the Indian followers of the expansionist Shawnee chief Tecumseh (1768–1813). In fighting along the Tippecanoe River, both sides sustained grievous casualties but Harrison prevailed and razed the Indians' village. The blow put an end to Tecumseh's hopes of forming a huge Indian confederacy to preserve the Ohio River as a barrier between whites and Native Americans.

In the War of 1812, Harrison won more military laurels when he was given the command of the Army in the Northwest with the rank of brigadier general. At the Battle of the Thames, north of Lake Erie, on October 5, 1813, he defeated the combined British and Indian forces and killed Tecumseh. The Indians scattered, never to offer serious resistance in the Indiana and Illinois region then called the Northwest.

Three decades later in 1840, Harrison campaigned for president as a simple frontier Indian fighter, living in a log cabin and drinking cider, in sharp contrast to incumbent Martin Van Buren—unfairly portrayed as an aristocratic dandy who preened himself before the mirror and sipped champagne. In 1841, Harrison became the ninth U.S. president on the slogan "Tippecanoe and Tyler, too," with John Tyler as his running mate. Harrison was more successful as a soldier than he was as a president: He contracted pneumonia and, barely a month after his inauguration, became the first president to die in office.

LOOMING WAR

Before turning over the presidency to James Madison in 1809, Jefferson had embargoed British imports until the dispute over impressment could be resolved. The move appealed to those who already felt resentment toward Britain, but it undermined Jefferson's popularity among the public as a whole. Thoughts of another war with England were especially unpopular in the Northeast, where New England relied heavily on trade with Europe.

Jefferson also took a few steps to prepare the young nation for war, including ordering a supply of .59-caliber flintlock musket rifles. But the new nation and its new Army were woefully unprepared. By Jefferson's time, the regular Army had grown slightly to 12,000 troops, but the numbers were inadequate for a growing frontier nation pushing its limits in new territory populated by Indians. To make matters worse, many of the Army's leaders were political hacks rather than experienced commanders. In contrast, Britain's professional military and naval forces ruled the high seas and much of the world. Britain, however, may have lacked some of the will: Businessmen wanted the former colonies as a market and supplier and preached cautiously against too greatly antagonizing the Americans. The Americans did not fear, and the British did not expect, that Britain would subdue the U.S. and return the new nation to colonial status. The issues of the coming conflict were smaller than that, but plenty of blood would be shed anyway.

> Caliber is a measurement of the diameter of the muzzle of a rifle or pistol. A .44 caliber pistol is $^{44}/_{100}$ of an inch in diameter at the muzzle.

Harrison's campaign against Tecumseh in Indiana quieted things in the Northwest and pushed the Indian issue to the background. But the country wanted war with England.

During the winter of 1811–1812, Madison's government detected and laid before Congress evidence of efforts by England to cause disaffection in the American northeast and encourage the region's secession from the union. On May 30, 1812, Britain formally rejected a roster of complaints by the U.S. concerning impressment of Americans, seizure of vessels, and refusal to negotiate these issues. After a strong and vigorous debate of several days, Congress agreed that war should be declared and that the president should immediately recruit 35,000 men for the regular Army as well as raise 50,000 volunteers. Congress also directed the president to call out 100,000 militiamen for garrison duty.

Maj. Gen. Henry Dearborn (1751–1829) of Massachusetts, who had been Jefferson's secretary of war, became the senior officer in the Army beginning January 27, 1812, and continued in that role until June 15, 1815. Dearborn was respected as a Revolutionary War veteran, but his service as the nation's top soldier quickly became little more than nominal. He was one of a number of elderly generals, mostly political appointees, who held the top positions in the Army at the beginning of the War of 1812; unlike Dearborn, most of them were removed as the war progressed. Dearborn stayed and served in the field with some distinction, but Madison often made decisions and issued orders without Dearborn's input.

It was now too late to prevent war. Belatedly, the British offered to negotiate the issues and, in fact, revoked the Orders in Council. The

French also revoked their decrees when they learned that neutral trade would not be punished. The only real issue remaining was that of impressment of American seamen. In Washington, Madison and other leaders decided that, with the exception of the use of privateers, America could not contest England on the high seas, so only an invasion of Canada would impact English policy. While an attempt to conquer Canada was being pondered, in the latter half of 1812, naval commander Stephen Decatur won a series of sea victories that boosted morale but had little impact on Britain's ability to fight.

During the War of 1812, British intelligence officers had a handy source of information about military movements by American soldiers: American newspapers. Journals in the U.S. routinely published details of troop movements and letters from officers that revealed the whereabouts of Army units. In 1814, most editors ignored an order by the Army's adjutant general forbidding publication of military information in newspapers.

TO CANADA

At the outset of the war, American forces deployed to the border of Canada, with Dearborn leading forces from Maine to Lake Champlain, Col. Stephen Van Rensselaer (1764–1839) commanding the center region, and Maj. Gen. William Hull (1753–1825) commanding the Michigan territory. The three forces were to cooperate in the objective of attacking Montreal.

In July 1812, Hull led the American Northwestern Army to invade Canada. Hull was a hero of the Revolutionary War who had fought in almost every major battle and had also helped to put down a farmers' uprising, Shays' Rebellion, in 1787.

At Detroit, Hull, with 2,000 men at his disposal, was isolated from other American forces by 200 miles of wilderness. He asked for reinforcements and recommended that Lake Erie be secured before the British could do so. His requests could not be accommodated, and he had to make do with resources at hand. The British under Gen. Isaac Brock, the governor of Upper Canada, moved energetically and quickly to surround Detroit. The British also aroused the Indian tribes, some of them Tecumseh's followers, against the Americans. Brock set up artillery across from Detroit and demanded its surrender. When that was refused, the British crossed the river on August 16, 1812, with several hundred Europeans and 600 Indians.

Dr. William Beaumont (1785–1853), an Army surgeon and veteran of the War of 1812, was the first person to directly observe human digestion while treating a man with a horrific shotgun wound to the stomach. Beaumont's 1833 book *Physiology of Digestion* described 128 experiments that revolutionized medical knowledge.

Hull dumbfounded both the British and his fellow Americans by surrendering without a fight. He also surrendered the entire Michigan Territory, opening up the northwest frontier to Indian and British attacks. A subsequent court-martial condemned Hull to be shot for cowardice, but Madison remanded the execution because of Hull's Revolutionary War service and his advanced age (almost 60).

The second disaster for the American cause in 1812 came about in the center sector. Van Rensselaer collected a force of New York militia near Niagara and, on October 13, crossed the Niagara River and attacked and took the British fort at Queenstown. British General Brock arrived with reinforcements but failed to retake the Fort and was killed in the attempt. Van Rensselaer went back across the river to get more troops across. The militiamen refused, arguing that they could not be ordered out of their own state.

As a result, the British reinforced their attacking force and defeated the Americans in Queenstown, killing or capturing all. Among those captured was 26-year-old Lt. Col. Winfield Scott (1786–1866), who would be nearly 75 when he commanded the Union armies at the outbreak of the Civil War. A future American commander in chief who had volunteered for this fight, Van Rensselaer resigned his commission in disgust, ending military action in the year 1812—but not the war named for that year, which would last until 1815.

YORK FIGHTING

In April 1813, American forces under Dearborn captured the city of York (Toronto) and burned government buildings there. They were blamed for the burning of the Parliament building. During the fighting, the explosion of a powder magazine killed Brig. Gen. Zebulon Pike, of Pike's Peak fame.

In May 1813, American forces under Brig. Gen. Winfield Scott took Fort George, forcing a British withdrawal from Lake Erie. Fighting on Lake Erie persisted into September. Oliver Hazard Perry defeated a British naval force on September 10, 1813, and wrote to Madison, "We have met the enemy and they are ours." The following month saw William Henry Harrison (see earlier sidebar) achieve a victory over British and Indian forces.

In November 1813, American forces under Maj. Gen. James Wilkinson—who replaced Dearborn in the field—were defeated at Montreal. Had things gone differently, Wilkinson might have been able to annex Ontario as part of the United States. The following month, another American force abandoned Fort George and burned the nearby village of Newark. The British were outraged and attacked Fort Niagara, killing the defenders and then burning every town and house, including Buffalo, Lewistown, Youngstown, Manchester, and Black Rock.

Former Brig. Gen. John Armstrong (1758–1843), secretary of war from 1813 to 1814, created a model for the future with the Army's first cohesive set of regulations. Armstrong was blamed for failing to fortify Washington from British attack. When the British returned to Chesapeake Bay in 1814, he was forced to resign.

JACKSON VS. INDIANS

While the war with Britain went on, Maj. Gen. Andrew Jackson (1767–1845) of the Tennessee militia waged the Creek Indian War. Despite serious problems of supply and a mutinous spirit among his militia troops, Jackson repeatedly inflicted heavy losses on the Creek, building up to March 17, 1814, when he achieved a decisive victory in the Battle of Horseshoe Bend, Alabama. The battle was earmarked by its savagery: Jackson's troops suffered 49 killed and 154 wounded, including some who died later, but they wiped out at least 800 of the 1,000 Indians opposing them.

In July 1814, an American advance from Plattsburg, New York, led by Wilkinson, had been checked just beyond the Canadian border in March. But on July 3, 3,500 men under Brig. Gen. Jacob Brown (1775–1823) seized Fort Erie across the Niagara in a coordinated attack with Commodore Isaac Chauncey's fleet, designed to wrest control of Lake Ontario from the British. Fort Erie surrendered to Brown without a shot being fired.

Almost simultaneously, Scott fought the Battle of Chippewa, 15 miles north of Lake Erie. Scott's brigade (1,300 men) of Brown's command unexpectedly confronted a large British force on July 5, 1814, near the Chippewa River. Scott's well-trained troops broke the enemy line with a skillfully executed charge, sending the survivors into a hasty retreat. British losses were 137 killed and 304 wounded; the Americans lost 48 killed and had 227 wounded.

The British retreated toward Burlington Heights. British and Americans clashed at Bridgewater, also known as Lundy's Lane, opposite Niagara Falls on July 25, 1814. Though his men occupied strong positions and could have held them, Scott led them in the attack. After 5 hours of hard fighting with 800 men lost on each side, the British withdrew, as did the Americans, who ran out of ammunition. Almost all of the American officers were wounded or killed. The victory was especially gratifying to the Americans because the British were seasoned veterans of the Wellington Peninsular War. Unfortunately, however, in the second battle for Fort Erie, the new American commander Gen. George Izard was incompetent and, fearing attack from reinforced British forces, retreated from gains made in Canada.

In September, an American success on Lake Champlain forced the British to abort a planned offensive south from Canada. In the Battle of Plattsburg, also called the Battle of Lake Champlain, Gen. Alexander Macomb held Plattsburg, New York, with 3,000 men. Facing threat of invasion by British Gen. George Prevost from Canada, Macomb called upon Vermont and New York militia units and obtained an additional 3,000 men. Twelve thousand veterans of Wellington's army reinforced Prevost. The Americans withdrew behind the natural barrier of the Saranac River south of Plattsburg. The Americans repulsed them, and the British lost 2,500 men and the British Fleet. The British retreated in disorder, abandoning the wounded and equipment.

> The Model 1795 Springfield Arsenal .69-caliber musket was the first standardized U.S. shoulder arm made in a government arsenal. Much like the Revolutionary-era muskets it replaced, it was a smoothbore muzzleloader derived partly from the French Charleville musket, which had been provided in large numbers (23,000 or more) as military assistance during the Revolution. In addition to the U.S. arsenal, which turned out examples from 1795 to 1814, private manufacturers including Eli Whitney produced the weapon.

The .69-caliber musket was replaced by the similar Charleville-derived Model 1812 Flintlock Musket, produced by the Springfield Armory in a quantity approaching 30,000 during 1814–1816. The M1812 was a .69 smoothbore, with a barrel 41 inches in length.

BLADENSBURG

Peace negotiations began in August 1814, but so did the Battle of Bladensburg, Maryland, when British troops marched almost unopposed into Washington. The British still had plenty of flexibility. Because the American navy was weak, the British fleet had been able to blockade American ports from Maine to Chesapeake Bay, where the British had complete freedom to maneuver as they chose. With a naval squadron that included 5,000 troops, British commander Adm. George Cockburn plotted to sow unrest by offering to rescue all slaves and transport them from the mainland to the Caribbean or Canada. The American side hesitated to call out the militia without knowing Cockburn's intention and deliberately left the city of Washington undefended. The British landed troops at the Patuxent River and advanced on Washington. A small number of American forces met the advancing British at Bladensburg, just east of Washington, on August 24, 1814. The Americans were quickly routed. The British advanced into the city and, in retaliation for the earlier American torching of York, burned a number of public buildings, including the White House, the Capitol, the Library of Congress, the buildings housing the State and Treasury Departments, and the Navy Yard. President Madison and his cabinet sought safety in Maryland.

The Potomac squadron anchored off Alexandria, Virginia. The city spared itself by paying a ransom of 16,000 barrels of flour and 1,000 hogsheads of tobacco.

But it was not the victory it appeared to be. The British were able to march into Washington, but they could not take Baltimore, where the beleaguered Americans mounted a strong defense. It was now September 1814. On the scene was 1st Lt. Francis Scott Key (1780–1843), a lawyer and a member of the D.C. Militia who had traveled under military orders to Baltimore to arrange for the release of a physician being held by the British. Detained on a British ship in Baltimore harbor, Key watched the

British bombard Fort McHenry. The commander of the fort, Maj. George Armistead, had asked for a flag so big that "the British would have no trouble seeing it from a distance." While watching it, Key was inspired to write the poem that later became the national anthem. Ultimately, the star-spangled banner continued to wave and the British were foiled in Maryland, just as they had been in Canada—but they still had an army in the Deep South, aimed at the Gulf Coast.

Andrew Jackson took his forces to New Orleans. The Treaty of Ghent (Belgium) was signed on Christmas Eve, 1814, for the purpose of ending the war. The treaty established a clear border between Canada and the United States, and left untouched other issues between the combatants, including the impressment of citizens into the British forces—not an issue because the British no longer needed sailors to fight France. Jackson was right to fight the January 8, 1815, Battle of New Orleans, since the Ghent treaty explicitly called for continued hostilities until ratification by both governments, which did not occur until February 1815.

The city of 20,000, so recently French, had little loyalty to the United States, and its defenses were in poor condition. Jackson declared martial law and set about immediately fortifying New Orleans. He called for volunteers to fight—accepting free blacks and convicts as well as privateers, including the infamous smuggler Lafitte.

The fighting in Louisiana was really a series of battles for New Orleans, beginning in December 1814. Jackson's adversary was Maj. Gen. Sir Edward Pakenham, the 37-year-old brother-in-law of the duke of Wellington and a much-decorated military hero. Pakenham had about 14,000 troops at his disposal, perhaps 8,000 of whom were committed to combat. Jackson's army never numbered more than a few thousand and was poorly equipped, but the men admired Jackson's charisma.

One of the first infantry weapons with a rifled barrel (unlike a musket) was the Kentucky rifle, actually developed in Pennsylvania. It was used by Andrew Jackson's troops in the 1815 Battle of New Orleans.

For the final skirmish in the series at New Orleans, Jackson assembled his troops behind a natural bottleneck between the Mississippi River and the Rodriguez Canal. Pakenham had no choice but to advance into fog against Americans who enjoyed superior defensive positions. Advancing British troops fell beneath volleys of American fire, some becoming fog-shrouded obstacles for the men behind them. Seeing his troops falter, Pakenham cried "Onward!" and "Onward, lads," only to fall, mortally wounded. The British turned and retreated after suffering 1,971 men killed and wounded, while the Americans lost just 71 men. The British withdrew through Lake Borgne and into the Gulf, and were soon gone. The American victory in the Gulf region forced the British to recognize United States claims to Louisiana and West Florida and to ratify the Treaty of Ghent, which ended the war. The Battle of New Orleans also marked Louisiana's incorporation into the Union.

According to Army figures, a total of 528,274 men served in the Army during the War of 1812, including 56,652 regulars and 471,622 volunteers. However, some of these numbers measure enlistments rather than men, meaning that some soldiers were counted more than once. The official casualty total for the Army during the war is 1,950 killed and 4,000 wounded. However, the first figure may be low because it covers only fatalities listed in official records. The figure for the wounded, although a round number, is again a total from official records and is not an estimate. No total was recorded for soldiers who died of disease.

INDIAN FIGHTER

James Monroe, who had been a young soldier tending the Marquis de Lafayette's wounds during the Revolutionary War, served as the nation's fifth president from 1817 to 1825. In foreign policy, he enunciated the Monroe Doctrine, responding to the threat that the more conservative governments in Europe might try to aid Spain in winning back her former Latin American colonies. John Quincy Adams, the son of the nation's second president, followed Monroe to become its sixth president from 1825 to 1829.

With the War of 1812 over, American military men returned their attention to the Indian tribes that peopled the land. In 1817, Polk dispatched Jackson to begin a war of questionable legality that would be America's longest conflict until Vietnam. On the ruse that Florida, which belonged to Spain, was being used as a refuge for escaped slaves and criminals, Jackson launched a military campaign against the Seminoles—a collective term for all Florida Indians, meaning "wild people" or "runaways." Jackson took over the region he invaded. The conflict he began, the First Seminole War, resulted in U.S. acquisition of Florida.

> The American soldier has always carried a weapon and sought a better one. From the musket to the M4 carbine, the soldier has always needed to aim and shoot—but has often been behind soldiers in other armies.
>
> In the Revolutionary War, Colonial soldiers carried a mixture of flintlock muskets. Some were .75-caliber British "Brown Bess" models, and some were French Charleville .69-caliber muskets—both able to mount a bayonet, which was more important than the musket itself as the primary weapon of the infantryman in the 1770s. At Breed's Hill, when Colonial soldiers ran out of ammunition, most had no bayonets to fight with. They had to turn and flee as Redcoats charged into their midst with cold steel.
>
> After the Revolution, the U.S. inaugurated its two arsenals at Springfield, Massachusetts, and Harpers Ferry, Virginia (now West Virginia), and manufactured a standard infantry musket, the U.S. Model 1795 musket. Soon existing flintlock muskets were modified to become percussion muskets. Still, these weapons had to be loaded at the muzzle, even though the technology to produce a breech-loading weapon had existed for years.
>
> The U.S. did not keep up with developments overseas; by 1840, the German army was manufacturing breech-loading, bolt-action, cartridge-loading rifles.
>
> The development of the Minie ball improved the accuracy of rifles up to 200 yards, producing a devastating increase in firepower. The Minie ball was actually a lead bullet with a hollow tail that followed a straighter course than the spherical musket ball. Soldiers could now fire a rifle as rapidly as a smoothbore weapon, but from farther away. The increased range now given to the infantryman was responsible for much of the horrific carnage of Civil War fighting. Because it was no longer practical to close to within arm's length, the increased range of Minie ball–firing weapons also meant that bayonet fighting became infrequent between 1861 and 1865.

BETWEEN WARS

Andrew Jackson, also called "Old Hickory" (and, by his detractors, "King Andrew"), took office as the seventh U.S. president in 1829. His nickname derived from the standard ramrod for a flintlock rifle during this period—metal-tipped, but made entirely of hickory wood, which enjoyed a reputation for never bending.

Jackson proclaimed his belief that government duties could be "so plain and simple" that offices should rotate among deserving applicants. He was an unabashed expansionist. Jackson was rough-hewn, a quality to Americans, and was a national hero for defeating the British in the Battle of New Orleans. As national politics polarized around Jackson and his opposition, two parties grew out of the old Republican Party: the Democratic Republicans, or Democrats, adhering to Jackson; and the National Republicans, or Whigs, opposing him.

Jackson was an ardent proponent of "removal"—a popular term—of Native American peoples from the Southeast, especially those of five tribes that had reached a high level of civilization: the Cherokee, Chickasaw, Choctaw, Creek, and Seminole tribes. Jackson easily won passage of the Indian Removal Act in 1830 that uprooted thousands from their lands. It was no coincidence that these Indians resided on lands that were fertile for the growing of tobacco and cotton. The First Seminole War suppressed one group that Jackson and his supporters had picked for "removal." The U.S. government moved tens of thousands from other tribes and seized their land.

Though not a warlike people, the Seminoles continued to resist long after the government sought to move them to Oklahoma. After Jackson became president, the conflict, only simmering at that point, heated up again into the Second Seminole War.

Brig. Gen. Zachary Taylor (1784–1850), called "Old Rough and Ready," fought in Florida's swamps for a time until he was replaced by Gen. Walker Keith Armistead in 1840. Army and Navy troops sought out the Seminoles, undeterred by the forbidding Florida Everglades, using flat-bottomed boats, canoes, and bloodhounds. The American public became increasingly critical of the inhumane methods and had ceased to support the effort by April 1842, when the last battle pitted Brig. Gen. William Worth (1794–1849) and 400 soldiers against a mere 40 Seminoles near Lake Ahapopka. (Worth also became a veteran of the Mexican War and a hero in Texas, where Fort Worth was named for him.)

Ultimately, more than 10,000 troops served in three Seminole Wars (1817–1818, 1835–1842, 1849–1858), often viewed by Native Americans as a single, continuous conflict. A total of 1,466 American soldiers died, 328 in combat. Surviving Seminoles were uprooted and shipped west.

With the possible exception of Taylor, who fought recklessly and sustained high casualties, none of the Army officers in the Seminole conflicts emerged with a good reputation or future career prospects.

> Battlefields of the nineteenth century were heavily forested, so military scouts preceding an army moved through the woods and marked the best path by hacking pieces of bark from tree trunks, creating blazes. From them we get the term *trailblazer* and the phrase "blazing a trail."

WAR WITH MEXICO

In 1845, journalist John L. O'Sullivan coined the phrase "manifest destiny" to express the almost religious fervor many Americans felt toward expanding their nation westward. In keeping with the expansionist mood, it was perhaps inevitable that Americans would fight a new war not for their independence, not on principle, but for the naked purpose of seizing territory and annexing it. It was a war for which, as would be typical through history, the Army was not well prepared.

In 1845, on the eve of war with Mexico over the annexation of Texas, the Army had an authorized strength of 8,613 and actual troops numbering only about 7,200, including generals and staff officers. There were two regiments of dragoons—no other cavalry—along with eight 10-company regiments of infantry, and four of artillery, of which one company in each regiment was mounted as a light horse or horse battery, also called the "flying artillery." There was also a corps of 45 officers of engineers, among them Capts. Robert E. Lee (1807–1870), George B. McClellan (1826–1885), and George G. Meade (1815–1872). For three decades, this Army had fought no one but a few Indian tribes.

The previous year, the House of Representatives voted on a measure to abolish the new military academy at West Point. The Jacksonian era was the time of the common man, and the mood of the nation was distrust of any aristocracy, including a military one. Jackson, now aging and infirm, had been followed in the presidency by Martin Van Buren, from 1837 to 1841; William Henry Harrison, for a few weeks in 1841; and John Tyler, who held the office from 1841 to 1845—all the eighth, ninth, and tenth presidents, to some degree Jacksonians, distrusted nobility. In Tyler's penultimate year in office, a measure to deny the military academy's appropriations was defeated by just a single vote. Most of the Army's great captains and heroes in the Mexican War, the Civil War, and the Spanish American War were alumni of West Point's Long Gray Line.

Still, a candidate for public office had better chances as a watchdog of the people's money than as a supporter of the military. For most of the nation's history, this was the American way, and it continued until 1948, when Harry S. Truman became the last presidential candidate to campaign on a pledge to reduce military spending. In 1845, with limited funding and even less support in the swamp along the Potomac River that had become Washington, the Army was stretched to its limit. Small detachments of troops were underequipped and overworked against the Indians on the frontier while pulling lethargic garrison duty at home.

On the other side, Mexico was a nation of eight million people. The Mexican Army had only recently reshaped itself after a preposterous situation in which it had 24,000 officers in a force of 44,000 men. Even on the eve of war, with its strength around 32,000, including the 9,000 militia that were always kept under arms, Mexico had more than 200 generals. This was a top-heavy and corrupt arrangement, but many elite units were well trained and highly disciplined, and many troops were veterans of Mexico's recent struggle for independence from Spain.

The Mexican army had 12 battalions of regular infantry, most of them armed with muskets gotten secondhand from the British army, and 12 regiments of cavalry, nearly all of them lancers. Three brigades of artillery were equipped with an inefficient gun of French design and manned by troops with little training. The typical Mexican soldier was an Indian or a poor laborer, sometimes kept in check by being tied or handcuffed, and desertion rates were high. Still, Mexican troops seemed inexhaustible on the march and often fought with considerable courage.

"POLK'S WAR"

On April 24, 1846, Brig. Gen. Zachary Taylor—"Old Rough and Ready"—positioned 3,500 troops on the north bank of the Rio Grande and peered across the river. Taylor held an order from President James K. Polk (1795–1849) to invade and occupy much of the territory on the Mexican side. Taylor was 51 years of age, and his military experience was limited to a short period of campaigning against the Seminoles three decades earlier, where Taylor's actions had been characterized more by brutality than shrewdness.

Polk became the nation's eleventh president in 1845. Following the forgettable Whig administration of John Tyler, Polk was a slight Tennessee lawyer and Democrat cut from the mold of Andrew Jackson and rooted in expansionism and manifest destiny. Polk campaigned on the argument that Texas should be "re-annexed" and all of Oregon should be "re-occupied." Polk also favored acquiring California. Whigs like Henry Clay opposed Polk's expansionist views, and Clay himself came within a narrow margin of defeating Polk in the campaign for the nation's top office. Clay would not have authorized the Mexican War. Some believe he might even have been able to mediate the deeply rooted tensions that soon would lead to the Civil War.

To be sure, Polk had a considerable following. Polk linked the Texas issue, popular in the South, with the Oregon question, attractive to the North. Even before Polk could take office, Congress passed a joint resolution offering annexation to Texas—giving the new president free rein to wage war on Mexico.

With his closely related expansionist position on Oregon, Polk appeared to be risking war with Great Britain. The 1844 Democratic platform called for the United States to annex Texas, as it did on March 1, 1845—ending Texas's nine years as a republic with broad support by Texans, who overwhelmingly favored joining the Union. Polk's platform also claimed the entire Oregon area, from the California boundary northward to a latitude of 54°, 40', the southern boundary of Russian Alaska. Extremists proclaimed "Fifty-four forty or fight!" Polk, aware of diplomatic realities, knew that no course short of war was likely to get all of Oregon.

Polk offered to settle the Oregon question by extending the Canadian boundary, along the forty-ninth parallel, from the Rockies to the Pacific. When the British declined, Polk reasserted the American claim to the entire area. Finally, the British settled for the forty-ninth parallel, except for the southern tip of Vancouver Island. The treaty was signed in 1846. Polk was not eager for war with Britain and was relieved to avoid it, but he had no such reluctance about war with Mexico.

The annexation of Texas was likely, but Polk's efforts to acquire California proved elusive. Polk sent an envoy to offer Mexico up to $20 million for California and the New Mexico country. Since no Mexican leader could cede half his country and remain in power, Polk's envoy was not received. To bring pressure, Polk sent Zachary Taylor to the disputed area on the Rio Grande. On April 26, 1846, Mexican forces killed 16 of Taylor's cavalrymen on a foray across the Rio Grande. The general sent a report to Polk: "Hostilities may now be considered as commenced." Congress declared war.

PALO ALTO BATTLE

On May 8, 1846, with his "flying artillery" providing an enormous advantage over a numerically superior Mexican force, Taylor defeated troops led by Gen. Mariano Arista in the Battle of Palo Alto. The victory immediately prompted newspaper reporters to tout Taylor as the next Whig president. Much of the credit for the battlefield success belonged to the "flying artillery," which performed so well that young Lt. Ulysses S. "Sam" Grant (1822–1885) said that he and his fellow infantrymen were largely spectators. The Americans killed or wounded about 500 Mexicans, with the loss of just 9 men. Mortally wounded in the fight was Maj. Samuel Ringgold (1795–1846), who was largely responsible for creating and fielding the mobile artillery force.

Taylor launched a campaign against Mexican forces, crossed into Mexico, and halted at Matamoros in early summer. Once supplies and reinforcements arrived, and his ranks were filled out with volunteers, he marched on Monterrey. Among his many soldiers was artillery 2nd Lt. Abner Doubleday (1819–1893), later a leader at Gettysburg and still later credited with inventing the game of baseball. Taylor had 6,200 men in all, but an entrenched force of 10,000 defended Monterrey.

Taylor led the attack on Monterrey from the east. He sent Brig. Gen. William Worth with a strong detachment to make an assault from the west. Worth captured the key defensive position of Federation Hill on September 21 and Independence Hill the following day. Meanwhile, progress into the city was slow, difficult, and costly, despite help from volunteer Texans who were experienced in this kind of fighting. Taylor thrust into the city on September 21 and, in hard fighting, drove the garrison into the Citadel (Black Fort). Blockaded on all sides, Gen. Pedro de Ampudia surrendered three days later. The Americans lost 488 soldiers, including 120 killed; the defenders suffered 367 casualties. After achieving a clear victory over a tenacious foe, Taylor allowed surviving Mexican troops to pass through his lines and escape. Militarily, it was a huge strategic error. It was also a decision that infuriated Polk.

SANTA ANNA

Hoping to bring about a leadership change that would resolve the situation with Mexico to his liking, President Polk allowed the return to Mexico, through the U.S. naval blockade, of one-legged Gen. Antonio Lopez de Santa Anna (1802–1854), the exiled leader who had besieged the Alamo before Texas became first independent and then a state. Arriving in Mexico City, Santa Anna immediately double-crossed the American president, proclaiming himself the savior of his nation. Polk, already unhappy with Taylor, vented much of his anger on Old Rough and Ready, transferring nearly all of Taylor's troops to the command of Maj. Gen. Winfield Scott.

Taylor retained command of almost 5,000 men, however. On February 22, 1847, Santa Anna's forces attacked them at Buena Vista. Though the Mexican general had 14,000 men in the battle, Taylor was able to repel them and achieve a modest victory. It was a very close thing, however, and again superior American artillery made the difference.

One leader in the Buena Vista battle was cavalryman Col. Jefferson Davis (1808–1889), who had reconciled with Taylor after a feud over Davis's marriage to Taylor's daughter—by this time, deceased. In later years, critics accused Davis of forming too high an opinion of his own military genius during this battle in Mexico, with unpleasant results for the Confederacy. Also on the scene at Buena Vista was Lt. Col. Braxton Bragg (1817–1876), to become a figure in the Confederacy in just a few years.

As for the forces under Scott, they were being led by a man with combat experience dating to 1812. Enamored with the trappings of rank, Scott was dubbed "Old Fuss and Feathers," with some calling him a martinet. On March 9, 1847, he pulled off a landing and an easy victory at Vera Cruz, helped, no doubt, by a staff that included Capt. Robert E. Lee. After skirmishing and defeating Mexican troops and accepting the surrender of 3,000, troops in Lee's sector discovered that the fleeing Santa Anna had left behind his wooden leg. Scott's troops lost just 63 killed at Vera Cruz.

Scott could have marched on Mexico City immediately but balked when 3,000 of his troops complained that their enlistments were up. He was also deterred by the approach of the yellow fever season. After months of delay, Scott advanced on the Mexican capital in August 1847, and Santa Anna prepared to defend it. A key battle took place at Chapultapec, the Mexican military academy, where junior officers under Scott included Grant, McClellan, and the Virginia mountaineer Capt. Thomas J. Jackson (1824–1863), who was not yet called "Stonewall." While some of Scott's Americans struggled with great difficulty against a force of just 600, mostly cadets, at Chapultapec, others stormed the gates of Mexico City where engineer troops under McClellan blasted holes in the walls of buildings to facilitate the attack. The walls of Chapultapec were more difficult to breach, and at one juncture 1st Lt. Lewis Armistead (1817–1863) and James Longstreet (1821–1904) both sustained wounds, while 1st Lt. George Pickett (1825–1875) came behind them and scrambled up a ladder to the top. Armistead, Longstreet, and Pickett were well acquainted two decades before their names rallied Confederate troops at Gettysburg.

The five-month campaign from Vera Cruz to Mexico City led by Scott—later to be a figure of some ridicule at the start of the Civil War—was one of the most brilliant successes in the Army's history. The duke of Wellington wrote, "His campaign was unsurpassed in military annals."

While the campaign continued in Mexico, American troops prevailed in New Mexico and California. Their successes ensured the defeat of Mexico and the annexation of vast lands by the United States.

> The Mexican War (1846–1848) taught important lessons to the Army, including a generation of junior officers who met later as generals in the Civil War.
>
> Most important was the value of leadership. Thanks to the Military Academy at West Point, New York, the United States had a cadre of professional officers the equal of any in the world at the art of war. The future of the Academy was rarely questioned after Gen. Winfield Scott's victory at Mexico City ended the fighting.

Planning was crucial. In one battle in which lava fields proved difficult to traverse, engineer officer Capt. Robert E. Lee prepared by learning the terrain, enabling troops to clear physical barriers, outflank the Mexicans, and attack by surprise.

The war taught the importance of the field artillery, the "King of Battle." American artillery reached farther than Mexican guns and was more accurate. To attack American positions, Mexican troops had to run through a veritable hell of artillery fire.

Another lesson was about rifling. Both infantry weapons and cannons worked better with rifling in the barrel. Most troops were still using muskets rather than rifles, and artillery was still smoothbore, but this would change in short order.

An important invention was the percussion cap, developed by a Scottish cleric who found, when duck hunting, that his prey would fly away at the initial flash of a flintlock. Replacing the flint (which was useless in rain), the percussion cap made muskets, rifles, and pistols easier to load, less delicate, and less likely to expose the shooter's location.

WAR'S END

During the Mexican War, the Army grew from a few thousand to 115,000 men, about 1.5 percent of whom died in the fighting. The official total of soldiers who served is 116,597, including 43,300 regulars and 73,297 volunteers. Casualties included 1,044 killed in action, 505 who died of wounds and 3,393 who were wounded. As in previous wars, the number of soldiers killed by disease was not tallied, but the figure is well above 10,000. The Army also lost 361 soldiers to accidents, an official total that is probably low, and 50 to executions. The nation had a new cadre of career officers who had learned about combat by being in the middle of it. The Army learned a great deal about leadership, training, weapons, and tactics from the Mexican War (see earlier sidebar), but the larger result that emerged from the war—a vastly expanded United States—contained the seeds of a greater conflict.

In 1848, the Treaty of Guadalupe Hidalgo ended the war with Mexico. The treaty reaffirmed Texas as part of the United States. It gave the United States the future states of Arizona, Nevada, and Utah, and it ceded New Mexico and California in return for $15 million and American assumption of the damage claims. The war ensured that the United States would expand from coast to coast, but it did little to settle the differences within the growing nation—especially those over slavery.

The nation was divided, not over any moral question about slavery, but over whether the new territories would be free or slave states. The agrarian South, which relied on slave labor for its products, did not want the country's slave states to be outnumbered by states where slavery was not practiced.

Zachary Taylor, the nation's twelfth president from 1849 until his sudden death in 1850, had no ready plan for the newly acquired territories or for the nation's differences over slavery. Taylor urged settlers in New Mexico and California to draft constitutions and apply for statehood, bypassing the interim stage of becoming territories.

Southerners were furious, since neither state constitution was likely to permit slavery. Members of Congress were dismayed, since they felt Taylor was usurping their policy-making prerogatives. In addition, Taylor's solution ignored two acute side issues: the Northern dislike of the slave market operating in the District of Columbia, and the Southern demands for a more stringent fugitive slave law.

In February 1850, President Taylor held a stormy conference with Southern leaders who threatened secession. He told them that, if it was necessary to enforce the laws, he personally would lead the Army. Anyone "taken in rebellion against the Union," Taylor vowed, would hang.

Taylor's death that year allowed passage of the Compromise of 1850. The Compromise admitted California as a free state but placed no restrictions on slavery in New Mexico (which was given territorial status), Utah, and Texas. It included a strong Fugitive Slave Act wanted in the South, which endangered even freed African Americans who had been living safely in the North for years, and led to unrest and violence. Millard Fillmore (1800–1874), the thirteenth president, a lawyer with no military experience, signed the legislation that brought about the Compromise of 1850. Fillmore appointed Daniel Webster to be secretary of state, thus proclaiming his alliance with the moderate Whigs who favored the Compromise.

The Compromise of 1850 was intended to settle the slavery controversy, but it functioned only as a temporary truce.

WEAK FACES

Franklin Pierce (1804–1869), like his predecessor, not a military man, handily defeated Whig General Winfield to become the fourteenth U.S. president in 1853. At his 1853 inauguration, Pierce said the United States might have to acquire more new territories for the sake of security—a gesture toward expansion that angered Northerners, who called him a cat's paw of Southerners eager to extend slavery into new regions. While some believed the storm had passed—the Compromise of 1850, they felt, would prevent the Union from being torn asunder—Pierce was ineffectual. On his watch, a handful of Washington politicians created a new political party, the Republicans.

Also during Pierce's term, the Kansas-Nebraska Act reopened the question of slavery in the West. This measure, the handiwork of Sen. Stephen A. Douglas (1813–1861), was aimed at organizing western territories through which a railroad might run. Trouble arose because Douglas provided in his bills that residents of the territories could decide the slavery question for themselves. This led to a rush into Kansas, as Southerners and Northerners vied for control. Shooting broke out. The violence killed more than 200 and can be viewed as a prelude to the Civil War. At the end of his administration, the Democrats did not even renominate Pierce, preferring the similarly innocuous James Buchanan (1791–1868).

When Gen. Stephen W. Kearny (1794–1848) moved 1,600 troops into New Mexico in June 1846, he began the swiftest and most effective campaign of the Mexican War. Kearny seized New Mexico easily and continued to California, where he fought and lost the Battle of San Pasqual against Mexicans commanded by Captain Andres Pico. The battle did give Americans a legitimate claim to the territory, and, thanks to Commodore John D. Sloat, John C. Frémont, and others, this Mexican province eventually came under American control.

Buchanan served as the fifteenth president from 1857 to 1861. Another ineffectual Democrat, he is remembered mostly as the only American chief executive never to marry. Buchanan could not handle the stresses on the nation that were building toward the Civil War; by the time Abraham Lincoln became president in 1861, he may have known that war was inevitable. In his inaugural address, Lincoln said, "In your hands, my dissatisfied fellow countrymen, and not in mine, is the momentous issue of civil war." Referring to secessionists, he added, "You have no oath registered in Heaven to destroy the government, while I shall have the most solemn one to preserve, protect, and defend it."

Throughout much of the 1850s, the nation had a small frontier Army, whose purpose was to guard against Indian tribes. But it was not the same Army as before the Mexican War. Communications were altered forever by the advent of the field telegraph. Rifled barrels, more powerful explosives, and lighter guns made weaponry more lethal.

CHAPTER 4

THE CIVIL WAR (1860–1865)

On April 12, 1861, Confederate gun batteries fired upon Fort Sumter, the Union bastion in the harbor at Charleston, South Carolina. Thus began the worst war ever fought in the Western Hemisphere. A week later, President Abraham Lincoln (1809–1865), who served as the nation's sixteenth president from 1861 to 1865, issued a proclamation declaring a blockade of Southern ports from South Carolina to Texas.

The Civil War, it's called today. At the time, it had other names. The War of the Southern Rebellion was the term used in the North at the time. To many in the South, it was called the War of Northern Aggression. Even today, Americans are sharply divided over virtually every aspect of the war, including its name.

It was a war that shaped the Army, changed the Army, and brought the nation firmly to the era of modern industrial warfare. In military terms, the war was a clash by armies using old tactics even though warfare had been made bloodier by the advent of new weapons.

When the Civil War began, the Union Army consisted of just over 16,000 troops, stretched from the Atlantic coastline to the

Canadian border and along the expanding frontier territories. The Army's own figures showed that on January 1, 1861, the Army numbered 1,098 officers and 15,259 enlisted men organized into 19 regiments (10 infantry, 4 artillery, 2 dragoon, 2 cavalry, and 1 mounted rifles). Of the 198 company-size units in these regiments, 183 were scattered at 79 posts along the frontiers. The other 15 units manned posts along the Atlantic Coast and the Canadian border, and the arsenals.

Neither army initially had draftees. Both had senior officers who had been junior officers during the fighting in Mexico. Both had officers and common soldiers who had no idea what they were getting into. The last war that most Americans had fought began in 1812, 49 years before. The last predominately ground war had been the American Revolution, and there were few alive with memories of it.

CAUSING A WAR

Among the causes of the Civil War were unfinished disagreements left over from the original Constitutional debates—the power of the states versus that of the federal government, and the issue of slavery. The compromises of 1820 and 1850 did not adequately address how slave states and free states would be balanced. The South wanted to ensure that at least a one-third portion of the Senate represented slave states. This could block major portions of legislation, such as an amendment to end slavery. Abolitionists were committed to reducing the South's hold on a blocking voting group and ending slavery by Constitutional amendment.

All of this was exacerbated by the encouragement of antislavery and slave-supporting factions across the nation with John Brown's raid and hanging; the Supreme Court's Dred Scott decision, which treated slaves as property; and the 1852 publication of *Uncle Tom's Cabin*, by Harriet Beecher Stowe, which emphasized the brutal nature of slavery instead of the myth of Negro happiness on Southern plantations.

The causes of the Civil War will be debated as long as humans live. It was about slavery to many, and yet both sides fielded valorous soldiers who had no stake in the issue. A combination of factors led to secession and to war—the issue of states' rights as opposed to a strong central government, slavery (a minor issue to many Southerners who did not own slaves, and to most Northerners who did not care about the plight of the slaves), and the tensions and rivalries between an agrarian society in the South and an industrial society in the North.

The people of the South did not want those in the North telling them how to conduct their affairs. There was no way to compromise, and war came. To cynics, it was a conflict in which wealthy businessmen supported Lincoln in order to prevent a large free-trade zone (the South) from existing next to a tariff-protected fledgling industrialist region (the North). Ultimately, the cause of the Civil War was the election of Abraham Lincoln as president, the spark that ignited the secession of South Carolina. Lincoln thought secession was illegal and was willing to use force to defend federal law and the Union.

The two sides in the Civil War sought different goals. The Union (the North, the Federals) wanted to bring back into the fold all of the states that had seceded, a task which almost certainly required invading and holding terrain. The Confederacy (the South, the Rebels) merely wanted secession to become an accomplished fact and to remain separate and apart, a task that could be achieved by tiring the North of the willingness to fight—as might have happened, for example, had Gen. Robert E. Lee won at Gettysburg.

The South lost the war because it lacked the resources for a long-term conflict and a strong central government. The North created a strong central government because it won the war. While the North's goal was to preserve the Union, it succeeded instead in creating a nation. Before the war, distances were great and travel was inconvenient and consumed time. Consider riding a horse from Louisville or Nashville or Atlanta to Washington, D.C., to participate in government. Governing from state capitals was much more efficient than from Washington just by virtue of the distance from the constituency. After the Civil War, the parochial governments of the states were no longer subordinate to the strong central government that became the norm.

To the casual student, the Civil War is rife with problems of terminology. In many cases, the two sides had different names for the same battle, beginning with the First Battle of Bull Run (the North's term), alias First Manassas (the South's). Nor did the two sides make it easier for us later to understand the names of their military formations. Both armies had a top soldier (on the Union side, called the "general-in-chief" by historians, but known as the "commanding general" by the Army's own history office), who was not always the same leader as the general in the field. The "Army of the Potomac" was the main Union army in the eastern theater of the war, and the "Army of Northern Virginia" was the main Confederate force. But after the war began, the North also had its own "Army of Virginia." Despite the training that most had received at West Point, both sides also had an excess of indecisive, incompetent generals who exercised poor leadership or none. There were repeated changes in leadership before the two top generals emerged in the highest jobs in their respective armies—Ulysses S. Grant and Robert E. Lee.

BEGINNING A FIGHT

On February 8, 1861, the Confederate States of America adopted a constitution; the following day, Jefferson Davis, a veteran of the Mexican War, became President of the Confederacy. On March 4, Abraham Lincoln was inaugurated as President of the United States. Remarkably, even at this late juncture, not all the Southern states had seceded. South Carolina, Florida, Alabama, Georgia, Louisiana, and Texas had already withdrawn from the Union. But others were still waiting and planning.

It was only after the Confederacy seized Fort Sumter in Charleston harbor that Virginia, Arkansas, North Carolina, and Tennessee also seceded from the Union. It may have been the opening shot of the war, but the actual battle at Fort Sumter was brief and largely symbolic. South Carolina militia under Brig. Gen. Pierre G. T. Beauregard (1818–1893) bombarded the garrison. After 34 hours of barrage, with neither supplies nor reinforcements in sight, the commander of the fort surrendered without a single casualty.

One way of looking at Fort Sumter is to see it as a seizure rather than the start of a war: All other federal property in the seceding states had been captured without incident, most being readily handed over by the caretakers. Only in Charleston harbor did the Union make a stand against a takeover of its property. Instead of making plans to retake the fort, Lincoln began raising 15,000 troops for an invasion. This prompted wavering border states to move toward secession and contributed to the Union's loss of Robert E. Lee and other key players who didn't necessarily support secession but weren't going to fight their own people at home, either.

Lee could have been the Union's top soldier. Urged by 75-year-old Gen. Winfield Scott, general-in-chief of the Army—gout-stricken and too overweight to mount a horse—President Lincoln requested Lee to take command of Union forces in the field. But by then, Virginia had decided to secede, an especially damaging loss to the Union, given Virginia's size and proximity to Washington, D.C. Torn by conflicting loyalties, Lee elected instead to accept a commission in the Virginia state forces, which were 40,000 strong by the time they were transferred to the Confederate Army on June 8, 1861. The Confederate government, initially situated in Montgomery, Alabama, was moved to Richmond.

In the Confederate Army, eight men eventually reached the rank of full general. Listed in rank order, they are as follows:

Samuel Cooper
Albert S. Johnston
Robert E. Lee
Joseph E. Johnston
Pierre G. T. Beauregard
Braxton Bragg
E. Kirby Smith (Provisional Army)
John B. Hood (Provisional Army, with temporary rank)

FIRST BULL RUN

July 21, 1861, marked the battle known as First Bull Run in the North and as First Manassas in the South. Some 32,000 Union troops commanded by Brig. Gen. Irvin McDowell (1818–1885) set forth, with McDowell expecting to bring a swift and easy end to the Southern rebellion. They ran into 25,000 Confederate troops led by Beauregard on the south bank of Bull Run in Manassas, Virginia. By the standards of battles that came later, this was an engagement of only modest size, but it changed the thinking of the Army and the divided nation.

The common soldiers on both sides were enthusiastic young volunteers in bright new uniforms. Many were certain they were about to participate in the only battle of a very short war. Most on the Union side were "90-day men," whose enlistments were soon to expire. They foresaw easy victory—a quick march to Richmond, 80 miles to the south, followed by a quick end to the Confederacy. On the other side, the troops from the South needed only to hold out, since the Southern states were seeking merely to secede, not to conquer the North.

Both sides were confident. McDowell was under strong pressure from Lincoln to achieve success and expected to succeed even though his troops were poorly trained and equipped.

Like their opponents, the Confederate troops were more colorful than capable. But although they were little trained and unready, they put up a strong fight. Beauregard planned to attack across the river on his right, turning McDowell's left flank, but instead he absorbed an assault by McDowell to the Confederates' left and center. Gen. Thomas Jackson earned his nickname as "Stonewall," by holding his position under heavy Union fire. Jackson's demeanor inspired General Bernard Bee to shout to his troops, "Look, men, there is Jackson standing like a stone wall! Let us determine to die here, and we will conquer!" It was largely a battle of amateurs, and the outcome was in doubt as late as midafternoon.

That was when Confederate reinforcements arrived belonging to the Army of the Shenandoah under Gen. Joseph E. Johnston (1807–1891). Johnston, who was senior in rank to Beauregard, hastily pulled his troops out of Harpers Ferry, Virginia—until then, the Confederacy's northernmost bastion—and rushed to the scene by rail. Amid his precipitous departure, Johnston burned bridges and destroyed a considerable amount of rolling stock, to prevent both from being useful to the North. The move angered many in adjacent Maryland, dampening support for the South by many in that wavering state.

Johnston's troops and those led by Col. Jubal Early (1816–1894) came on the field at Manassas in late afternoon and helped push back the Union right flank. A brigade led by Brig. Gen. James Longstreet (1821–1904) also took the field against McDowell's federal troops.

In the end, Union troops turned tail and ran for Washington. The Union suffered about 2,700 casualties; the Confederates lost about 1,900. The Confederate side rounded up about 1,600 prisoners. In the early days of the war, there would be intermittent prisoner exchanges; they would cease later in the conflict, and thousands would suffer terribly in captivity. Beauregard told his superiors that the Union side also lost "thousands of fugitives" who ran from the battle, deserting under fire.

In Washington, the Union was stunned. No more would ladies and gentlemen climb aboard their carriages and travel to Centreville, overlooking the battle, to picnic and observe. Their picnic was, of course, disrupted: A few died and the rest scurried back to Washington in panic. Lincoln's Secretary of War, Edwin M. Stanton (1814–1869), always something of a worrier in any event, feared the capital would fall within range of the South's field artillery. Five days after the battle, Stanton wrote to Lincoln, "The capture of Washington seems now to be inevitable."

Could the South have seized the initiative and followed fleeing federal troops into Washington? Confederate soldiers possibly could have entered the capital, seized Lincoln and his cabinet, and dictated an armistice that would have made Southern secession a fact of life. The capture of Washington in any form would surely have brought the Confederacy the support from Europe it desperately wanted and needed.

It was the first of at least two occasions when the opportunity presented itself and was not taken. Confederate President Jefferson Davis, who had conferred with Beauregard and Johnston on the battlefield before returning to Richmond, later noted that he possessed no communication to explain why Rebel forces were prevented from "prolonged vigorous pursuit of the enemy to and beyond the Potomac." The quote reflects enmity between Beauregard, who felt he had been given inadequate supplies and support, and Davis, who faulted Beauregard for dithering—a dispute that Johnston stayed out of. Davis later claimed that he had ordered the generals to pursue Union forces, a claim both denied.

The two sides still had little idea of the magnitude of the conflict they were embarking on.

DEVELOPMENTS IN 1861

First Manassas occurred due to political and social pressures to end the war quickly (both sides thought it would be a short war) and was fought by green troops who had received little, if any, military training.

First Manassas brought about a fundamental change in the way Americans perceived war, and not just on the part of those Washingtonians who had expected to watch the fight while picnicking. Afterward, some soldiers would still compose sentimental ballads, write flowery letters, or create artistic pictures of the romance and glory of war, but none who had been on a battlefield would again see war as anything but noise, horror, stench, strife, and death. Within the Army, professional officers had known much of this all along, but the common soldier was still to learn.

Lincoln replaced McDowell as Commander of the Department of the Potomac, meaning all troops in the Washington area, with 35-year-old Maj. Gen. George B. McClellan, a vigorous and strong-headed military figure who was also a saddle designer. Lincoln believed McClellan could restore the morale of the beaten Union Army and rebuild it for future operations. McClellan achieved exactly that after a meeting with the president while he continued lobbying for the higher position of Army general-in-chief. Soon afterward, the temporary enlistees in the ranks were gone, replaced by troops on three-year enlistments who became the core of what was soon called the Army of the Potomac. Credit for transforming an amateur Army into a real one belongs in large measure to McClellan, who organized, imposed discipline, and took care of the obvious first priority by reinforcing Washington so that it would not be vulnerable to attack. A month after his appointment, McClellan designated his force the Army of the Potomac and had molded it into a formidable fighting machine, more than 100,000 men strong.

In the East, there followed many months of inactivity for the main armies. The action shifted to the West, where the next fight began on August 10, 1861. The Battle of Wilson's Creek in Missouri was a defeat for Union forces led by Gen. John Frémont (1813–1890), called "The Pathfinder of the West" for his explorations in California. Wilson's Creek was a small but costly duel: The Union force of 5,400 men lost about 1,200; the Confederate force, twice as large, also lost about 1,200 in battle. As for Frémont, he commanded the Western Department of the Union Army, but his failure to defend Missouri removed from the war a border state that had not yet joined the Confederacy. In due course, Lincoln removed him from the position.

BALL'S BLUFF

McClellan, worried that Johnston's Confederate Army might cross the Potomac near Leesburg, Virginia, sent the 6,500-man division of Brig.

Gen. Charles P. Stone (1824–1887) to Poolesville, Maryland, to guard river approaches to Rebel-held Leesburg. An official Army history tells us that the opposing armies had some contact with little hostility: Confederate and Union pickets sometimes traded newspapers, tobacco, and other items by making small rafts and allowing them to drift across the Potomac to the other side. They occasionally shouted to each other in friendly conversation and less often fired shots at each other, but mostly they waited.

> Civil War soldiers slept in conical Sibley tents, named for Confederate Gen. Henry Sibley (1811–1891). The tents were meant for 12 soldiers, lying on straw, but they often held twice as many. Six-man and two-man tents also were used. Troops without shelter often dug "gopher holes" for warmth while sleeping.

McClellan ordered Stone to move closer to Leesburg, pondering a possible takeover of the city. After sparring and maneuvering by both sides, on October 21, 1861, Stone's Union troops faced off against Confederate forces in the Battle of Ball's Bluff, named for the 100-foot-high ground overlooking Harrison's Island on the Potomac. With 1,600 men, Confederate Brig. Gen. Nathan G. "Shanks" Evans (1824–1868) halted Stone's badly coordinated attempt to cross the Potomac with 2,000 Union soldiers at Harrison's Island and capture Leesburg. Stone probably had the troops and the momentum to take the city, but inadequate communication between commanders and logistical problems hampered his effort, and he found himself reeling backward instead of seizing ground.

The Confederate counterattack drove the Federals over the bluff and into the river. The Rebels captured more than 700 Federals. Ball's Bluff marked the only time a member of Congress was killed in action. Lincoln's friend and Illinois native Sen. (and Col.) Edward Baker (1811–1861), who had moved to Oregon before being elected to the Senate, was shot six times in the head. One of the president's sons was named Edward Baker Lincoln.

This Union rout, coming on the heels of First Manassas, had severe ramifications in Washington. It encouraged distrust and doubts among the officer corps, including the suspicion by many that West Pointers were Southern sympathizers. In a war where careers rose and fell, Ball's Bluff made Stone the target of public and congressional criticism. A few months after the battle, the Army arrested him in the middle of the night and confined him for 189 days without conferring charges. Stone did not fight again in the Civil War, but in 1886 he received recognition as co-designer of the 150-foot pedestal that supports the Statue of Liberty in New York Harbor. On the other side, Evans was later court-martialed for drunkenness and acquitted. Although he fought aggressively at both First Manassas and Ball's Bluff, Evans never had a significant role in the war.

The Union defeat at Ball's Bluff prompted establishment of the Congressional Joint Committee on the Conduct of the War. Congressional oversight of military conduct on the battlefield became a permanent part of the American system. Ball's Bluff prompted Lincoln to remove the hefty, ailing Scott from the top job in the Army. Although McClellan was in many respects a student of Scott's, he was also contemptuous of Scott and had sharpened his campaign for the job of general-in-chief. McClellan got the nod from Lincoln on November 1, 1861. Soon afterward, however, McClellan became ill, one of many factors that contributed to a period of little military activity in the winter of 1861–1862.

1862

While a period of inactivity marked the conflict along the eastern seaboard, on February 6, 1862, Brig. Gen. Ulysses S. Grant began a campaign in the Mississippi Valley. Grant's troops captured Fort Henry, Tennessee, on the Tennessee River. Grant then advanced cross-country to assault Fort Donelson, near Nashville. On February 16, after the failure of an all-out attack aimed at breaking through Grant's lines, the fort's 12,000-man Confederate garrison surrendered. This was a major win for Grant and a catastrophe for the South. It ensured that Kentucky would stay in the Union and opened up Tennessee for a Federal advance along the Tennessee and Cumberland rivers. For Grant's opponent, the tall, powerfully built Maj. Gen. Albert S. Johnston (1803–1862), Fort Donelson meant the loss of about a quarter of his army and more than half the state of Tennessee. Promoted to major general, Grant was dubbed "Unconditional Surrender"—a word play on his initials and also the terms of surrender he had demanded at Fort Donelson—within the Army.

> In 1862, Union soldiers began to see the first U.S. paper money, in minimum $5 denominations. The "greenback" (a pejorative term), not to be confused with a "gumback" (a postage stamp, also used as currency), was the work of Treasury Secretary Salmon P. Chase, the namesake of Chase Manhattan Bank.

Another of Grant's adversaries was Brig. Gen. Simon B. Buckner, one of many West Pointers and Mexican War veterans to have joined the Confederate Army. Buckner was the older half of an incredible father-and-son story. He was born 122 years before his son, Lt. Gen. Simon B. Buckner, became the highest-ranking American killed by enemy fire in World War II. Father and son were born in 1823 and 1886, graduated from West Point in 1844 and 1908, and died in 1914 and 1945.

Fighting continued in the West on April 6–7, 1862, when the Battle of Shiloh pitted Grant's 58,000-man Army of West Tennessee against the 55,000 troops of the Confederates' Army of the Mississippi under Albert Johnston. Grant had moved his troops, many of them new recruits, south along the Tennessee River to Pittsburg Landing for training and field exercises. Johnston concentrated his forces near Corinth, Mississippi, hoping to engage Grant before he could be reinforced, but he was delayed by heavy rain and bad roads.

Those around him were beginning to appreciate Grant, who, despite his shaggy look and casual manner, had the mind of a master strategist—just what was lacking in the Union Army elsewhere. As he maneuvered near Pittsburg Landing, Grant's objectives were to gain control of the Mississippi and split the Confederacy, isolating the South's leaders from their western sections. By drawing out the foe and winning on the battlefield, he could begin the process of carving the Confederacy in two.

Grant was in contact by telegraph with Maj. Gen. Henry W. Halleck (1815–1872), the overall Union commander on the western front—dubbed "Old Brains" by some. He knew from Halleck's telegrams that additional Union forces under Maj. Gen. Don Carlos Buell (1818–1898) were en route to support him. Halleck ordered Grant to sit tight until Buell could arrive. But first, Johnston attacked Grant on the inevitable "good ground" that commanders were always searching for. At this juncture, soldiers on both sides may still have been enamored with the romance of war. If they were, it died in the bloody horror of Shiloh.

Begun on a Sunday morning and named for a church near the fighting, Shiloh was the first of the great battles in which men used ancient tactics, only to be cut to pieces by modern weapons. The commanders on both sides had been steeped in Napoleonic doctrine that stressed marching shoulder to shoulder into the muzzles of the enemy's guns, an infantryman's weapon being less important than the shock value of a frontal assault and its inevitable bayonet charge to follow. This made sense as long as smoothbore muskets were inaccurate beyond 60 yards, field artillery had a range of only 600 yards, and the bayonet was the soldier's primary weapon. But the Civil War introduced the rifled musket and the Minie ball (and, in smaller numbers, the magazine-fed repeating rifles), meaning that a soldier could shoot and kill from 200 yards or farther. Field batteries could shoot half a mile or more. At Shiloh, Johnston rode up and down the ranks before the attack, urging his men to use cold steel. In fact, the bayonet was eclipsed by the bullet during the Civil War and was rarely used with much success. Johnston's own fate was an ironic testimony to how times had changed.

Military developments during the American Civil War included rifled muskets, breach loaders, cartridge rounds, repeating rifles, Gatling guns, rifled cannons, ironclad ships, balloons, and submarines.

Federal forces fought back stubbornly as they recovered from their initial surprise. Johnston fell in the fighting, shot from his horse, and his second-in-command, Beauregard, took over.

Late on the first day and into the night, Buell's troops arrived on the scene, too late for the initial clashes in which the Confederate side prevailed at staggering cost.

Witnessing fugitives from Grant's army cowering under the riverbank, Buell claimed that it was only his army that saved Grant—a point still being debated.

Grant's forces lost 1,751 killed, with 8,408 wounded and 2,885 wounded or captured. Losses on the Rebels' side were almost identical but uneven. The Confederate forces' 6th Mississippi volunteers lost 70.5 percent of their 425 troops. When losses on both sides were combined, they exceeded all the men killed in the Revolution, the War of 1812, and the Mexican War. Just days after the battle, Secretary of War Stanton ordered "a salute of 100 guns from the United States Arsenal at Washington in honor of these great victories" in the Shiloh clashes—but while Shiloh was a win for the North, it was scarcely a moment for pomp and ceremony.

> Confederate troops sometimes painted logs black, set them at an angle, and used them to represent real cannons. The fake guns got the name Quaker Guns because they couldn't be used in combat. They fooled Gen. George McClellan near Manassas in July 1861.

PENINSULA CAMPAIGN

On March 11, 1862, Lincoln relieved McClellan as general in chief of the Army but kept him in command of the Army of the Potomac. Lincoln temporarily left vacant the post of general in chief. Like all presidents up to this juncture in American life, Lincoln was personally involved in all aspects of military operations as commander in chief.

Lincoln also was well served by the dour, humorless Stanton, who had maneuvered himself into position to replace an inefficient and controversial Simon Cameron (1799–1889) as secretary of war. Cameron's strong views on aggressive war measures, which included his desire to arm fugitive slaves, drew heated opposition not only from other Cabinet members, but from Lincoln himself. Stanton did not at first have great rapport with Lincoln, but the president recognized Stanton's organizational skills. The pair became fast friends. Stanton often took the liberty of warning the president that he should allow himself to be guarded, to ensure his personal safety. Lincoln, in turn, pointed out that no American president had ever been assassinated. Stanton became the first modern administrator to run the Army, developing a centralized organization that oversaw the war effort, kept generals in tow, and guided procurement and acquisition. He defined the role of secretary of war as it would continue until just after World War II.

Constantly prodded by Lincoln and Stanton—who had once been a close advisor—McClellan waited until April 4, 1862, to launch his Peninsular Campaign aimed at seizing Richmond.

Even then, he moved at glacial speed, hindered by his own cautious nature and hampered because Brig. Gen. J. E. B. Stuart was harrying his

Union troops relentlessly. On May 4–14, McClellan's advance into Virginia enabled him to seize Yorktown and Williamsburg as well as the Confederates' White House near Richmond.

McClellan's inability to advance on Richmond and bring the war to a swift conclusion has been the stuff of debate ever since. His Army of the Potomac outnumbered the Army of Northern Virginia, but he was plagued by a Napoleonic siege mentality: He habitually overestimated the Confederate forces he faced and underestimated his ability to move expeditiously against them. Hesitant and cautious, McClellan paused, awaiting reinforcements and allowing his momentum to transform itself into inaction. His moment came and went.

On June 2, 1862, Robert E. Lee took command of the Army of Northern Virginia, succeeding Joseph E. Johnston. Lee attacked McClellan in the Seven Days' Battles (June 25–July 1). McClellan's dawdling, followed by his defeat in the Seven Days' fighting, led to Lincoln's decision to relieve him of command. Most of McClellan's troops were reassigned to the newly constituted Army of Virginia under Maj. Gen. John Pope (1822–1892). To fill the vacant position as general in chief of the Army, Lincoln chose the lackluster Halleck, but the president continued to be very much his own commander, with considerable help from Secretary of War Stanton.

On August 9, 1862, in the Battle of Cedar Mountain, Virginia, Lee sent Confederate forces under Stonewall Jackson to fight Union troops led by Maj. Gen. Nathaniel Banks (1816–1894). After a flurry of fighting seemed certain to produce a Union victory, Confederate reinforcements under Brig. Gen. A. P. Hill (1825–1865) turned the tide. The Confederate victory shifted the combat zone from the Peninsula to Northern Virginia, giving Lee the initiative over Pope. Like so many who came out second best in battle, Banks spent the remainder of his military career being criticized for the loss.

SECOND MANASSAS

Northern Virginia, of course, included the much-trod land around Manassas. On August 28, 1862, the second major battle there began when Jackson attacked a Federal column passing along his front at Brawner Farm and fought the Union troops to a standstill. This was the start of

Second Bull Run (Second Manassas), in which Lee, Jackson, and James Longstreet defeated Union troops under Pope. On August 30, Longstreet commanded 28,000 men who counterattacked Union troops in the largest simultaneous assault of the war, crushing the Federals' left flank and driving them back to Bull Run. Pope retreated to Centreville, probably faster than circumstances dictated, and many of his troops skedaddled all the way back to Washington. The Union suffered 13,830 casualties; the Rebels lost 8,350. It was the decisive battle of Lee's Northern Virginia campaign and a triumph for the South. In the aftermath of Second Manassas, Lincoln sacked Pope and reinstated McClellan as commander of the Army of the Potomac. It was yet another opportunity for McClellan, who, despite his reputation for caution, was beloved by his troops.

Lee spared Richmond by prevailing in the Seven Days' Battles and at Second Bull Run. In fact, in a mere three months, the situation between the opposing capitals was reversed. McClellan had been within eyesight of Richmond with 100,000 men, while McDowell threatened the capital with another 30,000 troops at Fredericksburg. There were 30,000 more Union troops in the Shenandoah Valley and in northern Virginia. In a stunning reversal in a short time, Lee pushed the front lines more than 100 miles northward, all the way back across the Potomac River and into western Maryland. It was the only time in the Civil War that so much territory changed hands so fast, and it was a harbinger for the North—until the opposing armies met next, at Antietam Creek.

TO ANTIETAM

After Second Manassas, as well as the victory at Ball's Bluff near Leesburg, the Peninsular Campaign that deflected the Federals from capturing Richmond, and tactical victories at Cedar Mountain and Ox Hill, Robert E. Lee crossed the Potomac and invaded Maryland and Pennsylvania, using the Shenandoah Valley's Blue Ridge Mountains to screen his movements. He probably expected to be on fertile ground: Maryland was a southern state that had remained part of the Union when Lincoln had its legislature thrown into jail to prevent a secession vote. At Frederick, Maryland, he split his army, sending Stonewall Jackson to seize the Federal garrison at Harpers Ferry, to free up his supply routes along the Shenandoah Valley. With his remaining troops, Lee marched northwest to Hagerstown.

McClellan learned that Lee's force had broken into two parts and attacked near Frederick on September 14. This action wiped away Lee's rear guard and forced him to fall back to Sharpsburg, where his troops formed behind Antietam Creek. On September 15, the Harpers Ferry garrison surrendered to Jackson, who then was able to move quickly to rejoin Lee at Sharpsburg 15 miles away.

Thus, Lee's first invasion of the North culminated on September 17 at Sharpsburg, Maryland, when the Battle of Antietam took place. Lee was later criticized for picking this spot to stand and fight, against the advice of his trusted subordinate, Longstreet—though the equally trusted and combative Jackson supported the decision.

The Rebels were seriously outnumbered. The Union Army consisted of no fewer than 75,300 troops confronting 37,330 Confederate soldiers. Lee meant to take the offensive, but, incredibly, a copy of his orders fell into Union hands, allowing the resurrected McClellan to anticipate his strategy.

At daylight on the morning of September 17, a corps of McClellan troops led by Maj. Gen. Joseph "Fightin' Joe" Hooker (1814–1879), having crossed Antietam Creek, launched a furious attack on Lee's left flank, assaulting troops led by Jackson.

Attacks and counterattacks swept across a cornfield and around the Dunker church. Union assaults eventually pierced the Confederate center, but the Federals failed to follow up on their advantage. Covered by cannon fire from Jackson's artillery, the Confederates retreated while Union troops fell back. Fresh Rebel soldiers arrived in time to repel a second Union frontal attack across Antietam Creek led by Maj. Gen. Ambrose Burnside (1824–1881), a Rhode Island political leader and a veteran of successful occupation of Rebel positions in North Carolina.

Just to the rear of the battle, observing the fight while guarding Union mules and supplies, Quartermaster Sgt. William McKinley (1843–1901) reacted to the violence as it unfolded. The future president led two mule teams with wagons of rations and hot coffee over rough terrain under fire from Confederate field batteries and riflemen. One of McKinley's mule teams fell amid the chaos, but he fed numerous troops under fire before returning to the rear.

By the end of the day, the battlefield was littered with corpses, and it was clear that McClellan had met Lee head-on and forced him to pull back. Although the fighting had actually been inconclusive, in symbolic terms, it was a monstrous defeat for the South, which had been hoping that a victory here would bring recognition and support from the European powers.

Antietam was the costliest one-day combat ever waged in the Western Hemisphere. Union forces lost 2,108 killed, 9,549 wounded, and 753 captured or missing. Confederate losses were nearly as great—in all, 22,726 were killed or wounded. On November 5, 1862, Lincoln again relieved McClellan as commander of the Army of the Potomac for his failure to pursue Lee into Virginia. Lincoln replaced McClellan with Burnside, while Halleck remained as Army general-in-chief. The choice of Burnside disappointed the hard-fighting Hooker, who wanted the job and credited Burnside with having "a brain the size of a hickory nut." Because it was deemed a win for the North, Antietam enabled Lincoln to issue the Emancipation Proclamation, which on January 1, 1863, declared free all slaves in states still in rebellion against the United States. Detractors of the Northern cause say Lincoln didn't need Antietam to issue the proclamation, which was intended as a strategic move to incite slave revolts and runaways, but doing so had a much greater impact because it gave Lincoln a moral cause to send young men to war—a far more noble cause than high tariffs in the industrial Northeast.

NEW ARMY

Although it was still changing commanders almost as fast as a game of musical chairs, under the leadership of Lincoln and Stanton the nation was developing its first modern Army. There was really no choice, now that the war would be long and the Union would be able to prevail only by overwhelming and overrunning the South. The Army introduced a serious, closely monitored logistics and supply system. It issued food rations to soldiers for the first time and introduced canned rations, a significant innovation. The Army issued rifled muskets and rifles to troops and used far-reaching artillery pieces with rifled barrels. Thanks to the railroad and the telegraph, and in spite of the absence of a decent road system, the Army boasted modern transportation and communications. Given the larger industrial base and population of the North, the Union probably did not face the prospect of losing the war again—except, perhaps, at Gettysburg, where fate intervened—and American soldiers would no longer be entirely amateurs.

These successes were the work of men in Washington, not of Burnside, the new head of the Army of the Potomac—renowned for his "muttonchop" facial hair and as the inventor of a carbine, but not especially as a commander. In November 1862, Burnside sent a corps to occupy the vicinity of Falmouth near Fredericksburg, Virginia. Burnside fielded over 100,000 troops against Lee, who reacted by digging in on the high ground behind Fredericksburg with 72,500 Confederate soldiers. After Union engineers laid five pontoon bridges across the Rappahannock while under fire, the Federal army crossed over, and on December 13, Burnside mounted a series of futile frontal assaults in what became known as the Battle of Fredericksburg. It was one of the few occasions during the Civil War when troops fought in harsh winter conditions, and casualties were horrendous.

"Muttonchop" was the Civil War term for the style of facial hair later called "sideburns," in a reversal of the name of one of the less successful Union Army leaders, Maj. Gen. Ambrose Burnside.

On the Federals' left flank, a Union division under Maj. Gen. George G. Meade briefly broke Stonewall Jackson's line but was repelled. On December 15, Burnside called off the assault. Burnside initiated a new offensive in January 1863, again ignoring the season, only to have his troops bog down in the winter mud. This became known as the "Mud March." Coupled with other failures, it prompted Lincoln to relieve Burnside—finally turning the Army of the Potomac over to Fightin' Joe Hooker in January.

FIGHTING IN 1863

In the West, the Confederate side's Army of the Mississippi was reorganized under Maj. Gen. Braxton Bragg (1817–1876) and was renamed the Army of Tennessee. On January 2, 1863, elements of this Confederate force halted the Union's advance toward Chattanooga, Tennessee, preventing the North from seizing the Confederacy's rail center. The Battle of

Murfreesboro, or Stones River, Tennessee, pitted Bragg against the North's Maj. Gen. William Rosecrans (1819–1898), commander of the new Army of the Cumberland, who had already ousted Bragg from Kentucky. Rosecrans was unable to prevail over Bragg at Murfreesboro or to move on to Chattanooga. However, Bragg eventually had to withdraw, and Rosecrans then transformed Murfreesboro into a fortress. Rosecrans was now secure in Tennessee but was constantly harried by Confederate raiders, including cavalrymen like Brig. Gen. Nathan Bedford Forrest (1821–1877). In July, Forrest seized Murfreesboro, destroyed Union supplies, and tore up railroad track in the area, while also diverting Federal troops from a drive on Chattanooga. Later in the year, Bragg would be in position to return to Kentucky in force.

On May 2–4, 1863, at the Battle of Chancellorsville, Virginia, Lee defeated Hooker's Army of the Potomac. Fightin' Joe Hooker, beloved by the common soldier but given short shrift by historians, boosted morale in the Army of the Potomac by pressing his officers to adopt new tactics to replace massed human assaults. He reorganized, formed a cavalry corps, and set forth to engage Lee's army. Hooker split his force, sending cavalry to disrupt Lee's line of communications with a raid on Richmond. Lee reacted by sending a division to dig in at Chancellorsville. Reinforcements under Stonewall Jackson marched to help block Hooker's advance. The Union troops paused near Chancellorsville after a rapid, stealthy march to the front in which Hooker brilliantly positioned 115,000 men without initially being detected. But Hooker's cavalry diversion foundered, and even after he deployed troops in positions that should have allowed him to crush Lee in a pincer movement, Hooker's main force was stalled without cavalry to warn of Lee's approach. Thus began the opening major battle of the 1863 military campaign in the East.

Though he had just 58,000 troops, or about half the strength of Hooker's force, Lee refused to accommodate the Federal commander by doing the obvious and retreating. The Rebel general posted troops at Fredericksburg and sent others to meet Hooker head-on. The clash came on May 1, 1863, at Chancellorsville, which was not a town, but a simple crossroads in thick underbrush dubbed "The Wilderness." For two days, the opponents thrusted and parried. On the third morning at 6:00 A.M., Jackson's Confederates burst out of The Wilderness to push the unsuspecting Union force back. Jackson's forces marched around Hooker's army, giving Lee the chance he needed to turn a sure defeat into possibly the most brilliant Confederate victory of the war.

Late on May 3, after a successful action that ripped up a Union flank and took numerous prisoners, Stonewall Jackson was riding in front of his lines when his own sentries inadvertently shot and seriously wounded him. That night, a doctor amputated his left arm just below the shoulder. Lee later noted that Jackson had lost his left arm, "but I have lost my right arm." Jackson died a week later.

On May 3, filling in for Jackson, Brig. Gen. J. E. B. Stuart initiated the bloodiest day at Chancellorsville by attempting to reunite his troops with Lee's. Hooker ordered a tactical withdrawal that, viewed in retrospect, may not have been necessary. At a critical juncture in the battle, Hooker was knocked unconscious and perhaps badly hurt when a Confederate cannon ball drove a wooden piece of a structure into him, inflicting a powerful blow from head to toe. Meanwhile, in a separate action, Union troops assaulted Fredericksburg but were isolated when Lee reacted. About 2,000 men became casualties in Second Fredericksburg, but the Federals drove from these positions the very badly outnumbered Confederates, who regrouped west and southeast of town.

Hooker, until then the model of the aggressive combat leader, seemed in a daze after being struck. Later, he blamed his loss at Chancellorsville on himself, a finding with which most historians would agree—but there is evidence he might simply have been too badly wounded to exercise command. For Robert E. Lee, Chancellorsville was a great victory. The battle also demonstrated how warfare was changing: Lee employed new, more mobile, and flexible tactics—although he would return to the traditional massing of troops at Gettysburg within two months. The combination of Chancellorsville and Second Fredericksburg rates as the second-bloodiest battle of the Civil War, with 16,845 Federal and 12,764 Confederate casualties.

On June 24, 1863, Lee took his army across the Potomac and toward Pennsylvania. The following day, Maj. Gen. George E. Meade was put in command of the Army of the Potomac. Meade, described by a supporter as acerbic and testy, took over when Hooker asked to be relieved of command.

Meanwhile, the war continued in the West. On May 14, 1863, in the Battle of Jackson, Mississippi, Union Maj. Gen. William Tecumseh

Sherman (1820–1891) defeated the Confederates under Joseph E. Johnston. It was not a major victory. In fact, Sherman never commanded during a major Union victory. He was a practical military man who refused to participate in politics—foreseeing an aloofness from politics in the American officer corps that would become tradition for most of the twentieth century. He would later become known for waging total war against the Confederacy—also foreseeing the future with sharper vision than most.

On May 22, 1863, Grant, in concert with Sherman, began the long siege of the Confederate citadel at Vicksburg, Mississippi, the key to control of the Mississippi River. On July 4, the siege ended in victory, with Grant demanding an unconditional surrender and 29,000 Confederate troops laying down their arms. Grant was beginning to receive considerable notice in Washington. Told that the general liked to drink, Lincoln quipped that he wished he could bottle Grant's favorite libation and supply it to every officer in the Army.

GETTYSBURG

The most significant battle of the War Between the States came just weeks after Chancellorsville, a cavalry clash at Brandy Station, and a fight at Winchester, Virginia, on the northern side of the Potomac River and the Mason-Dixon line. Lee, with 75,000 men, was making his second invasion of the North and his only foray into Pennsylvania. Meade, with 83,000 men, was maneuvering to engage him. It is unlikely either general wanted or expected to fight at Gettysburg.

On July 1, a party of Confederate infantry headed to Gettysburg to seize much-needed shoes. Coming straight toward them was a division of Union cavalry. The Battle of Gettysburg began with Confederate troops attacking that Union cavalry division under Brig. Gen. John Buford (1826–1863) on McPherson Ridge, west of Gettysburg. The opening shot of the battle at Gettysburg was fired at 7:30 A.M. on July 1 by one of Buford's cavalrymen, Marcellus E. Jones. Outnumbered, Buford's troops fought valiantly, struggling to hold position, knowing that a corps under Maj. Gen. John Reynolds (1820–1863) was en route to reinforce them. In fact, Buford's horsemen actually managed to drive the Confederate army back. Often overlooked is the fact that light, mobile cavalry units like

Buford's were the result of innovations in the Army made months earlier by Hooker.

Arriving to back up Buford in late morning, Reynolds galloped into the fields west of Gettysburg. Leading his troops, Reynolds called, "Forward men! Drive those fellows out of that woods. For God's sake, forward!" He turned in his saddle and was shot in the head and killed instantly. The action by Buford and Reynolds is credited with enabling Meade to make a stand south and east of the town over the following two days.

A furious battle raged that first day over the ridges west of Gettysburg between two of Lee's corps and two of Meade's. Late in the afternoon, Union defenders gave way under relentless attacks, and the Rebels chased them through the town and to the high ground to the south. Maj. Gen. Winfield Scott Hancock rallied the fleeing soldiers and set up a defensive line on high ground. Lee recognized the natural strength of their position and sent a message to his II Corps commander, Lt. Gen. Richard Ewell (1817–1872), that it "was only necessary to press those people in order to secure possession of the heights"—the peak was called Cemetery Hill—and urged him to take the high ground "if practicable." Ewell, replacement for Stonewall Jackson, was eager and new, but did not know Lee well enough to interpret this as an order. Ewell was also under orders from Lee to avoid a general engagement. He did not believe the attack was "practicable" and left Union troops in command of heights that would prove impossible to seize later. It is often overlooked that Ewell probably had no choice, since the ridge was populated with thousands of Union blue and many cannons.

On the second day, Lee wanted to launch a direct attack to roll up the Union's left flank. Longstreet wanted the Confederates to force the enemy to attack first, or to sweep around the flank of the Union Army, but Lee insisted on the attack. He attempted to envelop Meade's forces, first striking the Union left flank at the Peach Orchard, Wheatfield, Devil's Den, and the Round Tops with Longstreet's and Hill's divisions, and then attacking the Union right at Culp's and East Cemetery hills with Ewell's divisions. By evening, the Federals retained Little Round Top, thanks in part to a heroic bayonet charge led by Col. Joshua L. Chamberlain (1828–1914), and had repulsed most of Ewell's men.

Col. Joshua Chamberlain was a hero of the Civil War but was known only to history buffs before Jeff Daniels portrayed him in the 1993 movie *Gettysburg.* The film reprised the largest battle ever fought in the Western Hemisphere and the pivotal moment when Chamberlain ordered a bayonet charge.

On the second day at Gettysburg, Chamberlain's regiment was assigned to defend Little Round Top, a hill at the flank of the Union Army's defensive line. Any attack that overwhelmed Chamberlain's regiment of just 386 men (down from 1,000) could give Confederate forces the high ground and enable them to defeat the Union army. Chamberlain's troops were desperately low on food, water, and ammunition.

Col. William C. Oates's 15th Alabama Regiment attacked Chamberlain. In their first skirmish, Chamberlain's 20th Maine opened fire and sent the Confederates scurrying for cover.

Oates regrouped. He ordered a charge up the hill. Chamberlain's soldiers withstood six attacks by the persistent southern troops. But the onslaught seriously threatened Chamberlain's left flank. As the 20th Maine's soldiers exhausted their last ammunition, the Confederates were about to overwhelm them.

A single word—"Bayonets!"—shouted by Chamberlain galvanized the Union troops. Chamberlain led his men charging down Little Round Top in a furious counterattack. Oates, unable to maintain his position, ordered a retreat off the hill. The Union Army's Brig. Gen. Stephen H. Weed soon reinforced Chamberlain, and the Confederate threat, which might have changed the outcome at Gettysburg, ended.

Chamberlain distinguished himself after Gettysburg. Wounded at Little Round Top, he was wounded five more times, twice so severely that his obituary was published. Six times, a horse was shot out from under him.

On August 11, 1893, Chamberlain was awarded the Medal of Honor for "heroism and great tenacity in holding his position on the Little Round Top against repeated assaults."

On the third day at Gettysburg, Lee decided to launch a bold frontal attack against the Union center. Longstreet believed Lee should sweep around the southern end of George G. Meade's Union position rather than strike the center of the line along Cemetery Ridge. Once Lee ordered the charge, Longstreet decided that it could not succeed and stubbornly refused to send in the Confederate reserves that might have carried the day. Pickett's Charge momentarily pierced the Union line, but George Pickett's troops were driven back and all but annihilated.

Gettysburg was the bloodiest battle ever fought on this half of the planet and wrought Union losses of 3,155 killed, 14,529 wounded, and 5,365 missing or captured, with Confederate casualties slightly higher in all categories. Lee failed to dislodge Meade or to achieve the battlefield success that might have enabled the Confederacy to force the Union to sue for peace.

Lincoln wanted remnants of Lee's army destroyed as they retreated westward through Hagerstown and Williamsport in Maryland. Instead, the battle ended. Meade, licking his wounds, failed to pursue Lee. The war might have ended at Gettysburg. It did not.

CHICKAMAUGA

In the furious two days of September 19–20, 1863, the two sides fought the Battle of Chickamauga. The word was the Indian term for "River of Death" and referred to a 4-mile stretch of Chickamauga Creek in northern Georgia just 12 miles south of Chattanooga. The Union's 58,200-man Army of the Tennessee, led by Rosecrans and Brig. Gen. George H. Thomas (1816–1870), was defeated by the 66,300-man Confederate Army of the Tennessee under Gen. Braxton Bragg (1817–1876). It was the only significant Confederate victory in the West and the only success for Bragg, known as a strict adherent to regulations who lacked initiative or flexibility. One of eight men to reach the rank of full general in the Confederacy, Bragg was often reluctant on the battlefield.

For much of the first day, the two armies surged back and forth, neither able to dislodge the other. The day ended inconclusively, and that night Longstreet arrived with additional troops to reinforce Bragg.

On the morning of September 20, the Federals pushed back repeated, aggressive attacks; by late morning, the fighting had shifted down the lines toward Bragg's center. A Union officer reported erroneously to Rosecrans that a gap existed in his line. Needlessly, Rosecrans ordered a division to withdraw and plug the alleged gap, thereby creating a real gap. Longstreet launched a massive attack at exactly that spot, and Confederate troops poured through the Union line. The Federals suffered heavy losses. A powerful stand by Thomas earned him the sobriquet "The Rock of Chickamauga," but the Union side, which might yet have made a new stand and won, retreated hastily to Chattanooga.

When Grant was given command of Union forces in the West on October 16, 1863, he replaced Rosecrans as commander of the Army of the Cumberland with Thomas. The battle for Chattanooga came two months later on November 23–25, 1863, and was a Union victory that set the stage for the Atlanta Campaign. Grant's forces, led on the battlefield by Thomas, drove Bragg out of Chattanooga, effectively splitting the South from east to west. The credit belonged to Thomas, who had fought side by side with Bragg in the Mexican War and now robbed him of any chance to reap the fruits of his temporary success at Chickamauga.

On January 14, 1864, Sherman began his march across the South by occupying Sheridan, Mississippi. His strategy was total war. Sherman destroyed or seized anything that might enable the enemy to continue fighting. He burned and destroyed railroads, buildings, and supplies. It was called a "scorched earth" policy, but Sherman was not barbaric or inhuman. He simply understood that modern warfare could no longer be conducted on the battlefield alone. Sherman did not seek to wage war against ordinary civilians. He did, however, seek to subdue the South's infrastructure, assets, and people. Sherman had no less a goal than to break the spirit of the South's social elite—not the everyday citizen, but the upper class that had begun, and now carried on, the war.

On March 10, 1864, Lincoln named Grant general in chief of the Union Army. Grant was the Union's fourth top soldier (after Scott, McClellan, and Halleck). Many historians believe that the Lincoln administration lacked an overall strategy for winning the war and that Grant was the first leader to come up with one. One of Grant's first steps was to confer with his most trusted subordinate, Sherman, on a new, coordinate strategy to overwhelm Rebel armies and bring the war to a conclusion, with Grant pressuring the Rebels from one direction and Sherman coming from the other. Grant (and Meade) would assault Lee's main force in the East and drive to take Richmond. As part of this assault, Grant would send the Army of the James under Maj. Gen. Benjamin F. Butler (1818–1893) in a sweep to the west to double back and strike Confederate defenses protecting Richmond. Meanwhile, Sherman would attack the Confederates' Army of the Tennessee and seize Atlanta, the bustling commercial center of the Deep South.

GRANT'S STRATEGY

On May 4, 1864, Grant launched his drive toward Richmond with 100,000 troops. The two great generals of the war—Grant and Lee—collided when the Army of the Potomac forded the Rapidan River and marched into "The Wilderness," 70 square miles of dense trees, clawing underbrush, and deep gullies. There, Grant came upon 61,000 Confederate troops. The Battle of The Wilderness in Virginia brought two days of bloody fighting (May 5–6). The fighting produced many wounded on both sides. Many soldiers lost their lives in brush fires ignited by shooting in the thick woods. The fighting produced no clear victory, but it resulted in a change of tactics by the North. In the past, every Union general had pulled back his troops after a major engagement. Instead of withdrawing, Grant kept coming, his eyes still on Richmond.

In fact, Grant advanced to the Spotsylvania, Virginia, courthouse, where his troops ran into a wall of Confederate resistance. Over the period from May 8 to 21, 1864, including a continuous 20-hour duel on May 11–12 that might have been the longest sustained combat of the war, Grant and Lee slugged it out in the battle of Spotsylvania. On May 19, the Federals turned back a Confederate attempt to turn the Union right flank at Harris Farm, inflicting severe casualties. The battle ended as it had in The Wilderness, with no clear winner, but with Grant purposely wearing down Lee's smaller army and continuing to advance.

Grant's plan attached new importance to the war that had been raging in the West and now turned toward the Deep South as Sherman marched on Georgia. While Spotsylvania was going on, on May 13–15, 1864, Sherman's army of 110,000 inflicted a defeat on the Confederate forces that remained intact and withdrew in good order, ready to continue fighting.

Northern hopes that 1864 might bring a decisive victory, now seemingly within reach, suffered a setback on June 3, 1864, in the Battle of Cold Harbor, Virginia. Under Grant, cavalry led by Maj. Gen. Philip Sheridan (1831–1888) and infantry in Meade's divisions came up against seemingly impregnable Confederate troops along a 7-mile stretch of terrain from Bethesda Church to the Chickahominy River. Grant ignored the strength of Lee's defenses and pressed the attack—the only attack, he said later, that he ever regretted. The resistance prompted Grant to abandon a direct drive toward Richmond and instead to move around the Rebel capital toward Petersburg, Virginia.

GRANT IN THE SOUTH

On June 15–18, 1864, Grant laid siege to Petersburg, in a maneuver that reminded many of his earlier effort against Vicksburg. Later that month and much farther south, Sherman suffered a setback in a June 27 battle at Kennesaw Mountain, Georgia.

With Grant and Sherman both deep into the Confederacy, from July 2–13, 1864, Confederate forces under Lt. Gen. Jubal Early marked the anniversary of Gettysburg by taking 8,000 troops into Maryland and carrying out raids near Washington, culminating in a battle at Monocacy, Maryland. Early's dash took him within eyesight of the Union capital, but he was slowed by Union Maj. Gen. Lew Wallace (1827–1905), an accomplished battlefield leader who later achieved fame as author of the novel *Ben Hur*. Early withdrew his forces in good order into Virginia.

Grant continued to hold Petersburg at bay. On July 30, 1864, the city was shaken by monstrous explosions. Burnside had been attempting to dig a 500-foot tunnel beneath Confederate lines and fill it with thousands of pounds of explosives. In a disastrous miscalculation, the explosives detonated amid Burnside's own troops, killing dozens and wounding hundreds. Although the disaster did open a hole in the Confederate lines, the Union forces did not exploit the gap effectively. Always a problem in the Union chain of command—Burnside was technically senior to Meade and junior to Grant, a status for which no slot existed—the "muttonchop" general was relieved and did not hold an important military job again.

Pressing his concept of total war, waged not merely against the foe's soldiers, but also against his supply lines and infrastructure, Sherman took Atlanta on September 2, 1864. Mobile, Alabama, had also fallen to the Federals. Sherman's soldiers seized Atlanta, a move that was popular in the North and that undoubtedly helped the incumbent during this election year. With some difficulty, Lincoln gained re-election to the presidency, defeating two of his former generals, Frémont and McClellan.

WAR'S END

Now the Civil War was winding down, more with a whimper than a bang. In the Northern theater, in September and October, Union forces under Sheridan twice defeated Jubal Early's Confederates while sustaining heavy losses. These battles swept the Rebels out of the Shenandoah Valley, which had been one of their last remaining strongholds.

At the opposite end of the fighting, Sherman torched Atlanta on November 15, 1864, and began his famous march to the sea (at Savannah) with 62,000 Union troops. With much of Atlanta in ruins and Georgia no longer useful as a Rebel military base, Sherman left the Confederacy with nowhere to fall back to—while Grant continued to knock on Richmond's door. More months were to pass and more soldiers were to die, but there was now only one possible outcome.

On April 9, 1865, Robert E. Lee surrendered to Grant at the home of Wilmer and Virginia McLean at Appomattox Court House, Virginia. Other Confederate generals surrendered their forces between April 9 and May 4. The Civil War was over after 630,000 deaths and more than a million casualties.

The Union Army's figures for the Civil War indicate that 2,128,948 men served, including 75,215 regulars, 1,933,779 volunteers, and 119,954 draftees (the Army's only conscripts in the nineteenth century). The official total for deaths is 359,528, although the Army says, "the actual number must be larger … because … many of the records are incomplete." This total breaks down to 67,058 killed in action, 43,012 who died of wounds, a staggering 224,586 who died of disease, and 24,872 accidental and other deaths. The Army has no official figure for the number wounded, but unofficial estimates reach at least 300,000. Official Army figures count 211,411 taken prisoner. These figures are for the Union Army only.

> The mournful burial tune "Taps" was composed in 1862 when a wounded Union general, Daniel Adams Butterfield (1831–1901), directed brigade bugler Oliver Wilcox Norton (1841–1890) to honor his 600 troops who died in a battle by playing some notes he had written on the back of an envelope. "Taps" was recognized by the Army in 1874 and adopted by the armed forces in 1891.

CHAPTER 5

THE INDIAN WARS AND THE SPANISH-AMERICAN WAR (1865–1902)

In July 1865, just three months after Robert E. Lee's surrender at Appomattox, the Army placed Gen. William Tecumseh Sherman in command of the Military Division of the Missouri, with responsibility for all territories west of the Mississippi. Thus began more than a quarter-century (1865–1895) in which the Army played the central role in waging war against, defeating, and altering the lives of the Native American peoples of the West. It was a period of almost constant fighting. The Army uses the term "the Indian Wars" to refer to this period. For Native Americans on the Western Plains, the period ended forever a traditional nomadic lifestyle and led to life on the reservation. For the American soldier, both infantry and cavalry, it was a time when tactics and weapons needed to be adapted to irregular warfare, and individual commanders had to prevail in spite of bureaucratic bungling, faulty logistics, and appalling climatic conditions.

The Indian Wars persisted under the terms of several presidents: the eighteenth, Ulysses S. Grant, who served from 1869 to 1877;

the nineteenth, Rutherford B. Hayes, from 1877 to 1881; the twentieth, James Garfield, briefly in office during 1881; the twenty-first, Chester A. Arthur, from 1881 to 1885; the twenty-second, Grover Cleveland, from 1885 to 1889; the twenty-third, Benjamin Harrison, from 1889 to 1893; and the twenty-fourth, Cleveland again, from 1893 to 1897. All of these leaders, to some extent, used the Army as a tool to assist in the expansion and settlement of the West and the repression of the Native Americans who lived there.

It should be noted that many whites saw themselves as benefactors, bringing civilization to the Indians, rather than as conquerors. A paragraph from Cleveland's second inaugural address is typical:

> Our relations with the Indians located within our border impose upon us responsibilities we can not escape. Humanity and consistency require us to treat them with forbearance and in our dealings with them to honestly and considerately regard their rights and interests. Every effort should be made to lead them, through the paths of civilization and education, to self-supporting and independent citizenship. In the meantime, as the nation's wards, they should be promptly defended against the cupidity of designing men and shielded from every influence or temptation that retards their advancement.

Before the post–Civil War era, battles with Indian tribes—with the exception of the particularly brutal Seminole Wars—were limited in scope and took place in circumstances that enabled Indians to withdraw or be pushed into vast reaches of as yet unsettled territory westward. By 1865, there were fewer open spaces to which Native Americans could retreat. The quest for land, gold, commerce, and adventure, interrupted by the Civil War, was now unleashed in full fury. There was no way to avoid confrontation between settlers and Indians or to avoid a series of wars that raged over the Great Plains, mountains, and deserts in the American West.

There were a million Native Americans living in what is now the United States when Columbus came to the New World. By the time Sherman took command west of the Mississippi, the Indian population was about 275,000.

Sherman's command was made up of infantry and cavalry regiments stationed in forts built at strategic points. The job of the infantry was to man the forts and to keep communication and supply lines open by protecting the roads, stagecoach mails, and telegraph lines. The job of the cavalry was to match the mobility of the mounted Plains warrior.

THE PLAINS WARS

Long before the Civil War, the once-friendly relations between Indians and settlers gave way to tension as more and more whites emigrated to the west. In September 1851, the U.S. put forth the Fort Laramie treaty, named for the fort that became an Army post in 1849. The agreement reserved land for the Lakota and held forth the hope of peace. There was, in fact, plenty of room in the western territories for the two sides to live in a cooperative manner, and the treaty seemed to offer good prospects. In exchange for goods and protection from the federal government, the tribes granted permission for forts and roads to be built on their land.

The commitments made by the white settlers were honored only in part. In 1854, 15 miles from Fort Laramie, Brevet 2nd Lt. John L. Grattan of the Army's G Company, 6th Infantry, shot and killed an Indian chief, Conquering Bear, over the alleged theft of a cow in what may have been a misunderstanding caused by an inebriated interpreter. In immediate reaction, Brulé and Oglala Sioux warriors killed or mortally wounded Grattan and 20 of his men, and efforts by friendly Indians to save the wounded were in vain. The Grattan Massacre marked the effective beginning of the Indian Wars on the Northern Plains.

In 1855, ordered to retaliate for the Grattan Massacre, dragoons under Gen. William S. Harney (1800–1889) collided with a band of Lakota led by Chief Little Thunder. Ironically, Harney was urging better treatment for the Indians, while Little Thunder was counseling against an Indian attack on Fort Laramie. Among Harney's troops were Lt. John Buford and Capt. Henry Heth, who would meet on opposite sides at Gettysburg.

In what became known as the Battle of Ash Hollow or Blue Water (both in Nebraska), Harney's cavalrymen killed possibly as many as six dozen Sioux, including Little Thunder, effectively quelling—for a time—one of many Indian efforts to resist the settlers. After the battle, a depot named

Fort Grattan was established near the mouth of Ash Hollow and was abandoned in the spring of 1856.

Symbolic of many brutal actions of the period, on November 29, 1864, Colorado volunteers under Col. John H. Chivington killed at least 130 Cheyenne at Sand Creek, Colorado. It was less a battle than the latest of many massacres. Many of the Indian dead were women and children, some of them sexually mutilated and scalped by Chivington's men, who later exhibited their trophies to cheering crowds in Denver. An important Indian leader, Chief Black Kettle (1829–1868), narrowly escaped the slaughter and continued to fight the white horse soldiers marauding Indian territory.

Wagon trains, railroads, and hardy settlers continued the push toward manifest destiny that uprooted Native Americans and seized their best terrain. The Union Pacific Railroad completed its link across the country in 1869, changing forever the way people and supplies would cross the vast nation. The Army continued to be the force behind the changes. One after another, the settlers breached agreements with Indian tribes. Even when a new Fort Laramie Treaty was signed in 1868, bringing a series of skirmishes called the Powder River War to an end, Native American tribes continued to fight and resist, while the new occupants of the land continued to tighten their grip.

THE LATE 1860s

Throughout 1868, Sioux and Cheyenne war parties ransacked ranches and settlements, attacked wagon trains, and tore down telegraph wires. That year, Maj. Gen. Philip Sheridan (1831–1888), who had replaced Sherman in command of the Department of the Missouri, launched winter campaigning—unusual in the Army's experience—to locate elusive Indian bands in the northwestern territories. Some of Sheridan's soldiers were elite troops under Maj. George A. "Sandy" Forsyth, armed with Spencer repeating rifles that gave them a new standard of firepower and accuracy. Some troops packed .50-caliber Springfield breech-loaded rifles that were even more lethal.

During Sheridan's campaign against the Indians in border regions of Kansas, New Mexico, Colorado, and Texas, the following military actions took place:

- A nine-day defense of Beecher's Island (Colorado) against Indians led by Roman Nose (1830–1868) in September 1868 by Forsyth's detachment
- The defeat of Black Kettle in the Oklahoma Panhandle on November 27, 1868, by Lt. Col. George A. Custer and the 7th Cavalry, an action that claimed the lives of both Black Kettle and Capt. Lewis M. Hamilton, grandson of Alexander Hamilton
- The May 13, 1869, crushing of the Cheyenne under Chief Tall Bull at Summit Spring (Colorado) by cavalrymen and Pawnee scouts under Major Frank North
- The assault on the Kiowa-Comanche camp in Palo Doro Canyon on September 27, 1875, by Col. Ranald S. Mackenzie
- The attack and rout of Greybeard's big Cheyenne encampment in the Texas Panhandle on November 8, 1875, by 1st Lt. Frank Baldwin's detachment, spearheaded by infantry loaded in mule wagons

LITTLE BIGHORN

The Army suffered the best-known defeat in its history when Plains Indian warriors overwhelmed the 7th Cavalry Regiment, led by Lt. Col. George A. Custer.

In 1875, the U.S. government ordered that all Indians on the Western Plains settle on assigned reservations by January 31, 1876. The Army would be sent to track down any violators.

Also in 1875, settlers in search of gold invaded the Black Hills of the Dakota Territory (today South Dakota), regarded as sacred by Native Americans. The Indians tried to resist and rebelled against the 1875 order.

The Sioux nation, including the northern Cheyenne and the Lakota, rose up in the Sioux uprising of 1876–1877, a rebellion that included the Battle of Little Bighorn in southern Montana.

There, Custer collided with one of the largest concentrations of native warriors ever assembled on the North American continent. Native Americans from several tribes gathered in Montana for summer feasts and to plot strategy, led by Hunkpapa warrior Sitting Bull (1831–1890). Oglala warrior Crazy Horse (1845–1877) was another of the Native American leaders.

Lt. Gen. Philip Sheridan, commander of the Army's Department of the Missouri, which was responsible for the northwest, planned to defeat the Indians by surrounding them with three columns of troops. Brig. Gen. George Crook (1830–1890) led a column northwestward from Fort Fetterman in the Wyoming Territory. Col. John Gibbon headed southeast from Fort Ellis in the Montana Territory. On May 17, 1876, the third column, the 7th Cavalry, left Fort Abraham Lincoln in the Dakota Territory, commanded by Brig. Gen. Alfred H. Terry (1820–1890) and including Custer.

Crook, with 1,049 soldiers, fought Crazy Horse in a day-long engagement on June 17. The Indians overwhelmed Crook's cavalrymen, killing 10 and wounding 34. Crook fell back to await reinforcements. Crazy Horse failed to follow up his advantage, left the field, and rejoined Sitting Bull on the Little Bighorn. By failing to advise his superiors of the strength of Indian forces, Crook contributed to the loss by Custer eight days later on June 25.

Custer disobeyed an order from Terry and split his regiment of 650 men total into 3 battalions, commanded by Major Marcus A. Reno (1834–1889), Capt. Frederick W. Benteen (1834–1898), and himself. He left behind with his pack train several Gatling guns (rotary machine guns), which—on their wheeled, horse-drawn carriages—would have been difficult to deploy in the hilly Montana terrain.

Custer was acting on flawed intelligence. Despite warnings to the contrary from his scouts, he estimated that 500 Indian warriors were nearby. In fact, up to 15,000 Indians were assembled, including about 2,500 Lakota and Cheyenne fighters.

Divided as they headed for fighting they did not expect, most of Custer's horse soldiers carried single-shot .45-caliber Springfield carbines and six-shot Colt revolvers. Many of Sitting Bull's warriors had percussion rifles of various types, but some had Winchester repeating rifles that were superior to the carbines carried by Custer's men.

The cavalry units led by Benteen and Reno were separated from Custer's soldiers. The Indians attacked them and forced them into defensive positions while Custer's men rode into Little Bighorn in searing heat, the temperature approaching 100 degrees.

The cavalrymen fell into a trap. Indian warriors surrounded Custer's troops and assaulted them with two successive frontal attacks, one led by Crazy Horse (Sitting Bull was not at the battle). In their final moments, soldiers shot their own horses to use them as shields. It was a futile gesture. The Indians killed the soldiers, one by one, to the last man.

The Indians stripped dead cavalrymen of their clothing and mutilated many bodies (though not Custer's) to prevent the soldiers' spirits from enjoying the next life. Apparently, the Indian warriors never knew Custer's identity. Contrary to paintings that depict him in blue, Custer was wearing buckskins rather than a cavalry officer's uniform.

The tidings of Custer's death reached U.S. leaders in Philadelphia, where they were celebrating the nation's Centennial on July 4, 1876. Many could not believe that Native American warriors had defeated the vaunted 7th Cavalry. The press portrayed the Indians as savages and called the battle "Custer's Last Stand." It went unnoticed that Custer had blundered badly by going into the fight in defiance of an order, ignoring intelligence, outnumbered, and unprepared.

Public outrage silenced those in the nation with moderate views who wanted fairness toward Indians. Although there was room in the West for everybody, by defeating Custer the Indians invited bloody retaliation.

The Cavalry now ruled the western territories, too powerful for the Indians. The Army captured Sitting Bull, who died in captivity, and then exhausted huge resources chasing the elusive war leader Geronimo and his Apaches in the Southwest. In September 1886, a cavalry troop under Capt. Henry W. Lawton finally captured Geronimo, the most persistent holdout against the Army. For the remainder of the nineteenth century, the Army inflicted one blow after another on the Indians, culminating in the 1890 Battle of Wounded Knee in South Dakota, when soldiers used 3.2-inch Hotchkiss field cannons and other weapons to kill about 300 Indians, including women and children. Little Bighorn was the Native Americans' greatest victory, but it was also their last. By 1895, with Wounded Knee behind, the Army was deployed more or less equally around the country on the basis of regional rather than operational considerations.

THE CHANGING ARMY

It was time for the Army to change. By 1890, the U.S., until now a provincial backwater, was emerging as a world power and a competitor on the international stage with the great powers of Europe. The U.S. was also ready to grab territory, just as the European nations were doing. More and more Americans supported frankly imperialistic ventures. The nation was turning its eyes from the Western frontier—which, according to the Census Bureau, ceased to exist in 1890—and was looking beyond its own shores. The Army and the Navy were now to be called upon to support American interests overseas.

In 1890, the Regular Army consisted of 25 regiments of infantry, 10 regiments of cavalry, and 5 regiments of artillery. In March 1898, the Army added two more artillery regiments. It would take the Spanish-American War to bring further changes and bring the Army to a size commensurate with U.S. ambitions. During this period, the Army adopted the .30-caliber Krag-Jorgensen rifle as its infantry weapon to replace the single-shot .45-caliber Springfield carbine. Most troops, however, continued to be equipped with single-shot weapons, long after the other armies of the world had given a repeating rifle to every soldier.

Americans viewed war as a glorious undertaking in the 1890s, but the Army soon learned that it was hopelessly unprepared for one. Organization, leadership, training, and equipment stockpiles had been downsized since the Civil War. The Army would be caught unprepared again, but after 1898, it never relied on a hollow garrison force.

The Army was behind in developing a modern rifle. The war with Spain in 1898 showed that the Krag-Jorgenson rifle couldn't measure up to other armies' high-velocity, clip-loading rifles. The Army replaced the Krag with the 1903 Springfield.

The Spanish-American War saw the Army's first large-scale use of machine guns. John Parker, 2nd Lieutenant of the 13th Infantry, employed 40-year-old Gatling guns at Santiago Heights, Cuba, even though soldiers weren't taught how to use the guns before the battle. Parker said that his three Gatlings "put 6,000 rounds apiece on the top of San Juan Hill in eight minutes."

Perversely, fighting in Cuba in 1898 reinforced the Army's doctrine favoring marksmanship over rapid fire, as well as its miserly emphasis on conserving ammunition. Long after other armies favored rapid fire, officers boasted that Spanish soldiers were firing in furious volleys while U.S. soldiers were taking careful, individual aim.

Throughout the nineteenth century, more soldiers died of disease than in combat. Troops in Cuba and the Philippines faced 100° temperatures, parasites, dysentery, and malaria. The era prompted reforms in the Army's Medical Corps; in the twentieth century, combat killed more soldiers than Mother Nature.

A U.S. soldier during the Philippine Insurrection wore blue shirt, khaki pants, and web boots, and lugged 75 pounds of gear, including Krag-Jorgenson rifle, 40 rounds of ammunition (in bands around the arms), a canteen, a poncho, and a shelter tent. The Army's cork helmet proved unsuitable in the tropics. Soldiers wore campaign hats instead.

WAR WITH SPAIN

On January 25, 1898, the battleship USS *Maine* arrived in Havana harbor, supposedly to protect the interests of Americans being brutalized by the Spanish governor. The president at the time was William McKinley, who had been a quartermaster sergeant at the Battle of Antietam decades earlier. When the *Maine* exploded on February 15 while anchored in Havana harbor, killing 260 crewmembers, newspapers in the U.S. stirred up war fervor. On March 9, Congress appropriated $50 million for the military. Soon afterward, McKinley delivered what amounted to an ultimatum to Spain. Prowar leaders in Washington kept pressuring McKinley until he called for war on April 11.

The Spanish-American War lasted from April 21, 1898, until April 11, 1899, although hostilities ended on August 13, 1898. During this period, 280,564 soldiers served in the Army, including 57,329 regulars and 223,235 volunteers. There was no draft.

When Congress declared war on Spain on April 25, 1898 (making it retroactive to four days earlier, the day Spain broke off diplomatic relations), Americans were united in patriotic fervor. The events leading to the sinking of the *Maine* stirred enormous public hatred toward Spain. There was nothing but support in the air when Congress passed the Volunteer Army Act, which created a 1st Volunteer Cavalry. Assistant Navy Secretary Theodore Roosevelt (1858–1919) resigned his post to become a lieutenant colonel of the "Rough Riders," led by Col. Leonard Wood (1860–1927).

This spirited band of horse soldiers was genuinely rough and ready for action, a colorful regiment of outdoorsmen, cowboys, and Ivy League athletes.

Wood was a man of many achievements, a surgeon, and a general, later to be credited with numerous innovations in the Army. He had critical roles in the fighting both in Cuba and in that crucial Spanish possession, the Philippines. As commander of the "Rough Riders," Wood joined with his friend Theodore Roosevelt in the attack on Santiago de Cuba. Wood was later military commander of Santiago (1898–1899) and military governor of Cuba (1899–1902). Sent in 1903 to the Philippines as the governor of the Moro province, he was promoted to major general. He helped crush the opposition to U.S. occupation there, although he was criticized for his ruthlessness. From 1906 to 1908, he commanded U.S. military forces in the Philippines.

Even before brief, fierce fighting in Cuba, Commodore George Dewey (1837–1918) defeated the Spanish fleet in Manila Bay on May 1, 1898. The battle in Manila was the first military action of the war. Opening with the famous quote "You may fire when you are ready, Captain Gridley," in Manila Bay, the Philippines Islands, Dewey's squadron of six vessels completely wiped out Adm. Patricio Montojo y Pasaron's Spanish fleet and the batteries surrounding Manila without a single U.S. casualty (the lone fatality was an engineer who died of heatstroke in a ship's engine room). However, the conquest of Manila itself became as much a political as a military one; the United States wanted to retain control itself rather than turn power over to the Filipinos, and was negotiating a separate surrender with the Spanish. That month, troops were embarking for both Cuba and the Philippines. Many American soldiers, eager to re-enact the heroism of their fathers in the Civil War, found themselves not winning a victory over Spanish forces in Cuba as they anticipated, but instead being shipped to the distant Philippines, eventually to fight the very Filipinos they ostensibly came to set free.

On June 10, 1898, a few hundred U.S. Marines landed at Guantanamo Bay, beginning the invasion of Cuba. On June 22, no fewer than 20,000 soldiers landed at the fishing village of Daiquiri, east of Santiago.

More than 100 years ago, the Army sent Maj. Walter Reed to Cuba to head a team of military doctors studying infectious diseases of military significance. Arriving in Havana in June 1900, Reed formed the U.S. Army Yellow Fever Commission with his assistants, Drs. James Carroll, Aristides Agramonte, and Jesse Lazear.

After preliminary studies, Reed's team pursued the possibility that mosquitoes carried the disease. Sadly, seeking conformation through self-experimentation, Lazear contracted yellow fever and succumbed to the disease.

Reed and his colleagues overcame this setback and proposed to Gen. Leonard Wood that they establish a new sanitary camp and seek human volunteers for further experiments. Wood approved and funded their proposal.

In what turned out to be the least risky but most unpleasant experiment, Pvt. Warren G. Jernegan and others slept for three weeks in a small house constructed for the experiments. All their clothing and bedding came from the yellow fever wards of the local hospital, where it was soiled by blood, vomit, urine, and feces from patients. Each night, Jernegan and the others slept amid this environment wondering if each little ache was the onset of yellow fever. After three weeks, Jernegan and the others remained well.

Jernegan volunteered for a new experiment, this time to be bitten by a mosquito carrying blood from a yellow fever patient. He was bitten twice but again escaped illness, this time because the causative agent hadn't had time to incubate in the mosquito.

The persistent Jernegan volunteered a third time and was injected with blood taken from a yellow fever patient. Within four days, he was ill with yellow fever. Jernegan survived and completed his three-year enlistment in November 1901.

Jernegan and 17 other volunteers thus played a pivotal role in some of the most significant research ever performed by the Army. Reed's commission proved that the mosquito was the vector of transmission. This led to control of yellow fever throughout Cuba and ultimately allowed for construction of the Panama Canal.

BATTLE IN CUBA

The overall commander of U.S. troops in the invasion of Cuba was Maj. Gen. William Rufus Shafter (1835–1906), a Civil War veteran who was later praised for quick and decisive actions taken by others on the battlefield but was criticized for being poorly prepared, underestimating the foe, and having no plan to cope with disease. Shafter launched what became a three-week siege to take the city of Santiago.

On June 24, 1898, Brig. Gen. Henry Lawton (1843–1899), the captor of Geronimo, and Brig. Gen. Joseph "Fightin' Joe" Wheeler (1836–1906), a former Confederate cavalry officer, joined Leonard Wood in fielding over a thousand infantrymen and Rough Riders at Las Guasimas, Cuba. The battle with Spanish forces went well for the aroused Americans and was covered by war correspondents who took notice of Theodore Roosevelt, beginning Roosevelt's legend as a hero. The quintessential Southerner, Wheeler is said to have urged his troops to "Give them Yankees hell, boys!" only to correct himself good-naturedly and say, "Of course, I mean the Spanish."

On July 1, Americans sustained heavy casualties in the Battles of El Caney and San Juan Hill, the two more accurately described in a single term as the Battle of Santiago Heights. Spanish resistance was stronger than Shafter expected. At El Caney, the 6,000 U.S. soldiers outnumbered their Spanish adversaries 10 to 1, but sustained 400 casualties nonetheless. At San Juan Hill, there was monumental confusion until Roosevelt led his assault first on Kettle Hill and then on San Juan Heights (see following sidebar). The heavy losses that day were not helped by the fact that American soldiers were still using single-shot rifled muskets; the entrenched Spaniards could fire eight shots from their 7-mm Mauser rifles in the time the Americans got off a single round. There was American firepower on the scene, however: The Battle of San Juan Hill marked the use of three Gatling guns that put 6,000 rounds atop the peak in eight minutes—one of the earliest massed uses of the machine gun.

After taking the hill, the Rough Riders continued their attack, seizing the heights overlooking the city of Santiago. The American victory led to the Spanish surrender two weeks later on August 13.

So far, in every war, more American soldiers had been felled by illness than by the enemy. This one was no exception. For the ordinary American soldier, Cuba was a tropical hell of heat, rainstorms, insects, land crabs, rotten food, and—as in all wars—disease. Yellow fever was always a problem in Cuba. The Philippines would soon bring other forms of pestilence.

Total casualties suffered by the Army during the Spanish-American War were 4,024, including 369 who were killed in action, 2,061 noncombat deaths, and 1,594 wounded. These figures are for the Army only and do not include other service branches. The Spanish-American War was over, but the Philippine Insurrection had just begun.

On January 16, 2001, the nation awarded the Medal of Honor to Col. Theodore "Teddy" Roosevelt for his July 1, 1898, charge up San Juan Hill in Cuba.

The Battle of Santiago Heights, also called the Battle of San Juan Hill, began with Roosevelt's cavalry pinned at the base of Kettle Hill. Roosevelt led his volunteers into action alongside Army regulars up Kettle Hill, one of two hills comprising San Juan Heights.

The citation for the award says that Roosevelt, "in total disregard for his personal safety, and accompanied by only four or five men, led a desperate and gallant charge up San Juan Hill, encouraging his troops to continue the assault through withering enemy fire over open countryside. Facing the enemy's heavy fire, he displayed extraordinary bravery throughout the charge, and was the first to reach the enemy trenches, where he quickly killed one of the enemy with his pistol, allowing his men to continue the assault. His leadership and valor turned the tide."

Army Gen. Joseph "Fightin' Joe" Wheeler, commander of U.S. Volunteers, recommended the award a few months after the action. Wheeler quoted a witness who said:

"... [A]t the base of the San Juan, or first hill, there was a strong wire fence or entanglement in which the line hesitated under grueling fire and where the losses were severe. [Roosevelt] jumped through the fence, and by his enthusiasm, his example, and courage, succeeded in leading to the crest of the hill a line sufficiently strong to capture it.

"Col. Roosevelt [later] placed his life in extreme jeopardy by unavoidable exposure to severe fire while adjusting and strengthening the line, placing the men in positions which afforded best protection; and his conduct and example steadied the men by severe but necessary measures to prevent a small detachment from stampeding to the rear."

THE PHILIPPINES

As part of the war on Spain, the Army landed troops at Manila in the Philippines. By the end of July 1898, some 13,000 volunteer and 2,000 regular troops, constituting the VIII Corps under Maj. Gen. Wesley Merritt (1834–1910), had reached the islands. Spanish troops and Filipino insurgents knew they were outnumbered by the Americans, but efforts by

Dewey and Merritt to secure their surrender failed because the Spanish government in Madrid insisted that the garrison should offer at least token resistance.

The Spanish colonial government in the Philippines surrendered to U.S. forces in August 1898, coinciding with the surrender in Cuba. The end to the war with Spain meant that the Philippines was now U.S. property, along with Puerto Rico and Guam.

But U.S. soldiers still faced a difficult campaign ahead. Tensions grew between U.S. and Filipino forces near Manila. The U.S. plan to keep the Philippines as a colony did not suit Filipino nationalist leader Emilio Aguinaldo and his army of nearly 80,000 troops. Aguinaldo had been fighting the Spanish and now proclaimed that the U.S. soldiers in Luzon were no longer allies.

Thanks to Aguinaldo, a fiery leader who lacked military acumen, the fighting over the next two years was dubbed the Philippine Insurrection, although today it is more commonly called the Philippine War. The fighting is divided into two distinct phases. During the first phase, the Army waged a conventional campaign through 1899, chiefly on the island of Luzon, and inflicted defeats on Aguinaldo's troops at every turn. The second phase was a looser, more ragged guerrilla campaign on various islands of the Philippine archipelago, with fighting in Luzon, the Visayas, Panay, and Samar.

Merritt's replacement as VIII Corps commander, Maj. Gen. Elwell S. Otis (1838–1909), was an able planner and leader. The highly regarded Merritt became the first U.S. military governor of the Philippines and then left for Paris to advise the U.S. peace negotiators. As for Otis, tasked with pursuing the U.S. policy called "benevolent assimilation," he attempted to negotiate with Aguinaldo, to no avail. Otis was not really benevolent, policy or no policy: His troops often burned and pillaged in their effort to put down the Filipino insurgency.

In May 1900, Lt. Gen. Arthur MacArthur (1845–1912) replaced Otis. MacArthur, remembered today mostly as the father of twentieth-century giant Gen. Douglas MacArthur (1880–1964), was very much his own man and added new emphasis to Otis's policy of harsh, punitive measures against the Filipino insurgents and their supporters. He was consistently faced with the challenge of employing the very conventional U.S. Army, patterned after a European model, in a decentralized and unorthodox war. It was the very problem the British had faced during the American Revolution and that the Americans would confront again in Vietnam.

For decades, Philippine leaders have been asking the United States to return the Bells of Balangiga.

Two church bells encased in a concrete outdoor display—trophies from the Philippine Insurrection that followed the Spanish-American War—occupy a place of honor near the flagpole at Francis E. Warren Air Force Base, Wyoming. Visitors who admire the bells often do not know their significance.

American troops were caught up in a local insurgency that followed the Spanish-American War in 1898. Tribal groups battled for key regions of the Philippines. As guerrilla warfare raged around them, American soldiers occupied the village of Balangiga in the island province of Samar in late 1901.

On September 23, 1901, hundreds of guerrillas armed with long bolo knives attacked the American soldiers at dawn and killed 32, including 3 officers and a first sergeant. Many of the Filipinos under Gen. Vincente Lukban dressed themselves as women to achieve surprise. The attack was signaled by an eerie and hostile sound—the ringing of Balangiga's church bells by the insurgents.

American troops rallied and took control of this disputed part of the Philippines. They killed hundreds in reprisal and seized two bells plus an old cannon, and brought them back to Fort D. A. Russell, Wyoming, now the site of the missile base. A third bell is retained by U.S. troops at Tongduchon in Korea.

As long ago as 1911, a U.S. Army officer questioned "the propriety of taking, even as a souvenir, a bell belonging to a church simply because a recreant native priest either used it or permitted it to be used to sound a signal of attack on American soldiers."

Other examples of war booty abound in the United States. In the National Air and Space Museum in Washington, D.C., tourists can see a Japanese Mitsubishi A6M5 Zero fighter that was seized by U.S. troops on Saipan in 1944.

PHILIPPINE SCOUTS

During MacArthur's tenure, the Army created the Philippine Scouts, a military component often overlooked in history even though the scouts served valorously from 1900 to 1949. These soldiers were Filipinos who enlisted as members of the regular U.S. Army. They were led by American officers or by Filipino graduates of West Point. They should not be confused with two other organizations with similar names, the Philippine Army and the Philippine Constabulary.

In 1901, Congress authorized the Army to enlist, organize, arm, and equip Filipinos for service. The Army organized 50 companies totaling about 5,000 men.

Because of the large number of dialects spoken in the Philippines, thought was given to organizing companies by languages. Experience soon demonstrated that differences in dialect were no obstacle, however, and, except for the Moro and Igorot tribes, the lingual differences were forgotten.

With a few exceptions, the Philippine Scout formations were segregated. By law, their service was restricted to the Philippines except in time of war. The first Scouts were recruited in company-size units during 1900 to supplement regular American forces suppressing the Philippine Insurrection in the Spanish-American War.

Many American officers who served with the Scouts during that difficult period later became famous. Capt. John J. Pershing, who was promoted to brigadier general after fighting at Lanao and Jolo, led the campaign against the insurrection. Douglas MacArthur and George Marshall served with Pershing as second lieutenants.

Turn-of-the-century fighting in the Philippines continued intermittently. In fighting against Moro insurgents on September 24, 1911, at Lapurap, Basilan, Pvt. Jose B. Nisperos was so badly wounded that he couldn't stand. His left arm was broken and lacerated, and he had suffered several spear wounds in the body. But, according to an Army report, he "continued firing his rifle with one hand until the enemy was repulsed, thereby helping prevent the annihilation of his party and the mutilation of their bodies." Nisperos became the first Pacific Islander and the first of two Philippine Scouts to be awarded the Medal of Honor. The Scouts were to reappear as an important part of South Pacific fighting in World War II (see Chapter 7).

FUNSTON IN ACTION

Acting on MacArthur's orders, on March 23, 1901, Col. Frederick Funston (1865–1917), commander of the 20th Kansas Infantry Regiment, set forth on a daring and unorthodox mission. Funston, typical of the National Guard leaders during the Philippine Insurrection, disguised himself as a prisoner-of-war and led a column of loyal Filipinos to reach the hideaway of the Filipino leader Aguinaldo and take him prisoner. The capture of Aguinaldo was a giant step forward for the Americans, but Funston's methods were later criticized by many, including author Mark Twain. An earlier action against the Filipinos by Funston won him the Medal of Honor, while seizing the nationalist leader earned him a promotion to brigadier general.

MacArthur became Military Governor of the Philippines in 1901. But soon afterward, President McKinley appointed William Howard Taft (1857–1930) as the civilian governor, and he and MacArthur clashed frequently. Taft, a future Secretary of War, future president, and future chief justice of the Supreme Court, developed a great affection for the people of the Philippines and carried out many important reforms that helped ease tensions.

Fighting diminished after Aguinaldo was taken, but Theodore Roosevelt—who became president in September 1901 with the assassination of William McKinley—did not officially end the war until July 4, 1902, and only then after awkward revelations about atrocities by U.S. troops.

Roosevelt's statement that the war was over had little impact on the island of Mindanao, where a separate military campaign persisted from 1902 through 1905. The Moros, a Mohammedan people in Mindanao and the Sulu Archipelago, who had never been completely subjugated by the Spanish, waged war against American troops. When the Army occupied former Spanish garrison points, the Moros raided villages, attacked soldiers, and resisted the American attempt to secure what was now a U.S. possession. Between July 1902 and December 1904, and again late in 1905, the Army dispatched a series of expeditions into the interior of Mindanao to destroy Moro strongholds. With some 1,000 men (including elements of his own 27th Infantry and a mountain battery), Col. Frank D. Baldwin invaded the territory of the Sultan of Bayan near Lake Lanao and defeated the Sultan's forces in the hotly contested Battle of Bayan on May 2, 1902. Capt. John J. Pershing (1860–1948) headed a similar expedition into the Lanao country in 1903, and Capt. Frank R. McCoy finally killed the notorious Moro outlaw, Dato Ali, in the Cotabato district in October 1905.

In May 1905, March 1906, and again seven years later, Army regulars had to cope with disorders too extensive to be handled by the local constabulary and Philippine Scouts on the island of Jolo, a Moro stronghold. The last fighting against U.S. soldiers took place in June 1913.

The Philippine Insurrection lasted from April 11, 1899 (dating from the cessation of fighting in the Spanish-American War), until July 4, 1902 (except in the Moro province, where it ended July 15, 1903). Total troops involved were 126,468, including 76,416 regulars and 50,052 volunteers. There was no draft. Total deaths of 4,165 included 777 killed in action, 227 who died of wounds, 2,572 felled by disease, and 589 accidental and other deaths. There were 2,911 wounded. These figures are for the Army only.

During this era, the Army also fought in China during what became popularly known as the Boxer Rebellion. The China Relief Expedition lasted from June 20, 1900, to May 12, 1901. The 5,000 troops who participated were all regulars. Total deaths of 102 included 33 who were killed in action, 18 who died of wounds, 47 who died of disease, and 4 who suffered accidental and other deaths. The Army lists no wounded or prisoners.

CHAPTER 6

THE NEW CENTURY AND THE FIRST WORLD WAR (1902–1941)

At the beginning of the most destructive century the world would ever know, the U.S. Army went through dramatic change. Most of the changes were the work of Secretary of War Elihu Root (1845–1937), the service's top civilian from 1899 to 1904, and Gen. Frederick Funston. Root was a brilliant administrator and attorney who had been first in his law class. He quietly relished the role of being a powerful force for change.

The United States was no longer a second-rate nation with the principal military task of policing a wild frontier. In fact, the frontier officially ceased to exist before the turn of the century (a conclusion of the 1890 census). In the twentieth century, the United States was emerging as a world power with global alliances and responsibilities.

Following the fighting in Cuba and the Philippines, a postwar investigating commission appointed by President William McKinley and headed by Maj. Gen. Grenville M. Dodge (1831–1916) found a serious need for reform of the Army's high command. Inefficiency was rampant inside the War Department. The Army's branches, the adjutant general's corps, the quartermaster corps, the artillery, and the infantry, were a collection of fiefdoms, each with its own way of doing things. In some cases, practices were not merely inefficient; they were corrupt.

There was general agreement in Washington that the Army needed a better way to prepare for war. The Spanish-American War and the Philippine Insurrection pointed to glaring problems, including the peculiar fact that the commanding general of the Army held no authority over the administration and supply of the Army. Every other country in the world had a general staff that oversaw every aspect of military operations.

Root was appalled at the behind-the-scenes turf fights among bureau chiefs who reported to the Secretary of War but not to the commanding general of the Army. After long study within the War Department, Root restored strictly military matters to the generals. He reduced the power of the bureau chiefs and established a general staff headed by a chief of staff who replaced the commanding general of the Army and acted as chief adviser and executive agent of the president on military policy. Despite the opposition of the incumbent commanding general and the bureau chiefs, Congress adopted Secretary Root's proposal in the Militia Act of 1903 (the Dick Act). Root went further, however. He established new standards for promotion, created the War College, enlarged West Point, and focused strongly on what became the National Guard. With advice from Funston and others, Root made the largest changes the Army would see until subsequent transformations in 1947 and 2002.

THE DICK ACT

Root's efforts and the Dick Act reorganized the militia as the Organized Militia (soon to acquire yet another name: the National Guard) and the Reserve Militia. Root brought National Guard training, organization, and weaponry in line with that of the regular Army. Control over Guard personnel remained, however, in the hands of the state governments, with the president authorized to federalize the Guard only in case of invasion or insurrection or to enforce federal laws of the Union. Later in the twentieth century, National Guardsmen would be federalized for longer periods in all of the nation's major wars, except for limited numbers during the Vietnam Conflict. Root won praise from many in Washington, including a future secretary of war, Henry L. Stimson (1867–1950).

It is interesting to note that the general staff created by Root no longer exists today. The Army's top soldier is still called the chief of staff, the term created by Root, but today he "owns" no troops, tanks, or guns, and he commands only his small Pentagon staff. Later in the century, in part due to distaste for the German model, the U.S. would dispense with the idea of a general staff.

Lt. Gen. Samuel B. M. Young (1840–1924), a Civil War veteran who had been a leader in the Battle of Santiago Heights, became the Army's first chief of staff on August 15, 1903. Although the duties of the incumbent have since changed and the general staff has been discarded, Young's installation as the nation's top soldier established an organizational format that continues to this day. Today the chief of staff, as the principal officer of the Army, is appointed by the president, with the advice and consent of the Senate, from among the general officers of the Army. He serves at the pleasure of the president for a period of four years and performs his duties under the direction of the secretary of the Army.

In 1905, the Army established the division, rather than the corps, as the basic combined arms unit. A division would have three brigades (each of two or more infantry regiments) along with artillery (provisional regiment), cavalry (regiment), engineers (battalion), and other support units. A typical division could have as many as 28,000 men. This continuing process of the Army redefining itself continued in the early years of the new century, even though the first officers occupying the chief of staff's slot were viewed as relatively weak figures.

On August 1, 1907, the Army created the Aeronautical Division of the Signal Corps. The nation's air arm remained part of the Army until the U.S. belatedly made its Air Force an independent service branch in 1947. The era from biplanes to jets is considered part of Air Force history and is covered in the *Alpha Bravo Delta Guide to the U.S. Air Force.*

Lt. Gen. Adna R. Chaffee (1842–1914) followed Young as chief of staff in 1904. Lt. Gen. John C. Bates (1842–1919) held the slot for just a few months in 1906.

Maj. Gen. J. Franklin Bell (1856–1919) served as the Army's chief of staff from 1906 to 1910, followed by Medal of Honor recipient and former

"Rough Riders" commander Maj. Gen. Leonard Wood from 1910 to 1914. Wood was the first truly effective chief of staff. He believed that a soldier, even an officer, could be trained in six months or less, and helped to create short-term officer-training programs that would be sorely needed for the remainder of the century.

William Howard Taft, the former governor of the newly annexed Philippines, replaced Theodore Roosevelt to become the twenty-seventh president in 1909.

THE PREWAR ERA

Continuing in the spirit of Root's reforms, between 1909 and 1914 Congress enacted numerous changes to the law governing the National Guard. The changes gave the president—always the commander in chief—authority to prescribe the length of federal service and to appoint Guard officers while the Guard was in federal service. Regular Army soldiers and National Guardsmen began to participate together in war games.

Between the Spanish-American War and World War I, the Army made considerable adjustment in response to new developments in munitions and equipment. Probably the most far-reaching changes came as a result of the development of the internal combustion engine, which made possible the truck, the airplane, and the tank. The impact on tactics, organization, and logistics was revolutionary. Still, the American soldier of the period before World War I was no better equipped than—and, in some cases, not as well equipped as—soldiers of other nations. In less than 15 years, the Army had transitioned from its first smokeless powder magazine rifle, the M1892 Krag-Jorgensen, to the improved M1903 Springfield, but rapid-fire weapons were entering service elsewhere and the United States was still relying on bolt action.

Though Americans had developed the machine gun, the Army relied on small numbers of inferior Colt models while the Germans possessed thousands of superior machine guns developed by the American inventor Hiram Maxim (1840–1916). The Army also was forced to use the French 75-mm cannon because it did not have a weapon of its own in this class. In the next great conflict, Americans would go to war using French aircraft, tanks, and automatic rifles.

In Cuba, a provisional government led by Army generals brought economic and political stability to the island. Among its greatest achievements were the discovery of the cause of yellow fever in 1900 and the subsequent elimination of the disease in Cuba by the Medical Department.

The Army built the Panama Canal, with the principal work being done by a commission composed of Army officers and headed by Col. (later Maj. Gen.) George W. Goethals (1858–1928), who pushed construction to completion in eight years. Both the corps of engineers and the Medical Department made major contributions to this project. The Medical Department controlled the malaria and yellow fever that had blocked earlier attempts to build a canal. The engineers' completion of this project freed the nation from the cost of maintaining large fleets in two oceans. At the same time, the canal established a requirement for constant protection by highly trained garrisons manning modern fortifications and weapons.

As the Army transformed itself from frontier duty to overseas deployment, the War Department developed a plan to station troops in overseas garrisons as a strong signal of America's commitment to defending Panama, Hawaii, Puerto Rico, Alaska, and the Philippines. By 1913, the Army had established 22 new camps and forts in the Philippines alone.

Taft occupied the White House until 1913, when Woodrow Wilson (1856–1924), the twenty-eighth president, succeeded him. The Army continued to evolve—and, in Europe, war clouds gathered.

Wilson was old enough to have personal memories of the horrors of war. He was the son of a Presbyterian minister who during the Civil War was a pastor in Augusta, Georgia, and during Reconstruction was a professor in the charred city of Columbia, South Carolina. Wilson brought many changes to the nation, including maneuvering through Congress the legislation that created a federal income tax, but his focus in his re-election campaign was on staying out of the conflagration sweeping Europe. The slogan "He kept us out of war" enabled Wilson to win re-election, although just narrowly.

SOUTH OF THE BORDER

Wilson was very conscious that the strategic Panama Canal would soon be finished and that the United States had strong interests in Latin America. Wilson and others in Washington were almost paternal toward those who lived south of the border. They were also distinctly uncomfortable about Mexico, the same country the United States had invaded six decades earlier.

Wilson found an excuse to have the Navy attack Vera Cruz in 1914, a move that destabilized the regime and empowered Pancho Villa (1878–1923), a bandit who fancied himself a general and enjoyed a wide following. When not fighting Emiliano Zapata (1879–1919) and his Zapatista followers, Villa used his forces to attack Americans.

He murdered a dozen Americans on a train inside Mexico. Then, on March 9, 1916, he led 500 Villistas who then sallied north of the border to kill a group of Americans in Columbus, New Mexico. Wilson sent Maj. Gen. John J. "Black Jack" Pershing to kill or capture Villa. Another officer who searched for Villa was a young Capt. George S. Patton (1885–1945).

American troops gained considerable experience in light, mobile warfare trying to track down Villa, but the Mexican proved too elusive. With 10,000 troops and 11 months of effort, the Army never once met up with Villa's main force. Eventually, it became obvious that the Army was going to be needed elsewhere, and in 1917 Wilson ordered an end to Pershing's expedition.

U.S. TO WAR

The official dates for U.S. participation in World War I are from April 6, 1917, until July 2, 1921, even though the armistice took effect and the fighting essentially stopped on November 11, 1918. It was not until much later, when the world was embroiled in World War II, that this conflict became known as World War I.

The war really began on June 28, 1914, when a student nationalist assassinated Archduke Francis Ferdinand of the Austro-Hungarian Empire in the Eastern European city of Sarajevo. The killing was the catalyst that stirred up resentments among Britain, France, and Austria's ally, Germany, headed by the autocratic young Kaiser Wilhelm. In early August, Germany declared war on Russia and then on France. On August 4, honoring a mutual defense commitment, Great Britain declared war on Germany while German troops drove through Belgium en route to France. The following day, a much-divided United States declared its neutrality, although many Americans volunteered to fight with British and French forces.

On September 5, 1914, the Battle of the Marne, fought with French and British troops on one side and Germans on the other, halted Germany's drive to take over Western Europe, but at enormous cost, with tens of thousands killed or wounded. The Marne fighting demonstrated vividly that nineteenth-century tactics were useless in the face of twentieth-century weapons, but military leaders were slow to adapt and the opposing armies settled in for a deadly stalemate in opposing trenches. News of the horrendous slaughter at the Marne helped strengthen those in the United States who wanted to see the country stay out of the war.

As Elihu Root had foreseen when he reorganized the U.S. Army, it was a new era, with hand-loaded muskets and chivalrous cavalry charges giving way to a roster of new and more lethal weapons, including the water-cooled machine gun, the tank, and the aircraft. Another innovation was the U-boat (submarine). On May 7, 1915, one of these torpedoed and sank the Cunard ocean liner the *Lusitania*, killing about 1,200, including about 120 U.S. citizens. The sinking fired up some tempers in the United States but had little impact on Washington's policy of maintaining neutrality. President Woodrow Wilson was quietly making plans to fight but was talking publicly of peace.

TOWARD WAR

Wilson's first Secretary of War after Root was Lindley M. Garrison (1864–1932), who served from 1913 to 1916 and would be a "hawk" in today's parlance. Garrison favored a military buildup and a harsh policy toward Mexico, as well as retention of the Philippines. He resigned after Wilson, attempting to hew to his peace pledge, refused to ask Congress to increase the size of the Army.

Though he pledged to keep the United States out of the horrors unfolding on European battlefields, Wilson knew that the United States might need to send an expeditionary force to Europe. He had chosen as his secretary of war the rather unlikely Newton D. Baker (1871–1937), a man who had served as a postmaster and as mayor of Cleveland but who had no military credentials and was, in fact, viewed as a pacifist. As things turned out, Baker would become a hawk, too, and would institute the draft and quadruple the Army to four million men.

Wilson and Baker concluded that the best man to command U.S. troops abroad was the diminutive, non–West Pointer Frederick N. Funston, a Medal of Honor recipient during the Philippine Insurrection and the fiery captor of the Filipino insurgent Aguinaldo. Funston led military relief efforts after the 1906 San Francisco earthquake and was one of the Army's reformers.

Secretary of War Baker was hosting a Washington function for President Wilson on the night of February 19, 1917, and left orders not to be disturbed. A young major, Douglas MacArthur, the son of Medal of Honor recipient Arthur MacArthur, happened to be the on-duty officer in the State, War, Navy Building when fellow officer Lt. Col. Peyton C. March (1864–1955) brought news. MacArthur later wrote, "About 10 o'clock March brought up a wire that General Funston, who had been informally selected to command an American Expeditionary Force if we entered the war, had just dropped dead in the St. Anthony Hotel in San Francisco." MacArthur drew the hapless job of hand-carrying the news to Baker's residence, where he presented it personally to Wilson. When the president asked who should replace Funston to command a U.S. expeditionary force, MacArthur replied that he could only speak for himself, but in his opinion it should be Pershing. It was an obvious choice, and it is unlikely MacArthur had any real influence on the decision that followed.

Long before Funston's death, Wilson was in the midst of a turnaround. Shortly after beginning his second term in 1917, Wilson completed this about-face. He concluded that America could not remain neutral in the world war. On April 2, 1917, he asked Congress for a declaration of war on Germany.

Reformed but far from ready, the Army attempted to make preparations. It had some valuable leaders—Funston until his death; Tasker H. Bliss (1853–1930), who served as chief of staff of the Army from September 1917 to May 1918; Peyton C. March, who favored limits on the powers of the chief of staff; and a somewhat lesser known John J. Pershing.

ARMY STRENGTH

The Army was 13,000 men below strength in April 1917, with just 127,588 soldiers on its rolls, plus about 5,000 Philippine Scouts. Also part of the nation's arsenal was the National Guard, which had about 174,000 soldiers, half of whom had been federalized. There were also about 15,000 Reserve troops. Thus, the total number of uniformed Americans was in the neighborhood of 335,000. This was a figure that in no way resembled the 4.1 million Americans who would eventually serve during the World War I era.

Up to this point in American history, no one had yet held the rank of full general (George Washington, for example, having reached lieutenant general). But after the United States entered World War I, the rank of full general (four stars) eventually was bestowed on Bliss, March, and Pershing to give them parity with French and British field marshals. With the death of Funston, Wilson and Baker's next choice for leadership was Pershing, who had fought well as a junior officer in Cuba and the Philippines and had led the incursion into Mexico aimed at capturing the troublesome Pancho Villa. They chose Pershing to command the American Expeditionary Force, or AEF, the "Doughboys."

"Doughboy," the popular term for the American soldier in World War I, was used by some at least a century earlier, but no one knows exactly why. One theory is that infantrymen cooking doughy flour and rice rations over a camp fire earned the "doughboy" appellation.

On April 6, 1917, four days after Wilson requested it, the United States declared war on Germany. The vote was 90–6 in the Senate, and 373–50 in the House. A dramatic increase in U-boat attacks by Germany, coupled with the interception of the Zimmerman telegram (which promised Mexico it would regain part of the United States if it entered the war on the German side), precipitated the American decision to join the fight.

GOING TO WAR

It was painfully apparent that the United States could not field a significant presence in Europe with an all-volunteer Army. On May 18, 1917, Congress enacted the Selective Service Law, authorizing the drafting of males between 21 and 30. The government sold war bonds, which were promoted by film stars Douglas Fairbanks (1883–1939) and Mary Pickford (1892–1979). Wilson decreed a "mobilization of every resource in the nation." The War Industries Bureau, under Bernard Baruch (1870–1965), took measures to control industrial production. The bureau oversaw a vast reorganization of the nation's infrastructure. Distribution of raw materials and sources of energy was organized in deference to the war effort, industries were converted, railways were placed under government control, and mining engineer Herbert Hoover (1874–1964) administered the organization of food for Europe.

> World War I was the first industrial war, a full-scale conflict that brought scientific advances, mass production, and nationwide mobilization of human and economic resources. U.S. industry was largely up to the task of producing war supplies, but the nation was never fully equipped to ship them overseas once they were made.

Wilson officially named Pershing to command the AEF. In May 1917, Pershing sailed secretly for Europe aboard a passenger ship, the *Baltic.* The Rainbow Division, so-named because it was composed of hand-picked National Guard units from 26 states and the District of Columbia, was assigned to move to Europe as the first of many units in Pershing's AEF. Officially, it was the 42nd Infantry Division, commanded by Maj. Gen. Charles Menoher, but its newly promoted chief of staff, Col. Douglas MacArthur, said that, "[It] stretches like a Rainbow from one end of America to the other." A serious and somber figure, Menoher was overshadowed by MacArthur during the fighting and just after the war by almost everyone when—as the only nonflyer to head the Air Service—he took the unpopular view that the nation's air arm should remain part of the Army.

The First Expeditionary Division, later designated the 1st Infantry Division and called the "Big Red One," was organized in May 1917 from regular Army units in service on the Mexican border and throughout the United States. The 1st Division's first elements sailed from New York and New Jersey in June 1917. Throughout the remainder of the year, the rest of the division landed troops at St. Nazaire, France, and Liverpool, England.

On the American Independence Day, July 4, 1917, Americans paraded through the streets of Paris to bolster French spirits. At the tomb of the American Revolutionary War hero Lafayette, one of Pershing's aides uttered the famous words, "Lafayette, we are here!" The 1st Division fired the first American artillery shell on the morning of October 23 and two days later sustained the first American casualties of the war.

The Rainbow Division arrived in France in November 1917 and entered the front line in March 1918, where it remained in almost constant contact with the enemy for 174 days. MacArthur eventually commanded the division, which participated in 6 major campaigns and incurred 1 out of 16 casualties suffered by the Army during the war.

Wood's replacement as Army chief of staff, Maj. Gen. William W. Wotherspoon, served only briefly and was followed by Maj. Gen. Hugh L. Scott, who served from 1914 until September 1917. Under Scott, on June 7, 1917, the general staff issued a plan to ship American troops to Europe at a rate of 120,000 per month beginning in August. It was an unrealistically high goal and would not be achieved until April 1918.

FIRST CASUALTIES

In later years, the Army would officially identify several names as representing the first casualties of the AEF. The very first was 1st Lt. Louis J. Genella, Medical Corps, who suffered a shell wound on July 14, 1917, while serving with the British at the front southwest of Arras.

The first AEF soldiers to be killed by the enemy were 1st Lt. William T. Fitzsimmons and Pfcs. Rudolph Rubino Jr., Oscar C. Tugo, and Leslie G. Woods, all of U.S. Base Hospital No. 5. They lost their lives on September 4, 1917, when the Germans bombed a British hospital in which they were on duty near Dannes-Camiers.

Continuing the Army's own grim roster of "firsts," the first battle casualties of an American unit while it was serving at the front were Sgt. Matthew R. Calderwood and Pvt. William F. Branigan, both of Company F, 11th Engineers, who were wounded by shellfire on September 5, 1917, while working on a railway near Gouzeaucourt.

Finally, the first American soldiers to be killed in action as members of an American unit were Cpl. James B. Gresham and Pvts. Thomas F. Enright and Merle D. Hay, all of whom perished when German troops raided American trenches at Bathelemont on November 2, 1917.

While the United States geared up for war, in November 1917, Bolsheviks overthrew the Russian government, creating a new regime that made peace with Germany. The United States did not recognize the government created by the Russian Revolution. In fact, Russia would become the battleground for a separate war waged on two fronts by U.S. troops from 1918 to 1920. Meanwhile, on December 7, 1917, America added a new belligerent by declaring war on the Austro-Hungarian Empire.

The procurement of horses and mules was a major problem during World War I, and a shortage always existed. Still, the United States and its Allies (Britain, France, and Spain) acquired 243,039 horses and mules in 1917 and 1918 at an average cost of $416.63 per animal.

On January 8, 1918, Wilson enunciated his "14 points," which included the formation of a league of nations. The European Allies paid little attention. As American doughboys began to arrive at European ports, pressure from French leaders resulted in France's Gen. Ferdinand Foch (1851–1929) being made supreme commander of Allied forces. Foch was soon made Marshal of France, a military rank that put him a notch above the Americans' Pershing. The Allies failed to define Foch's authority, however, and Pershing never lost sight of his goal for an integrated American Army.

Born in 1860, John J. "Black Jack" Pershing was a West Pointer (1886) who fought in frontier campaigns that culminated at Wounded Knee in 1890.

Pershing was the protégé of Lt. Col. Theodore Roosevelt. After he became president in 1901, Roosevelt wanted to reward then-Capt. Pershing. But the president lacked the authority to promote a captain to major, although he could appoint anyone he wanted a brigadier general. Roosevelt resolved the issue by elevating Pershing from captain to brigadier general, over the heads of 862 other officers.

In 1916, Pershing led U.S. troops into Mexico chasing the bandit Pancho Villa, a futile hunt dubbed the Punitive Expedition.

Pershing's nickname, "Black Jack," bestowed by cadets when he taught at West Point, was a cleaned-up version of an epithet that faulted Pershing for his positive attitude toward Negro soldiers during a stint with a black regiment.

In May 1917, Pershing was tasked with fielding Army troops in France, where both sides were pitted in brutal trench warfare.

Pershing resisted British and French efforts to absorb American "doughboys" into their own armies instead of forming an all-American force. Pershing also faced huge supply and logistics challenges.

Made a full general in October 1917, Pershing did a superb job of managing turf battles with the Allies, building a railroad system to support the AEF, and putting American troops into battle.

Pershing defied political pressures and assembled an AEF of 500,000 men. In September 1918, he led them in the reduction of the St. Mihiel salient, the first victory in an all–U.S. operation. When the war ended in November 1918, the AEF under Pershing had played a pivotal role.

In September 1919, Congress created the rank of General of the Armies, making Pershing the highest-ranking American ever to serve in uniform—surpassing even the five-star officers who followed in World War II. From 1921 to 1924, he was Army chief of staff. His memoir, *My Experiences in the World War,* won him the 1932 Pulitzer Prize for history. Pershing died in 1948.

PERSHING ORGANIZES

From his headquarters in Chaumont, Pershing sought to create what he called the 1st Army, an all-American fighting force, to be made up of several corps—each of which, in turn, was made up of several divisions.

At the start of a new year of conflict, Pershing now had eight American divisions, only three of which were in combat; both numbers would increase dramatically as 1918 unfolded. On January 15, 1918, Pershing formed I Corps, with headquarters at Neufchâteau, and placed his deputy, Maj. Gen. (later Lt. Gen.) Hunter Liggett (1857–1937), in command. Liggett thus became responsible for the 1st ("Big Red One"), 2nd ("Indianhead"), 26th, and 42nd ("Rainbow") divisions. Liggett was credited with understanding the everyday American soldier better than many commanders, but was also viewed by some as a rulebook soldier who might have benefited from greater flexibility.

The corps that eventually made up the American force were led by some of the most accomplished leaders in the Army. II Corps was part of French forces and never became part of Pershing's much-wanted 1st Army.

III Corps fell under the command of Maj. Gen. (later Lt. Gen.) Robert L. Bullard, who first headed the 1st Division in its initial action at Cantigny before moving up to the corps level. Bullard did a remarkable job of transforming troops that were less prepared and equipped than most into a fighting force.

IV Corps, formed later in the year, came under Maj. Gen. Joseph Dickman, who began the war as commander of the 3rd Division at Château-Thierry. Dickman was an innovator and a disciplinarian; he later replaced Liggett at I Corps and still later commanded the 3rd Army when it was created at the end of the war.

V Corps, also formed later in 1918, was initially led by Maj. Gen. George Cameron, who performed well but, after the Battle of Montfaucon later in the year, was so exhausted that he asked to be returned to his former (and lower) status as 4th Division commander. At the corps level, he was replaced by Maj. Gen. Charles P. Summeral, who was viewed as loud, hard driving, and ruthless.

VI Corps was not a genuine major command, a fact not even fully revealed to its commander, Maj. Gen. Omar Bundy. It was essentially a dummy created to deceive the Germans by giving the impression that the doughboys planned to attack in another location when the fight for the St. Mihiel salient was being organized.

In March 1918, Secretary of War Baker traveled to Europe, visited the front, and proclaimed himself "on the frontier of freedom." By then, Bliss—like Scott before him—was pushing mandatory retirement age (65) and was ready to retire as Army chief of staff. Baker replaced him with a rapidly promoted Maj. Gen. Peyton C. March (who apparently was performing the job weeks before he officially stepped into it on May 18, 1918). Historian John Eisenhower described March as "an odd sort of Army officer [who] never developed the social manners that were considered prerequisite for a successful military career." His belief in limited powers on the part of the Army chief was heartfelt. But his style, wrote Eisenhower, could be "ruthless and abrasive." To some, he was a troubleshooter; to others, he was a hatchet man. In fact, March would leave a significant mark on the Army.

DOUGHBOY ACTION

On April 9, 1918, German forces launched a major offensive in Flanders. Coincidentally, American doughboys had adopted "Mademoiselle from

Armentieres," an irreverent soldiers' song with disputed British origins, as their own, but Armentieres was the first town to fall to the Kaiser's troops.

Beginning May 31, 1918, as the Germans launched what was known as the third Aisne offensive, the 3rd Division was caught up in 41 days of unrelenting combat in the Battle of Château-Thierry, an action that actually encompassed three operations by Americans sent by Pershing to French Command. The three phases were the defense of the line at the Marne River, the battle of Belleau Wood (where the Aisne offensive was stopped by the 2nd Division and U.S. Marines saw their first large-scale action), and the capture of Vaux. The 2nd Infantry Division, known as the "Indianhead" division, took Vaux in vicious fighting after days of sparring that included a skirmish in which German mustard gas inflicted 400 American casualties. For the "Indianhead" soldiers, it was the beginning of a long and distinguished history: The division remains on guard in Korea today.

Yellow in color with a garlicky smell, mustard gas actually had nothing to do with mustard. This poison gas attacked the skin and eyes and caused severe blisters. If inhaled, it could damage the lungs. It often produced gruesome injuries but did not kill, meaning that additional soldiers were kept out of the fighting while they tended to casualties.

SECOND MARNE

After blunting the German offensive and striking back, Pershing's AEF, now 260,000 strong, was ready to achieve a turning point after years of nearly static trench warfare. Now came the Second Battle of the Marne—the first having taken place before the United States entered the war.

The successful defense at Château-Thierry produced a bulge in the battle line some 30 miles wide where German forces seemed especially vulnerable. In July 1918, when the Germans struggled to get on the offensive once again, Pershing's staff decided to withstand another attack, hope for heavy attrition on the part of the Germans, and then strike back once more.

On July 15, 1918, the 3rd Division began a difficult defensive effort against the Germans at the left extreme of the Marne line. Throughout July and August, the 2nd and 3rd Divisions were in especially heavy fighting. The turn of the tide came finally at Soissons, where U.S. troops assaulted

German forces and sent them reeling. At the end of July and the start of August, the 32nd and 42nd Divisions occupied positions abandoned by the Germans and drove toward the Ourcq and the Vesle Rivers.

In combat for the first time in mid-July, the 3rd Division readily earned the name it would use ever after: "Rock of the Marne." When surrounding units retreated, the 3rd Infantry Division stood fast and even gained ground, albeit with heavy casualties.

The 28th Division, called the "Keystone" division because it was composed largely of Pennsylvanians, went into battle in mid-July also. Soldiers of the division participated in six major campaigns, and Pershing called the unit the "Iron Division."

By August 6, 1918, the Aisne-Marne campaign had ended. Wiping out the Marne salient ended the German threat to Paris. The initiative now had definitely passed to the Allies. Moreover, the success of the offensive revealed the advantages of Allied unity of command and the fighting qualities of American units. The eight AEF divisions (1st, 2nd, 3rd, 4th, 26th, 28th, 32nd, and 42nd) in the action spearheaded much of the advance, demonstrating offensive capabilities that inspired new confidence in the war-weary Allied armies.

It was a costly effort. The Second Battle of Marne cost 30,000 Americans killed and wounded, casualties on the enormous scale that the British and French knew only too well.

> Except for four 14-inch naval guns, the First Army throughout its entire service on the Western Front in 1917 and 1918 did not fire a single cannon or shell that was made in America. Most cannons used by Americans were of French manufacture.

While the fighting was still underway, the Allies' supreme commander, Foch, convened the only conference of Allied commanders that he called during the war. Foch argued that the Allied offensive should reduce the three main German salients—Marne, Amiens, and St. Mihiel. This would improve command and control behind the lines and permit a final drive to win the war with a general offensive in the fall. The job of reducing the St. Mihiel salient was assigned to Pershing at his own request.

The Americans' good performance in the Aisne-Marne Offensive gave Pershing an opportunity to press again for the formation of an independent American army. After conferences in July 1918, Foch agreed to the organization of the 1st Army and to the formation of two American sectors—a temporary combat sector in the Château-Thierry region, where the already active I and III Corps could comprise the nucleus of the 1st Army, and a quiet sector farther east, extending from Nomeny (east of the Moselle) to a point north of St. Mihiel. The eastern sector would become the actual theater of operations for the American Army as soon as circumstances permitted concentration of AEF divisions there. Orders issued on July 24 announced formation of the 1st Army, effective on August 10; they designated Pershing as its commander and located its headquarters at La Ferté-sous-Jouarre, west of Château-Thierry. The operations officer for the all-American force was Col. George C. Marshall.

The U.S. had a diversion from World War I in August 1918 when American soldiers joined a Japanese invasion of the region around Vladivostok in Russia. American troops joined "White Russian" forces in a doomed effort against the Bolshevik revolutionaries.

ST. MIHIEL SALIENT

Pershing ended up bypassing the Château-Thierry region and building up 1st Army units in the vicinity of the St. Mihiel salient. Tentative plans for reduction of the salient called for the concentration of 3 American corps (about 14 American and 3 French divisions) on a front extending from Port-sur-Seille westward around the bulge to Watronville. Three American divisions would remain on the Vesle front. Meanwhile, Allied forces, including American units operating in other sectors of the Western Front, made significant gains in the preliminary phases of the great final offensives. American units fought in the Somme Offensive (beginning August 8) and battles at Oise-Aisne (beginning August 18) and Ypres-Lys (beginning August 19). These actions preceded the final effort by the doughboys in their all-American force in the St. Mihiel (beginning September 12) and the Meuse-Argonne (beginning September 26) campaigns.

In September 1918, with both the Marne and the Amiens salients eliminated, there remained a major threat to lateral rail communications behind

Allied lines, the St. Mihiel salient near the Paris-Nancy line. The 14 American and 4 French divisions assigned to the 1st Army for the operation contained ample infantry and machine-gun units for the attack. But because of the earlier priority given to shipment of infantry (at the insistence of the British and French), the 1st Army was short of artillery, tank, air, and other support units essential to a well-balanced field army. The French made up this deficiency by loaning Pershing over half the artillery and nearly half the airplanes and tanks needed for the St. Mihiel operation.

> All tanks operated by the Army in the war were of French or British make. American manufacturers were just beginning to produce tanks in quantity when the armistice took effect.

Foch and Pershing argued about details, and Pershing remained steadfast in his insistence that the 1st Army retain its American identity and not be broken up. The St. Mihiel offensive began on September 12 with a threefold assault on the salient. The main attack was made against the south face by two American corps. On the right was the I Corps (from right to left the 82nd, 90th, 5th, and 2nd divisions in line, with the 78th in reserve), covering a front from Pont-à-Mousson on the Moselle westward to Limey; on the left was the IV Corps (from right to left the 89th, 42nd, and 1st divisions in line, with the 3rd in reserve), extending along a front from Limey westward to Marvoisin. The Americans carried out a secondary thrust against the western face along the heights of the Meuse, from Mouilly north to Haudimont, by the V Corps (from right to left, the 26th Division, the French 15th Colonial Division, and the 8th Brigade, 4th Division in line, with the rest of the 4th in reserve). French forces made a holding attack against the apex, to keep the enemy in the salient. In 1st Army reserve were the American 35th, 80th, and 91st divisions.

In the St. Mihiel action, total Allied forces numbered more than 650,000—some 550,000 American and 100,000 Allied (mostly French) troops. In support of the attack, the 1st Army had over 3,000 guns, 400 French tanks, and 1,500 aircraft.

At least eight German divisions, plus two in reserve, defended the St. Mihiel salient. Now strained in manpower, the Germans began a step-by-step withdrawal from the day before the offensive began. Pershing's attack went well; on September 12, the American commander ordered a speedup of the assault. By the morning of September 13, the 1st Division, advancing from the east, joined hands with the 26th Division, moving in from the west, and before evening all objectives in the salient had been captured. At this point, Pershing halted further advances so that American units could be withdrawn for the coming offensive in the Meuse-Argonne sector.

This was the first major operation by an American Army under its own command. It took 16,000 prisoners at a cost of 7,000 casualties, eliminated the threat of an attack on the rear of Allied fortifications at Nancy and Verdun, greatly improved Allied lateral rail communications, and opened the way for a future offensive action that might prove decisive.

On September 20, the AEF had grown to the point that Pershing was able to form a 2nd Army. To command it, he chose Bullard, who had consistently performed well throughout the fighting.

He was known as Sergeant York, but he was a corporal during the battle in 1918 when 30-year-old Alvin C. York proved himself to be an Army of one.

York, a devout Tennessee native who disliked war, is credited with killing 20 German soldiers and capturing 132. His battlefield feat earned York the Medal of Honor.

After his platoon had suffered heavy casualties and three other noncommissioned officers had become casualties, York assumed command. Fearlessly leading seven men, he charged with great daring a machine-gun nest that was pouring deadly and incessant fire upon his platoon. In this heroic feat, the machine-gun nest was taken, together with 4 officers, 128 men, and several guns.

It was October 8, 1918. The last great offensive of the war was underway in the Argonne Forest. With his platoon under fire by a German machine-gun position, 1st Lt. Harry M. Parsons ordered Sgt. Bernard Early to attack the gun position with 15 men.

Early and his troops maneuvered behind the German gun nest and fixed bayonets. Preparing to charge, they inadvertently walked into German officers studying a map. Early's troops fired a few rounds, and the Germans raised their hands in surrender.

The machine gun crew, however, turned their weapon around and opened fire, killing six Americans and wounding Early and York's best friend in the platoon, Pvt. Murray Savage.

At one point, a German lieutenant and six men charged York's position. Now wielding a pistol, York—according to legend—killed all six.

After the war, York resisted celebrity until 1939, when—despite his church's view that movies were sinful—he reluctantly authorized a film about himself. Released in 1942, *Sergeant York,* starring Gary Cooper, became one of the top-grossing Warner Brothers films of the era and earned Cooper the Academy Award for Best Actor.

In May 2000, the U.S. Postal Service issued a commemorative stamp honoring York.

WAR'S END

Now U.S. troops fought in the final offensive of World War I, an attack that required both courage on the battlefield and incredible logistics skills, much of the latter provided by Marshall. Much as Americans would do in the Persian Gulf near the end of the century, in the Meusse-Argonne fighting they moved entire divisions, with all their weapons and equipment, over distances of 20 miles or more, merely to maintain contact with the foe and continue to press the fight. While some skeptics remained, it was now a proven fact that an all-American force under Pershing could hold its own and even turn the tide.

All this time, the Army was redefining itself. Peyton C. March, now a full general, pulled duty as Army chief of staff from May 1918 until June 1921. During his time as chief of staff, March established the primacy of the chief of staff in the Army hierarchy; he supervised the buildup of American forces in World War I, centralized control over supply, and created an Air Service, Tank Corps, and Chemical Warfare School.

On the eve of the armistice that ended World War I (in the eleventh hour of the eleventh day of the eleventh month), Pershing relinquished to Lt. Gen. Liggett command of the 1st Army with its one million doughboys. Liggett remained in command of the 1st Army until its inactivation in April 1919. The 3rd Army stood up on November 7, just days before the armistice, under Maj. Gen. Joseph T. Dickman. It eventually became the occupation force for Germany, and Liggett commanded it beginning in April 1919. By then, of course, the troops were coming home, parades were being held, flags were being waved, and—as inevitably happens in peacetime—the Army was being downsized.

Ammunition expended by the American Expeditionary Force during World War I included 181,391,341 rounds of .30-caliber (rifle), 120,901,102 rounds of .45-caliber (pistol), 2,274,229 rounds of 37-mm (cannon), 7,550,835 rounds of 75-mm (howitzer), and 2,724,067 grenades.

The total number of American soldiers in service during World War I was 4,057,101, a figure that included 545,773 regulars, 728,234 volunteers (including 433,478 National Guard members, 183,797 from the Reserve Corps, and 110,959 who voluntarily enlisted before call under the Selective Service regulations), and 2,783,094 draftees. Total deaths of 119,956 include 37,568 killed in combat (among them, 27 in American forces in Siberia), and 12,942 who died of wounds (among them, 8 in Siberia). Wounds totaled 193,663, but since some soldiers were wounded more than once, these occurred among 182,674 individuals (including 52 in Siberia). There were 4,416 soldiers taken prisoner. These figures are for the Army only.

For the 25 months from April 1917 to May 1919, the war cost the United States more than $1 million per hour. Its total expenditure, including loans to the Allies, was $22 billion, or roughly the entire cost of running the U.S. government from 1791 through 1914. At the time of the armistice, the cost was about $2 million per hour. The pay of officers and men amounted to only about 13 percent of this amount.

AMERICANS IN RUSSIA

After November 11, 1918, it was peacetime for most Americans, but not for all of them—and especially not for U.S. soldiers transplanted to Russia. From 1918 to 1920, these Americans fought in a faraway conflict that few understood. About 400 lost their lives.

U.S. troops were thrown into a counter-revolutionary war at both ends of Russia, near Archangelsk on the European continent and near Vladivostok on the Asian land mass.

In both regions, the Americans fought in harsh Arctic conditions. Their adversary was the Red Army, founded in January 1918 by Leon Trotsky, one of the Bolshevik revolutionaries on the verge of bringing almost seven decades of communism to Russia. The Red Army had seized Moscow and St. Petersburg the previous winter.

The misguided combat mission for U.S. troops began while other Americans were still fighting World War I in the trenches of Western Europe—a war from which Russia had dropped out.

The "Polar Bear Expedition" to Archangelsk, 600 miles north of Moscow, was justified to the troops as a measure to prevent Germany from opening a new front. About 5,000 members of the 85th Division from Camp Custer, Michigan, were placed under British command when they arrived in September 1918.

They found no Germans, but soon began to sustain casualties in wintry battles with Red Army troops.

World War I ended in an armistice on November 11, 1918. It was a defeat for Germany and Austria-Hungary, otherwise known as the Central Powers.

There were celebrations and victory parades. But in Russia, demoralized U.S. troops continued to fight the Bolsheviks. In 1919, one group attempted a short-lived mutiny, while another presented an antiwar petition to officers.

At the other end of Russia, the American Expeditionary Force in Siberia was made up of 10,000 troops from the 27th and 31st infantry regiments, transferred from the Philippines and the 8th Infantry Division from Camp Fremont, California. They remained under U.S. leadership, commanded by Maj. Gen. William Graves (West Point, 1889).

The Russian misadventure was undertaken with no clear vision of what the Army was supposed to accomplish. An Army fact book published decades later in 1949 gave this justification:

> The purposes of the expedition were threefold: To help the Czecho-Slovaks (who had been held as prisoners of war in Russia and were then in Siberia, liberated and partially organized); to steady any efforts at self-government of self-defense in which the Russians themselves might be willing to accept assistance; and to guard military stores which might subsequently be needed by any Russian forces which might be organized again to fight against the Central Powers.

The first reference was to 40,000 Czech troops who had been stranded in Russia when that country dropped out of World War I. The second purpose sounds almost incomprehensible today but refers to helping

"White Russian" anti-Bolsheviks in a futile and forlorn attempt to resist the Russian Revolution.

Calling for restraint on the part of his expedition, Graves clashed repeatedly with commanders of British, French, and Japanese contingents. His obituary by the Association of Graduates of the U.S. Military Academy says, "His administration of a distasteful duty won him the respect of the Russian people who felt that the restraint imposed on other commanders by Gen. Graves ... assisted in checking Allied intentions to dismember their country."

The soldiers' experience was miserable. Problems with fuel, ammunition, supplies, and food were rife. Horses accustomed to temperate climates were unable to function in subzero Russia. Water-cooled machine guns froze and became useless. The foe was an experienced Red Army that understood the climate and terrain.

Troops near Archangelsk were withdrawn in early 1919, but those in Siberia had another year to struggle.

Information on casualties in the Russian expedition is in dispute, but it appears that the Army lost approximately 150 soldiers in action, 50 from wounds, 150 from disease, and 50 from accidental causes. Six committed suicide.

Some believe that missing soldiers were left behind in Russia, making them the first missing-in-action in the twentieth century. The National Alliance of Families charges, "[T]he Bolsheviks held many American [prisoners of war] and other U.S. citizens against their will" and claims that the government did not try hard enough to win their release. In 1929, a War Department commission went to Archangelsk to recover bodies of U.S. soldiers buried there and to bring them home.

Soon after the U.S. troops were withdrawn from Russia, President Warren G. Harding (1865–1923), who had taken office as the twenty-ninth president in March 1921, called the expedition a mistake and blamed the previous administration. Harding, who was president from 1921 to 1923, is generally credited with doing too little to make many mistakes of his own. One opponent called Harding's speeches "an army of pompous phrases moving across the landscape in search of an idea."

THE ROARING TWENTIES

When Harding died in 1923, Vice President Calvin Coolidge (1872–1933) became the thirtieth president. He won election in 1924. In his inaugural address, he asserted that the country had achieved "a state of contentment seldom before seen" and pledged to maintain the status quo. He decided not to seek re-election in 1928. Neither Harding nor Coolidge had military experience, and neither had a significant impact on the Army.

By the time "Black Jack" Pershing completed his tour as chief of staff (in 1924), the Army was on a peacetime footing and a small cadre of soldiers was working to maintain readiness at the high point of the Industrial Age. The National Defense Act of June 4, 1920, charged the Assistant Secretary of War with planning for industrial mobilization and responsibility for the War Department's procurement, an acknowledgement that modern warfare demanded huge mechanized ground forces armed with sophisticated weapons and the ability to move over large fronts—in short, that the soldier needed to be supported by the entire national economy.

Maj. Gen. John L. Hines was Army chief of staff from 1924 to 1926; Gen. Charles P. Summerall served in this position from 1926 to 1930. Hines had commanded the 4th Infantry Division in World War I and was a seasoned but unimaginative soldier. Summerall later presided over the Citadel, that great Southern university that forged so many of America's officers. Neither general had much to work with in the Roaring Twenties; Army officers looked great with their Sam Browne belts and cavalry swords, but Army readiness lagged. At one point, the service decided it no longer needed tanks, a temporary decision that frustrated two middle-grade officers named Patton and Eisenhower. Soldiers still rode on horses, however.

Seeking to prepare the Army for future war, in 1923 the brass produced its first peacetime plan for mobilization. The plan called for 6 field armies with a strength rising from 400,000 on the day of mobilization (known as M-Day), to 1.3 million soldiers within four months and an increase every month thereafter. The plan recognized that the availability of supplies and equipment determined the rate at which troops could be absorbed. However, the plan amounted to what is known in modern jargon as an "unfounded mandate": It neglected the critical issue of the resources needed to create the supplies on which mobilization depended. It assumed that production would adjust to strategic plans, expanding when necessary and contracting when not. It also left unresolved the question of whether different plans were needed for different contingencies.

Two innovations took place as the nation surged toward the Great Depression. One was the establishment of the joint Army and Navy Munitions Board in June 1922. This board brought together the assistant secretaries of the Army and Navy, usually bitter rivals, to give the taxpayer a better way of procuring munitions used by both services.

The other innovation was the creation of the Army Industrial College, where a one-year curriculum enabled officers to study mobilization from a variety of perspectives. Faculty and students contributed to the preparation of the industrial mobilization plans that emerged in the 1930s. The establishment of the board and college showed an understanding that problems of mobilization transcended the Army as a single service branch.

A NEW DECADE

In March 1929, Herbert Hoover became the nation's thirty-first president, just in time for the stock market crash and the onslaught of the Great Depression.

When Gen. Douglas MacArthur became chief of staff in 1930, the nation was still trying to understand the stock market crash of the previous year. It was not a time to be looking for a lot of money from Congress, and while many armies now used automatic rifles, American soldiers were still lugging bolt-action 1903 Springfields. Depression-era retrenchment, most severe in 1933–1934, made it all but impossible to obtain new weapons or hardware for the American soldier.

In March 1933, Franklin D. Roosevelt (1882–1945) became the thirty-second president of the United States. Roosevelt cultivated MacArthur and had a correct, if somewhat distant, relationship with him.

MacArthur is credited with improving Army deficiencies in personnel and materiel, steering those plans for industrial mobilization and manpower procurement, establishing an Air Force headquarters, and administering Army control over the Civilian Conservation Corps. He is also the general who evicted the "bonus marchers" from Washington.

The "bonus marchers" were veterans of World War I who had been promised benefits they never received. When MacArthur violated orders and pushed an angry mob of them out of Washington and across the Potomac River into Anacostia where he burned their tents and shanties, the Army found itself fighting its own veterans.

> The "bonus marchers" were an impoverished, mostly homeless band of veterans of World War I who felt the government owed them cash. About 25,000 marchers, many accompanied by wives and children, descended on the nation's capital to petition Congress for payment of a $500 veterans' bonus promised in 1924 but not payable until 1945. They threw up a shantytown on the Anacostia flat across the Potomac River from Washington and dubbed it "Hoovertown," mocking President Herbert Hoover, whom they accused of not taking the Great Depression seriously enough.
>
> The marchers were not violent. But Hoover believed many of them were communists. Most, in fact, were everyday citizens, their economic circumstances typical in an era when one third of the work force was unemployed.
>
> On July 28, 1932, after two marchers were killed in a scuffle with police, Hoover ordered Secretary of War Patrick J. Hurley to have Army chief of staff Gen. Douglas MacArthur forcibly evict the veterans, assisted by his aide Maj. Dwight D. Eisenhower and soldiers from Fort Myer, Virginia, and Fort Washington, Maryland.
>
> Soldiers donned gas masks and fixed bayonets. They used tear gas, billy clubs, cavalry sabers, horses, and five lightweight Renault tanks to dislodge the veterans from the Capitol Hill region and push them back across the Sousa Bridge into Anacostia. No shots were fired.
>
> Ordered not to go into Anacostia, MacArthur disregarded the order, crossed the river, and trashed the veterans' camp, razing their shanties and setting fires.
>
> The Army's handling of the bonus march, coupled with Hoover's failure to grasp the seriousness of the Great Depression, led to a sharp drop in the president's popularity. Some historians believe that, had MacArthur followed orders, Hoover could have been re-elected in November 1932. Instead, he was defeated by Franklin D. Roosevelt.

THE ARMY IN THE 1930s

Throughout the 1930s, the Army maintained garrisons in exotic, remote locations, like Honolulu in the Territory of Hawaii; ran war-game exercises; and put into effect a series of industrial mobilization plans that started in

1930 and culminated in 1939, aimed at organizing industry and military procurement in wartime.

Gen. Malin Craig (1898–1945) replaced MacArthur as Army chief of staff in 1935. MacArthur went off to head the army of the Philippines and resigned from the U.S. Army.

Wedged by history into a four-year slot between two of the greats, MacArthur and Marshall, Craig is something of a mystery to historians. He believed in training and revived and vitalized the "staff ride," the Army's term for a field trip for training purposes by junior officers. He performed competently and well. He recognized the need to develop modern tanks (though the United States remained behind Germany and other nations), but he failed to grasp the growing importance of air power. Mostly, Craig is remembered only as the figure who reigned over the Army before Gen. George C. Marshall showed up.

That happened on September 1, 1939. Marshall had completed his long march from being a fresh junior officer (during the Philippine Insurrection in 1902) to becoming its top soldier. It happened on the day Germany invaded Poland, and England and France went to war with the Third Reich. It happened during the month recognized by most historians as the beginning of World War II. Japan had already been fighting in Asia for years, but now Germany attacked Poland. In Europe, the war was on. In the U.S., many were urging the nation's leaders to stay out of it.

Marshall might have seemed a curious choice to be chief of staff. Other officers were senior in rank. Marshall had never held a major combat command; many had expected the top job to go to Brig. Gen. (later Maj. Gen.) Adna R. Chaffee Jr. (1884–1941), an armor pioneer and the son of a former chief of staff. Just 10 months earlier, in a small White House meeting, Marshall had expressed disagreement with Franklin D. Roosevelt on the focus of the nation's military buildup. Marshall was especially displeased that American soldiers were still using 1903 Springfield rifles a decade after MacArthur had seen them as inadequate, and were still equipped with 75-mm howitzers when European armies had 105-mm guns.

Marshall took over an Army that was almost nonexistent. As pointed out by Thomas Parrish in *Roosevelt and Marshall: Partners in Politics and War*, the U.S. Army ranked seventeenth in the world, numbered just

174,000 soldiers against an authorized strength of 210,000, and was, to use Marshall's word, "ineffective." As Parrish put it, "Nine infantry divisions existed on paper, but only three were actually organized as such and none could claim even half strength."

On August 27, 1940, Congress approved calling 60,000 National Guardsmen to federal service. On September 14, lawmakers approved the Selective Service and Training Act, reinstating the draft in America. That month, while fighting raged in Europe, the Army grew slightly to a total strength of 291,031 soldiers, including 224,117 in the United States and 66,914 outside the continental United States. Marshall said on a radio broadcast that, "for the first time in our history we are beginning in time of peace to prepare against the possibility of war." The United States transferred destroyers to Britain, launched a lend-lease program, and began mobilizing industry. Initially, however, draftees were to serve for just one year—not enough to be much help if the United States should enter the growing war in Europe.

While it began drafting buck privates, the nation continued to turn out fresh, butter-bar second lieutenants. One of these, Harry Kinnard, graduated from West Point in 1939 and chose an assignment as a platoon leader in the 27th Infantry Regiment, or "Wolfhounds," of the Hawaiian Regiment. It was a December Sunday morning two years later when Kinnard looked out from his quarters at Schofield Barracks and saw Japanese Zero fighters hurtling overhead, strafing nearby Wheeler Field. He was watching the December 7, 1941, Japanese attack on Pearl Harbor.

CHAPTER 7

WORLD WAR II (1941–1945)

The U.S. role in history's most destructive war lasted from December 7, 1941, until August 15, 1945 (V. J. Day, for "victory over Japan"), with a formal surrender signed on September 2, 1945. The end of fighting in Europe (V. E. Day, for "victory in Europe") was May 8, 1945. By the time the United States was drawn into World War II in December 1941, the Army's strength had been increased from 190,000 to more than 1.6 million. Rated seventeenth in the world just two years earlier, the U.S. Army was growing rapidly but did not have the infrastructure, logistics, or weaponry to support rapid growth. Some of the contrasts were ludicrous: soldiers in basic training wearing new, clean fatigue uniforms that would be the envy of any army, but training with broomsticks because not enough real rifles were available.

The strength of the Army reached its highest point in September 1945, when the service boasted 8,268,000 military personnel and 1,881,000 civilians serving in some capacity, including 4,428,899 outside the continental United States. The totals included members of the Women's Army Corps, which was established on May 14, 1942. The Army's growth to more than eight million was one of the remarkable stories of America's role in history's greatest war.

A significant chunk of the Army was located in the territory of Hawaii, which was also home to the U.S. Fleet. The Army commander in Hawaii, Lt. Gen. Walter Short, had bolstered vigilance and clustered his aircraft together to discourage sabotage, undoubtedly aware that this made them vulnerable to air attack—but who would attack a necklace of tropical islands in the Pacific, far from anywhere?

Before dawn on December 7, 1941, the Japanese First Air Fleet, commanded by Vice Adm. Chuichi Nagumo, consisting of six aircraft carriers and 360 aircraft and positioned 220 miles north of Oahu, launched a first wave of 148 warplanes. A second wave of 170 planes followed. The attack was aimed at the U.S. Fleet, but it also struck all six U.S. airfields on Oahu.

Just moments before 8:00 A.M., Aichi D3A Type 99 "Val" dive-bomber pilot Lt. Kunikiya Hira, from the carrier *Shokaku*, dropped the first bomb on Hickam Air Field, hit Hangar 15, and set a B-24A Liberator bomber ablaze, killing two of its crew, who became the first American casualties of the war. The Pearl Harbor attack killed 2,403 people, most of them American servicemen, and wounded 1,104 others. The Japanese conceded the loss of 29 aircraft, of which U.S. fighter pilots downed 10. It was a "date which will live in infamy," in the words of President Franklin D. Roosevelt's next-day speech calling on Congress to declare war on Japan.

In the hours following Pearl Harbor, Japanese forces struck Guam, Midway, and British bases in Hong Kong and Singapore. The Japanese assault on the Philippines was a blow to Gen. Douglas MacArthur, who lost three dozen aircraft on the ground on December 8, 1941, and began a holding action that would end with Japan seizing the Philippines. The Japanese took Wake Island in the north Pacific on December 23, overwhelming a courageous but outnumbered American garrison.

THE PACIFIC WAR

After being besieged at Corregidor, on March 11, 1942, MacArthur withdrew from the Philippines, vowing, "I shall return." He left Gen. Jonathan Wainwright (1893–1953) in command of forces in the Philippines (see following sidebar). The beleaguered Americans withdrew to the Bataan Peninsula.

United States Army, Robert F. Dorr

General of the Army Douglas MacArthur in Manila, Philippines.

The garrison at Bataan, consisting of 76,000 American and Philippine troops, surrendered to the Japanese after valiant resistance on April 9, 1942. Their captors herded the men into the infamous Bataan Death March, forcing them to cover 100 miles without food or water and killing stragglers. Weeks later, Wainwright surrendered, and the Japanese faced only guerrilla resistance within the Philippines.

Lt. Gen. Jonathan M. Wainwright was the highest-ranking American held prisoner during World War II. He was captured when the Japanese overcame the last resistance at Corregidor and Bataan in 1942. Forty-three months later, he was hailed as a hero and President Harry S. Truman hung the Medal of Honor around his neck.

The Japanese attack on the Philippines on December 8, 1941, six hours after the strike on Pearl Harbor, caught the Americans unprepared. Wainwright was in command on North Luzon where the main assault came. He had more troops than the Japanese, but they were poorly trained and lacked modern equipment. MacArthur soon told Wainwright that they were going to be defeated and that any attempt to defend the capital, Manila, would merely risk needless bloodshed. MacArthur decided to withdraw to the Bataan Peninsula, and Wainwright's troops—many suffering from malaria and low on rations—fought a desperate delaying action.

President Franklin D. Roosevelt ordered MacArthur to depart from the Philippines. On March 11, 1942, he did, escaping with his family in a patrol boat to Mindanao and then in a B-17 bomber to Australia. When Japanese forces overran the Bataan garrison and forced its surrender, Wainwright and 11,000 troops held out on Corregidor, which finally fell on May 6, 1942.

As a prisoner, Wainwright was shuffled from Luzon to Formosa (Taiwan) and then to Manchuria. Finally freed in August 1945, he was able to attend the surrender ceremonies presided over by MacArthur in Tokyo Bay aboard the battleship *Missouri* on September 2. On his return to the United States, Wainwright was promoted to full general and was presented with the nation's highest award for valor.

Although the U.S. public was hungry for heroes, it often heard little or nothing about the real soldiers who struggled under desperate circumstances in the darkest hours of the Pacific war. One such soldier was an alumnus of the West Point class of 1941, which produced many of the Army's leaders during World War II. Alexander R. "Sandy" Nininger Jr. volunteered for assignment to the Philippines and arrived in Manila—a soft-spoken, intelligent lieutenant who became a human fighting machine when the chips were down.

As a platoon leader in Company A, 1st Battalion, 57th Infantry Regiment, Nininger became part of the II Philippine Corps under Maj. Gen. George M. Parker, who reported to MacArthur and then came under siege in the Malinta Tunnel on Corregidor. Nininger's primary function was to lead Filipino troops.

Although he worked hard to train his soldiers, Nininger initially was ordered to keep his platoon in reserve while other American and Philippine troops mounted a defense against advancing Japanese outside Abucay, a town on the east coast of Bataan.

On January 12, 1942, Nininger insisted on a chance to fight and attached himself to Company K while that unit was under attack by a huge Japanese force. He arrived on a battlefield littered with destruction, dead, and wounded. Told that many Japanese troops had overrun friendly positions and now occupied foxholes initially dug by friendlies, Nininger believed he had to set an example to Filipino soldiers who were led by American officers. It was a crucial decision for a 23-year-old who had been known at the military academy as a quiet youngster intrigued by art and literature.

Nininger gathered up grenades and ammunition, and slung a captured Japanese Nambu 12.7-mm light machine gun over his shoulder. He set forth on a furious assault that prompted another soldier later to dub him a "one-man army." Nininger charged straight into Japanese gunfire, drawing 100 yards, and then 200 yards, ahead of friendly troops.

Rushing at the Japanese, Nininger's tactic was to heave a grenade into their midst, then depress the machine gun, and sweep them with bursts of automatic fire. He repeated this cycle several times. Japanese snipers in trees and foxholes shot back at him repeatedly. Still, Nininger cleaned out several enemy foxholes before a Japanese rifle bullet struck him in the shoulder. Dazed, hurt, and bleeding, he plunged into dense jungle and continued his assault. He dropped the machine gun when its ammunition was expended and began fighting with his pistol. Ironically, the Colt .45 automatic had been inspired by an earlier American experience in the Philippines at the turn of the century.

Japanese bullets slammed into Nininger a second time, then a third. When the lieutenant attacked yet another foxhole, a Japanese officer and two Japanese soldiers swarmed over him, stabbing him from behind with their bayonets. Nininger killed all three with the .45. Then, mortally wounded, he fell to the jungle floor. The young lieutenant had slowed the Japanese advance all by himself. On February 10, 1942, Nininger's father was summoned to MacDill Army Air Field, Florida, to receive the first Medal of Honor awarded to an American soldier in World War II.

The Army's most famous antiaircraft artillery gun had its roots in a country that hasn't been in a war for 200 years. Sweden's Bofors company has manufactured cannons since 1883.

In 1937, the Army was thinking of replacing its 37-mm cannon (something that didn't happen) and became enamored of Bofors' 40-mm gun because it was lighter and had a greater muzzle velocity.

Before Pearl Harbor, the Army purchased two Bofors guns for testing. During the war years, Chrysler, Firestone, and the Pontiac Division of General Motors produced more than 34,000 Bofors cannons and mountings, of which the Army received 10,000. The Army assigned the designation M1 in May 1941.

Soldiers liked the Bofors cannon, with its open, funnel-shaped snout, because it was a simple and pragmatic design. It was the ideal defense against low-flying warplanes.

The heart of the design was the "autoloader" unit mounted on the gun body above and to the rear of the breech. A soldier could drop a four-round clip of cartridges into this unit in a split-second. The first round was loaded into the breech by operating a hand lever. The gunner sat on a steel seat and fired the weapon using a foot pedal.

Some Bofors cannons were mounted on vehicles. Retired Army Gen. Bruce Kingston was a second lieutenant in Korea in 1950 when ordered to take a company to the banks of the Yalu River. Kingston took along a pair of armored tracked vehicles, each with twin 40-mm Bofors M1 cannons. Impressed by their reliability and flexibility, Kingston said in an interview that the Bofors cannons were "magnificent."

As recently as 1955, Army air defense artillery units were using the Bofors to defend installations around the world. Today, missiles have replaced cannons in antiaircraft artillery units.

THE PHILIPPINE SCOUTS

Already renowned within the Army (if little known to the outside world) for their role in the fighting at the turn of the century, the Philippine Scouts—Filipino soldiers serving under U.S. officers or under Filipino graduates of West Point—made up the backbone of American forces in the Philippines before the war. With a prewar strength of 7,000, they comprised two infantry regiments, two field artillery regiments, a cavalry regiment, and other units. All were understrength when Japan attacked. In the fighting that followed, it would have been easy for Scouts to shed their uniforms and vanish into the general population. Yet, even when faced with death or capture during the defense of Bataan in early 1942, nearly all continued fighting.

Philippine Scout Sgt. José Calugas was caught up in an extraordinary action on the Bataan peninsula on January 16, 1942. The Japanese had bombed and shelled a friendly gun position until the gun was put out of commission and all the cannoneers were killed or wounded. Calugas, a mess sergeant—not a combat soldier—voluntarily and without orders ran 1,000 yards across the shell-swept area to the gun position. There he organized a volunteer squad that placed the gun back in commission and fired back, although the position remained under constant and heavy Japanese artillery fire. Calugas was awarded the Medal of Honor. In later years, he resided in Seattle, where he died in 1998 at age 90.

The value of the Scouts to the embattled forces in the Philippines was summarized by Wainwright:

> My Filipino soldiers were Philippine Scouts, fine fighters and equipped as well as our Army was equipping anybody else at that time. Many of them were sons of men who had fought against the United States in the Insurrection, but who had later been formed into the Scouts. They were tough, hard, well trained, and … [were] the nucleus of a good, proud, intelligent force.

As a component of the Army, the Philippine Scouts served until July 1, 1949, when they held their last muster and were officially disbanded. The independence of their country relegated them to the history books. That happened, of course, only after there was a war to be won.

JAPANESE ONSLAUGHT

By early 1942, Japan secured virtually all of the Philippines. In a stunning follow-up assault, the Japanese overwhelmed the last American resistance on the island of Java, but two bright moments occurred that spring. On April 18, 1942, Lt. Col. (later Gen.) James Doolittle led a B-25 Mitchell bomber raid from the deck of the carrier *Hornet* to the Japanese home islands. On May 8, 1942, the Allies wrapped up the Battle of Coral Sea, in which the Japanese suffered substantial naval losses. In early June, U.S. forces wreaked an important success in the Battle of Midway, a major naval action viewed as halting the Japanese advance in the Pacific.

In the first offensive of the war, Marines landed on Guadalcanal in the Solomon Islands on August 7, 1942. They were soon joined by Army troops who came to know the heat, stench, and disease of what looked outwardly like a tropical paradise. It took six months to secure the island.

To the American public of 1941–1945, Joe Louis was "the best known and most admired black man on earth," as one biographer described him. But the "Brown Bomber" and heavyweight champion was also Pvt. (later Sgt.) Louis. On January 10, 1942, the day after defeating Buddy Baer in a charity fight, Louis enlisted in the Army.

As war fervor boiled up in the U.S., Louis told reporters that the Japanese were "all lightweights." The *Chicago Tribune* wrote, "Joe has a date for a return engagement with Max Schmeling"—the German who had handed Louis his only professional defeat in 1936, and whom Louis had knocked out in a 1938 rematch. Schmeling was a hero in Hitler's Third Reich.

The irony escaped the public. Schmeling would have been more welcome in some American homes than Louis. Even while the U.S. prepared for war, the Army, like American society, remained segregated. It took a lawsuit to open up flight training to black Americans and a near-defeat—the Battle of the Bulge in December 1944—to get black troops into ground combat. The few who were given the chance rose to the occasion. The all-Negro 761st Tank Battalion was one of George S. Patton's finest armor outfits.

Although some criticized him for having an easy time of it, Louis was widely viewed as a symbol of American determination to win the war.

In 1943, he had a cameo in the film *This Is the Army,* starring Ronald Reagan. In 1944, the Army Signal Corps recruited director Frank Capra to produce a film, *The Negro Soldier.* Carlton Moss, an African American, wrote the script and played the lead. Moss used footage of Louis fighting Schmeling to convey the message that Americans needed to defeat the Axis.

Louis traveled 70,000 miles, fought 96 exhibition matches, visited 216 bases, and was seen in person by 5 million servicemen. According to biographer Richard Bak, "The needs of a country at war with the forces of fascism had humanized him, transforming him into a friendly, dignified … symbol of patriotism, national resolve, and racial unity."

INVADING EUROPE

On January 26, 1942, a small number of American soldiers arrived in Northern Ireland to begin a buildup in the British Isles. It marked the first time U.S. troops had landed in Europe since World War I. On February 9, in Washington, the first meeting was held of the U.S. joint chiefs of staff, the American component of the Anglo–U.S. combined chiefs of staff. This predecessor of today's joint chiefs—a defining creation in the saga of the U.S. armed forces—came about without any official order or proclamation. It simply happened.

As the joint chiefs evolved, the Navy's Adm. William Leahy became chairman and the Navy's Adm. Ernest King occupied theoretically equal seating with the Army's Marshall. Interestingly, the Army's air chief, Maj. Gen. Henry H. "Hap" Arnold, also had a seat at the table while the chief of naval aviation did not—a premonition of the independent Air Force that would be created in the postwar era.

In November 1942, the Army played a key role in Operation Torch, the invasion of North Africa that marked the first Allied offensive of World War II. Torch was aimed at establishing a foothold for future combat against Italy and Germany. It was hoped that a North Africa invasion would prevent German Field Marshal Erwin Rommel (1891–1944) from moving west to take control of the North African coast and the Suez Canal.

The combined American and British invasion force invaded territory belonging to Vichy France. Although under German control, Vichy was officially neutral. The invasion pitted the Allies' Lt. Gen. Dwight D. Eisenhower against Vichy's Adm. Jean François Darlan. On November 5, 1942, Eisenhower arrived in Gibraltar to set up headquarters for the Torch invasion. Three days later, three task forces began landing troops at North Africa beachheads. At the time, it was the largest amphibious operation ever undertaken.

Ike commanded a force of 107,000. Under Darlan, 100,000 Vichy troops were stationed in Algeria, Morocco, and Tunisia. Within the Vichy ranks were commanders and soldiers of various sympathies.

In advance of the landings, Eisenhower sent his deputy, Maj. Gen. Mark Clark, and three other officers on a top-secret mission to meet with French commanders. Clark's party landed by submarine and entered talks, seeking agreement from the Vichy not to resist the Torch landings. Clark's clandestine mission failed, and his party narrowly escaped.

> Soldiers who knew "Old Blood and Guts" Gen. George S. Patton Jr. say he might have been useless in peacetime with his brash, hard-charging personality.
>
> Patton was the American pioneer who grasped the importance of the tank as a military weapon and led the armored drive into Nazi Germany.
>
> Born in 1885 and graduated from West Point, New York, in 1909, Patton saw action during the U.S. expedition against Pancho Villa in Mexico in 1916. He accompanied Gen. John "Black Jack" Pershing to France in 1917 and

saw how the French and British were employing a new weapon, the tank. Patton established a tank training school and commanded a tank brigade.

In action during World War I, Patton suffered serious wounds when hit by German machine gun fire.

By July 1943, Patton commanded the U.S. 7th Army in the Allied invasion of Sicily. His "Old Blood and Guts" aggressiveness paid off there with a bold campaign that beat the British into Palermo. But a much-publicized incident in which he verbally accosted two ailing soldiers, one of whom he also slapped, nearly cost him his career.

When American forces broke through the German defenses in Europe, Patton's 3rd Army dashed eastward and exploited German weaknesses. At times, Patton's tanks moved so fast against the foe that it was a challenge to keep them supplied with fuel and ammunition. When the Allies advanced to the Rhine, the unorthodox Patton arranged to be photographed urinating into the river.

When Patton abruptly lost his life in a traffic mishap following victory in Europe, he was buried in the 3rd Army cemetery in Luxembourg.

Patton wrote a book, *War As I Knew It,* and is the subject of many biographies. In 1970, George C. Scott portrayed Patton's career in the award-winning film *Patton.*

Several museums honor the general. The Patton Museum of Cavalry and Armor was established in 1949 at Fort Knox, Kentucky.

The Western Task Force of U.S. troops under Maj. Gen. George S. Patton landed 34,300 men along a 200-mile front centered at Casablanca, Morocco. The initial landing went more smoothly than many had feared, but some Vichy troops resisted. It took two days for Patton to secure his beachhead.

As part of Patton's effort, soldiers under Brig. Gen. Lucian K. Truscott attacked Port Lyautey to seize the town's airfield. P-40F Warhawk fighters brought across the Atlantic by the Navy escort carrier USS *Chenango* (CVE-28) would use the airfield, as would L-4A Cub artillery spotter planes aboard the Navy carrier USS *Ranger* (CV-4).

Truscott's force encountered sporadic resistance, so fierce in some places that one of his battalions—the 2nd Battalion, 60th Regimental Combat Team, 9th Infantry Division, or "Go-Devils" under Maj. John H. Dilley—had to fix bayonets and engage in hand-to-hand fighting.

Torch's Center Task Force of 39,000 American soldiers under Maj. Gen. Lloyd Fredendall landed near Oran, Algeria. The landings encountered stiffer Vichy resistance, but troops established a beachhead and captured the Tafaraiu airfield by nightfall. U.S. aircraft began flying combat missions from the airfield the next day.

The Eastern Task Force of 10,000 U.S. troops under Maj. Gen. Charles Ryder, plus 23,000 British soldiers, landed at Algiers and quickly captured the town.

On news of the Torch landings, German troops were flown from Sicily to Tunisia, adjacent to the Allied forces, on November 9. Abetted by Vichy troops who were in sympathy with them, the Germans began a buildup that later led to months of hard fighting.

The fighting gave the world the advent of organic Army aviation—not the Army Air Force, which is today considered part of Air Force history, but the Army itself operating small spotter aircraft in direct support of the ground soldier. The morning after the initial landings, 60 miles from shore, three L-4A Cubs belonging to organic Army aviation took off from the *Ranger* and flew ashore, piloted by Capt. Ford E. "Ace" Allcorn and 1st Lts. John R. Shell and William H. Butler. A fourth L-4A pilot, Capt. Brenton A. Devol Jr., accompanied Butler in his plane's back seat. In the confusion of battle, Allcorn was wounded and shot down by friendly fire. The others were diverted to an emergency landing, where they were briefly Vichy prisoners. More Cubs shipped to the war zone in crates quickly became operational in North Africa, beginning a successful career for the Army's most famous fixed-wing airplane.

Operation Torch was quickly followed by the collapse of Vichy forces in the region and then new battles farther east with German troops. The United States initially allowed Darlan to remain the French leader in North Africa—infuriating Free French leader Gen. Charles de Gaulle, who was then in England—but Darlan was assassinated by a lone killer in December 1942.

Officers viewed Operation Torch as a vindication of a new Great War, but many—and most enlisted troops—belonged to a new generation: citizen soldiers, hastily trained and, until Torch, untested in combat. Operation Torch landings cost the Americans 556 killed and 837 wounded.

The war in Europe held priority in the January 14–24, 1943, Casablanca Conference when Roosevelt and Britain's Winston S. Churchill convened to set strategy for the forthcoming invasion of Europe. The U.S. wanted to make it happen quickly; the Allies felt an invasion of North Africa needed to come first. Their thinking prevailed.

The Pentagon Building was constructed by a brilliant, egotistical Army engineer who would have flunked today's weight standards for soldiers.

Lt. Gen. Leslie R. Groves Jr., born in Albany, New York, in 1896 and fourth in his 1918 class at West Point, served in France during World War I and took engineering courses afterward.

Biographer Stanley Goldberg wrote that "Groves was despised and hated by many of those who had to work under him. In the military, Groves was commonly described as 'the biggest S.O.B. I ever worked for,' a remark sometimes delivered with grudging admiration."

Groves always dismissed allegations that construction of the world's largest office building—designed with five sides and an open center so that an employee could readily walk from any part of the building to another—entailed waste and mismanagement.

The Pentagon became headquarters of the new Department of Defense in 1947 and currently boasts 23,000 employees.

In September 1942, Groves became the head of the Manhattan Engineer District. Made a brigadier general, Groves oversaw basic atomic bomb research at universities and supervised building plants at Oak Ridge, Tennessee, and Hanford, Washington.

Groves's towering achievement was the secluded Los Alamos, New Mexico, laboratory where a city of rude wooden buildings rose in secrecy and scientists built the atomic bomb. By 1944, he was responsible for $3.5 billion in expenditures, as well as a secret labor force of 125,000.

Groves's relationship with J. Robert Oppenheimer, the civilian head of the scientific team, was often abrasive but characterized by mutual respect. Both stood in the desert near Alamogordo on July 16, 1945, when Oppenheimer's team detonated a plutonium bomb like the one that would be dropped on Nagasaki, Japan, on August 9. The uranium bomb dropped on Hiroshima on August 6, 1945, was not tested in advance.

Groves was promoted to major general in December 1944. He continued to head the atomic establishment created during wartime until January 1947. He was then named the chief of the Army's Special Weapons Project. Groves died in 1970 at age 74.

THE WAR IN THE MEDITERRANEAN

Once the Americans came up against crack German forces, their unreadiness was apparent. During February 14–25, 1943, at Kasserine Pass in Tunisia, Rommel's Afrika Korps inflicted a stunning defeat on U.S. troops. But the Americans, now under Lt. Gen. George S. Patton, were able to regroup and prevent Rommel from advancing. The Americans soon linked up with British troops under Field Marshal Bernard Montgomery (1887–1976), who had uprooted Rommel in Egypt.

Patton's and Montgomery's forces converged at Tunis on May 7, 1943, leading to the surrender of German and Italian troops in North Africa. The Allies eventually captured almost a quarter-million enemy troops and inflicted over 100,000 casualties. The Army sustained 17,000 killed and wounded in North Africa.

The 7th Army, the first numbered field army to see action in World War II, was activated at sea in July 1943, on the invasion convoy off Sicily, with Patton in command. Eisenhower was the overall commander of the Sicily invasion. On July 10, the 7th Army assaulted the beaches of southern Sicily in the Licata, Gela, and Pozzallo areas, with the British 8th Army on its right. In the following weeks, U.S. troops fanned out to the south and west, conquering most of western Sicily and taking Palermo on July 22.

At the "Trident" Conference in Washington in May 1943, Roosevelt and Churchill agreed that an invasion of Italy would remove that country as a factor in the war. This would bolster Allied morale and threaten German control of the Balkans. They agreed on the importance of Sicily, the largest island in the Mediterranean. Again Eisenhower was supreme commander, Britain's Montgomery commanded the 8th Army, and Patton commanded the 7th.

Brig. Gen. (later Gen.) Matthew B. Ridgway (1895–1993) had never used a parachute when the division he commanded, the 82nd, became an Airborne unit. Improvising step by step, Ridgway went on to become a leading Airborne commander of World War II. He made jumps and glider assaults. He even rode in a glider being put through stunts, to reassure his soldiers.

Ridgway was in charge when the 82nd Airborne Division dropped into Sicily. Though he did not jump with the troops on that occasion, feeling that he could best direct the action from afar, he came ashore quickly and joined the fight. His deputy, Brig. Gen. James Gavin, noted that he was "right up front every minute—hard as a flint and full of intensity."

The Sicily fighting had moments of intensity, too. Allied troops then pressed Germans and Italians into northeastern Sicily, to complete the conquest of the island with the capture of Messina on August 16, 1943. The Seventh Army, with a strength of 195,617, claimed to have killed or captured no fewer than 112,000 enemy troops. Now the Allies could control Mediterranean shipping and held a base from which to launch the offensive on Sicily itself.

United States Army, Robert F. Dorr

Audie Murphy poses with his 33 awards and decorations, including the Medal of Honor.

On September 9, 1943, the U.S. 5th Army undertook Operation Avalanche, the invasion of Italy at Salerno, with one American and one British corps and additional units. Ridgway's paratroopers jumped and fought at Salerno. By late in the month, troops began a long, hard drive up the Italian peninsula, seizing Naples on October 1. The Italian winter stalled the advance, but after Mussolini was forced out, a new Italian regime changed sides and declared war on Germany.

From November 28 to December 1, Roosevelt, Churchill, and Russia's Josef Stalin (1879–1953) met in the Tehran Conference in Iran, the first meeting of the trio. They discussed progress in the Mediterranean and, in particular, the coming Allied invasion of Europe.

Lt. Gen. Mark Clark took command of the 7th Army on January 1, 1944, and began planning for the invasion of southern France. When Clark moved up the ladder, command of the 7th Army passed to Lt. Gen. Alexander M. Patch. The 5th Army's IV Corps made its famous "left hook" amphibious landing at Anzio, where the U.S. advance stalled (see sidebar) on the road to Rome.

The German stronghold at Monte Cassino in central Italy fell on May 18, 1944, after months of aerial and artillery bombardment. The Allies' siege of Cassino had been an undertaking of dubious value to the war effort. Soon afterward, the troops who had been bogged down following the Anzio landing were finally able to seize Rome on June 4.

The world's attention shifted to northern Europe with the D-Day landings on June 6, 1944, but the war in the Mediterranean theater continued. On August 15, 1944, the 7th Army, together with other U.S. and French units, assaulted the beaches in the St. Tropez–St. Raphael area of southern France. This second front in France was opened against relatively little resistance. Within a few short weeks, the Allies controlled all of the region. On August 27, French troops liberated Paris. Eisenhower and other Allied leaders arrived in the French capital two days later.

In Italy, the final major assault was launched in the spring of 1945 when the 5th Army crossed the Po Valley. German forces in Italy surrendered unconditionally on May 2, 1945.

On January 22, 1944, the U.S. 5th Army landed on Italian beaches near the one-time resort cities of Anzio and Nettuno. In Operation Shingle, the brass hoped to make an "end run" around at Cassino. Without meeting the fierce resistance expected on the beaches, the first waves charged inland.

American and British units gained their first day's objectives by noon. The ease of the landing was noted by one paratrooper of the 504th Parachute Infantry Regiment, 82nd Airborne Division, who recalled that D-Day at Anzio was sunny and warm, making it hard to believe a war was going on.

By landing 30 miles south of Rome, the Allies created a beachhead that Adolf Hitler called "an abscess." Had the Army moved quickly, it might have quickly seized Rome and split up German defenders. But Maj. Gen. John P. Lucas, commander of the 5th Army's VI Corps and of the 36,000 invasion troops, was too timid. He decided not to advance inland until he had gotten 70,000 more U.S. and British troops ashore.

Lucas's boss, Gen. Mark Clark, conveyed vague orders to move toward the Alban Hills 20 miles inland and eventually to link up with the 5th Army to the south. In what became a relentless controversy, neither general interpreted these orders as specifically charging VI Corps with the immediate capture of the Alban Hills. That sealed the doom of thousands of GIs. When the Germans finally began pouring fire into the troops on the beachhead, they inflicted horrendous casualties.

Among thousands caught on the beachhead because of Lucas's caution, cartoonist Bill Mauldin of the "Willie and Joe" series listened to German cannons crashing and watched American soldiers caught in artillery barrages around him. An artillery barrage pulverized a building housing war correspondents and wounded several, among them correspondent Ernie Pyle. Some of the lethal firepower came from Anzio Annie, a railway-mounted 280-mm German gun that fired a 561-lb projectile. Lucas's failure to move decisively resulted in American and some British troops being mauled in a counteroffensive that cost at least 29,000 casualties. The Allies ultimately liberated Rome, but Anzio was a missed opportunity, a place where many GIs died needlessly.

D-DAY

Following months of preliminary planning by the Allies, in December 1943, Gen. Dwight D. Eisenhower was notified of his selection as Supreme Commander of Allied Expeditionary Force. A subsequent directive prescribed Ike's task as follows: "You will enter the continent of Europe and, in conjunction with the other United Nations, undertake operations aimed at the heart of Germany and the destruction of her armed forces." Eisenhower selected as his chief of staff Lt. Gen. Walter B. Smith, who had been an aide to Marshall in Washington. Eisenhower, Marshall, and Smith all excelled at a job that was difficult for a soldier: juggling the conflicting demands of Allied leaders and forging a fighting force consisting of the armies of many nations.

United States Army, Robert F. Dorr

Supreme Commander of Allied Expeditionary Force and future president Dwight D. Eisenhower.

The date for an assault on Nazi-occupied Europe, code-named Operation Overlord, had to be repeatedly set back because of shortages of men, materiel, and munitions, but Eisenhower finally chose the first week of

June 1944. He picked June 5 as D-Day. The initial assault was to be made on a five-division front in Normandy. Bad weather forced further postponement of the invasion date, but on June 5, Ike made the "irrevocable" decision that the invasion of France would take place the following day.

The landings were preceded by tremendous air and naval bombardment. Allied air units flew over 100,000 sorties during the 24 hours of June 6. Airborne assault forces went in by parachute and glider on both flanks of the Normandy invasion some 5 hours before 176,000 seaborne troops first set foot on the 5 beaches.

When the 82nd and 101st Airborne divisions dropped behind the invasion beaches on the night of June 5–6, 1944, Ridgway jumped into battle with his troops. Ridgway subsequently became commander of the XVIII Airborne Corps (17th, 82nd, and 101st Airborne divisions) and planned combat drops that eventually became unnecessary as ground forces advanced toward Germany.

The D-Day landing marked the greatest amphibious assault in history. It was a remarkable achievement of logistics, planning, and synchronized military action. No fewer than 176,475 men, 3,000 guns, 1,500 tanks, and 15,000 other assorted vehicles landed in German-held Normandy across the 5 assault beaches or by glider and parachute in the fields of France.

Omaha was the code name for the second beach from the right of the five landing areas of the Normandy invasion. It ran for 6 miles, with a 100-foot cliff at its western extreme. "Bloody Omaha," assigned to the U.S. V Corps commanded by Maj. Gen. Leonard T. Gerow, was also the beach where everything went wrong.

"None of the plans survived initial contact with the enemy," said Tim Kilvert-Jones, 43, of Fairfax, Virginia, a retired British Army major, in an interview. Kilvert-Jones, who works in the United States as a defense consultant, instructs U.S. Army units in "lessons learned" in past battles.

"The Germans were highly effective soldiers, sited in well-prepared defensive positions on a naturally fortified escarpment overlooking the landing beach."

Few battles compare with Omaha Beach for their challenges to American troops. The 16th Regiment of the 1st Infantry Division ("the Big Red One") and the 116th Regiment of the 29th Infantry Division made the initial assault at Omaha. The 16th Regiment landed at Omaha's Easy Red and Fox Green sectors at 6:30 A.M. The sectors drew their names from the military phonetic alphabet.

Soaked, cold, and overloaded with equipment, the men of the 16th Regiment encountered so much German resistance that, hours after the landing, they believed they had failed.

Amphibious Sherman tanks fitted with flotation screens that were supposed to support the 116th Regiment sank instead in the choppy waters of the English Channel after being offloaded too far from shore. Nearly every man in those tanks drowned. Only 2 of the 29 Shermans made it to the beach. Except for one rifle company, no element of the 116th came ashore where it was planned.

"The Big Red One's" 16th Regiment bogged down and fought for its life on the Easy Red sector of Omaha Beach near Colleville-sur-Mer. For two hours, soldiers huddled behind the seawall. The beach was so congested with dead and dying that there was no room to land reinforcements. Col. George Taylor, regiment commander, told his men, "Two kinds of people are staying on this beach! The dead and those who are going to die! Now let's get the hell out of here!" The troops moved inland.

Rangers at Dog Green sector of Omaha Beach—re-created half a century later in the Steven Spielberg film *Saving Private Ryan*—had to improvise without any of the air and armor support they'd been promised.

Farther west, approaching in tricky coastal waters after being delayed by a navigational error, Rangers under Col. James E. Rudder had to come ashore on a bullet-raked shingle shelf under the face of a 100-foot cliff, scale the cliff, and attack German coastal artillery batteries. The location was Pointe du Hoc, on the extreme western end of Omaha Beach. Rudder hadn't believed the magnitude of the task at first. "The first time I heard about it," he told a superior officer, "I thought you were trying to scare me."

At Omaha, heavy bombers of the 8th Air Force dropped bombs 3 miles from their intended targets, missing fortified German bunkers.

Gen. Dwight D. Eisenhower prepared a statement of regret he would issue if the Germans pushed his troops into the sea. He never had to read it. The issue was never in doubt at Juno, Gold, and Sword beaches, taken by British and Canadian troops, or at Utah Beach, taken by Americans.

At Omaha, thanks largely to junior U.S. officers and noncommissioned officers—by tradition, exercising greater initiative than their counterparts in other armies—Gerow's V Corps overcame horrendous difficulties and seized the beach.

By the end of what German Field Marshal Erwin Rommel called "the longest day," the final outcome of World War II was never in doubt again.

In June 1944, Allied troops captured the French port of Cherbourg, which had been badly booby-trapped and sabotaged by the withdrawing Germans. American troops broke out of the beachhead at St. Lô, France, in late July and swept north toward the German frontier. Meanwhile, in mid-August, American and French troops landed in southern France from the Mediterranean and moved north through the Rhone Valley to link up with Allied troops already on the continent. The 9th Army began operations on the continent on September 5, containing German forces pocketed in Lorient and St. Nazaire. The 9th Army then acquired responsibility for all U.S. combat forces in the Brittany Peninsula.

The Army's own official history benignly dismisses the October 1944 airborne attacks on Arnhem as "only partially successful." The 1st Allied Airborne Army lifted, airdropped, and resupplied more than three divisions in Operation Market over the period of September 17–26, 1944, in an operation aimed at the seizure of bridges and vantage points in Arnhem, Nijmegen, and Veghel in Holland.

Early in October 1944, the 9th Army moved east to take up a position on the Siegfried Line in the Ardennes between the 1st and 3rd Armies.

On December 16, 1944, the Germans launched their counteroffensive in the Ardennes. In the resulting Battle of the Bulge, named for the bulge created in the center of the line, Allied troops struggled to contain the attack. This meant two weeks of intense fighting in snow, fog, and severe cold. The 15th Army first went into action in the midst of the battle, commanded by Lt. Gen. Leonard T. Gerow, who had earlier been the corps commander at Omaha Beach. The 7th Army, which had moved north into Europe from the Mediterranean theater, fought defensive actions until its troops could be resupplied and launch a counterattack. The 1st Allied Airborne Army supplied the besieged 101st Airborne Division at Bastogne, Belgium, by air and also transported the 17th Airborne Division by air from England to the continent.

During the Battle of the Bulge, when parts of the 101st Division were surrounded by German troops at Bastogne, Belgium, a German officer approached under a white flag to demand the surrender of the Americans. Lt. Col. Harry Kinnard, on the staff of division commander Maj. Gen. Anthony McAuliffe, suggested that McAuliffe respond to the German ultimatum with the word "Nuts!" That one-word reply by Americans unwilling to yield has become part of the lore of the Army.

More than one million men fought in the Battle of the Bulge, often called the largest land battle of World War II (a characterization that excludes the Soviet Eastern Front). In scope and number of participants, few battles in history were costlier. At its conclusion, 19,000 U.S. soldiers had been killed and 62,000 wounded.

DEVELOPMENTS IN 1945

In early February 1945, Roosevelt, Churchill, and Stalin held the Yalta Conference in the Crimea to discuss the Allies' demand for unconditional surrender by Germany and Japan, and to make plans for the postwar United Nations. Roosevelt was now in his fourth term and had served longer than any other American president.

On March 7, 1945, after finding a single bridge intact, U.S. soldiers crossed the Rhine River at Remagen and elsewhere to the south and north. By the end of the month, all German troops had been pushed back to German soil and the once-invincible German forces were now fielding old men and teenagers. Allied forces fanned out and raced rapidly to link up with Soviet troops on the Elbe. Fighting ended with the German surrender of May 7, 1945.

At the time of the German surrender, Eisenhower had under his command 90 divisions: 61 American, 13 British, 10 French, 5 Canadian, and 1 Polish, plus numerous additional units representing several nations.

On April 12, 1945, Roosevelt suffered a massive cerebral hemorrhage and died at his Warm Springs, Georgia, retreat. Former World War I National Guard artillery officer and combat veteran Harry S. Truman (1884–1972) became the thirty-third president. Only a fortnight later did briefers tell Truman about the U.S. effort to develop an atomic bomb.

On May 4, 1945, less than nine months after pulling up stakes in Italy, 7th Army troops crossed Brenner Pass and joined up with 5th Army troops on Italian soil. In 262 days of continuous fighting, the 7th Army had advanced over 1,000 miles from the beaches of southern France.

Was Gen. Mark W. Clark "a lightweight with an egotistic streak," as fellow West Pointer Gen. Omar Bradley called him, or was Clark one of the towering military figures of the twentieth century?

Clark was aloof, but friends admired his competence and addressed him by his middle name, Wayne. He graduated from the military academy in April 1917. Wounded in fighting in the trenches in Europe, he received awards for his service in World War I. In July 1942, he arrived in England to take command of the emerging Army Ground Forces in Europe.

Clark led the 5th Army, from the landing at Salerno and the seizure of Naples to the drive for Rome and the January 1944 invasion of Anzio. Reluctance to seize the advantage at Anzio frustrated Clark, who had been so thinned by providing forces for the landing that he was unable to push his remaining troops across the Rapido River to link up with invasion troops. Clark advanced in Italy slowly, perhaps prolonging the conflict, but he ultimately liberated Rome. He was appointed 15th Army Group commander in December 1944 and ran the Italian campaign until victory in May 1945.

Clark was one of the few American generals to enjoy cordial relations with his French counterparts—even Charles de Gaulle, whose arrogance made Clark seem mild-mannered by comparison. In later years, he was the only American leader who could persuade South Korea's cantankerous president, Syngman Rhee, to accept an armistice agreement—something about which Clark himself had strong personal doubts.

Clark shelved plans to retire and replaced Gen. Matthew Ridgway as commander of U.S. and Allied troops in Korea—a changeover that occurred during a riot by North Korean prisoners of war that Clark put down with force. Clark remained in command to become the American officer who inked the Korean armistice agreement July 27, 1953. For the rest of his life, he resented having been the only American general ever to sign a cease-fire in which a clear victory had not been achieved.

THE PACIFIC OFFENSIVE

The U.S. 6th Army, which dubbed its headquarters the Alamo Force, seized the Kiriwina and Woodlark islands in July 1943 and began a tortured 2,700-mile advance toward the Philippines. The 10th Army was formed in June 1944 under Lt. Gen. Simon Bolivar Buckner Jr. (son of a Confederate general of the Civil War).

The 6th Army's progress was marked by the following: capture of the western end of New Britain and of Saidor (December 1943–February 1944), seizure of the Admiralty Islands (February–May 1944), landings at Hollandia and Altape (April–August 1944), the seizure of Biak (May–August 1944), and several actions leading up to the occupation of Leyte that began in October 1944. On October 20, MacArthur waded ashore at Leyte Island, fulfilling his pledge to return. Three days later, the naval Battle of Leyte Gulf was a major defeat for the Japanese, moving the Allies closer to regaining control of all of the Philippines.

On August 10, 1944, U.S. troops regained control of Guam after three weeks of heavy fighting. The advancing Americans also took the island of Tinian. Saipan, Tinian, and Guam were to prove crucial as B-29 Superfortress bases for the final air assault on the Japanese home islands.

SAIPAN

The Pacific Islands campaign was touted as a Marine Corps effort, and the Marines often—but not always—were in the first wave. In most of the island-hopping operations, however, the Army also had a vital role. Symbolic of the soldiers who fought was Sgt. Thomas A. Baker, who made a point that he was fighting for his buddies, "not for the flag or anything like that."

Baker was a sergeant in Company A, 105th Infantry, 27th Infantry Division, on embattled Saipan in the Mariana Islands. Marines landed on the island's infamous Red Beach One near Aslito airfield on June 15, 1944, followed by Army troops on their right flank. Long afterward, the island's 30,000 Japanese defenders resisted. Some Japanese squirreled themselves away in caves and kept fighting. Some chose suicide over surrender.

Army soldiers and Marines fought side by side on the island, but their leaders were not always in harmony. Marine Lt. Gen. Holland "Howlin' Mad" Smith so disliked the performance of Army Maj. Gen. Ralph Smith (no relation) that he relieved the Army general of his duty and took personal command of the soldiers.

Baker, who hailed from Troy, New York, was a private on June 19 when his advancing company was halted in its tracks by automatic weapons fire from fortified enemy positions looking down from higher ground. With Japanese Nambu machine guns and rifles blazing away at him, Baker seized the initiative, grabbed a 2.5-inch bazooka (rocket launcher), and scrambled to within 100 yards of the foe. The Army's history office later noted, "Through heavy rifle and machine-gun fire that was directed at him by the enemy, he knocked out the strong point, enabling his company to assault the ridge."

As the fighting on Saipan persisted, Baker was promoted to sergeant, in part because of heavy casualties. Days later, while his company advanced across an open field flanked with obstructions and places of concealment, Sergeant Baker volunteered to take up a position in the rear to protect against surprise attack. He came upon two heavily fortified locations manned by 2 Japanese officers and 10 enlisted troops that the Americans had unwittingly bypassed. Again acting as an army of one, Baker charged and killed five of the enemy. He then advanced 500 yards and discovered six more Japanese troops who had concealed themselves behind American lines. Wielding his M1 Garand rifle, Baker dodged their gunfire and killed all six.

On July 7, 1944, Baker's perimeter was attacked from three sides by 3,000 to 5,000 Japanese. During the early stages of this attack, Baker was seriously wounded. He insisted on remaining in the line. He kept firing at enemy troops who got as close as 5 yards. When his ammunition ran out, the sergeant used his Garand as a club, swinging at onrushing Japanese in hand-to-hand combat.

During a few seconds of respite, a fellow soldier carried Baker about 50 yards to the rear. Then his helper was wounded. Baker refused to be moved any farther. He said he preferred to be left to die rather than risk the lives of his friends. At his request, Baker was placed in a sitting position against a small tree. A comrade, withdrawing, offered assistance. Baker refused and insisted that he be left alone. He asked to be given a pistol. When last seen alive, Baker was propped against a tree, pistol in hand, calmly facing the foe. Later, Baker's body was found in the same position, gun empty, with eight Japanese lying dead before him.

After 16,525 soldiers and Marines had been killed or wounded, Gen. Holland Smith announced Saipan secured on June 22, 1944. All but a thousand of the 30,000 Japanese defenders were dead. Sgt. Thomas A. Baker was posthumously awarded the Medal of Honor.

PROGRESS IN THE PACIFIC

On October 12, 1944, the 9th Army under Lt. Gen. Robert L. Eichelberger assumed control of all operational areas in New Guinea, New Britain, the Admiralties, and Morotai, making this numbered army responsible for 200,000 troops in 20 locations.

The 8th Army moved to the Philippines and took over responsibility for completion of the Leyte operation.

In January 1945, the 6th and 8th Armies began the drive toward Manila. In February, March, and April, the 8th Army executed amphibious landings to clear the Verde Island Passages and the San Bernardino Straits. The 8th Army assumed control of the entire Philippines on July 1, 1945, when it acquired responsibility for operations on Luzon. MacArthur proclaimed the recapture of the Philippines on July 5, after nearly 12,000 Americans died in a tortured 10-month campaign.

In the northern Pacific, plans to employ Buckner's 10th Army against Formosa were changed, and at the end of March 1945, this numbered army began the invasion of Okinawa. The Japanese stood back and allowed troops to come ashore; then they set forth to destroy the naval support, unleashing what became the bloodiest battle of the Pacific war, with 12,500 Americans killed and 37,000 wounded. Resistance increased after U.S. troops seized the adjacent island of Ie Shima on April 16, and ground and naval forces soon found themselves pitted against Japan's kamikaze, or suicide, forces. Buckner was killed by enemy shellfire on June 18, 1945, while observing an infantry and armor attack. Gen. Joseph W. Stilwell took over Buckner's command. Okinawa finally fell on June 21.

The Army operated 26 hospital ships during the war, with a total bed capacity of 26,755. Army ships were capable of handling between 286 and 1,628 sick and wounded. In addition to these, the Army operated three foreign-flag hospital ships commandeered by Gen. Douglas MacArthur early in the war. Many of these Army ocean-going ships were quite large. The Army hospital ship the *Thistle,* operated by the 206th Hospital Ship complement, was 432 feet in length and displaced 7,822 tons.

B-29 Superfortresses, which had already laid much of Japan's industry and infrastructure to waste, dropped atomic bombs on Hiroshima on

August 6 and on Nagasaki on August 9, 1945. Fighting ended with Japan's surrender on August 15, and a surrender ceremony was held on September 2 in Tokyo Bay. MacArthur, now titled Supreme Commander of Allied Powers in Japan, presided over the ceremony on the deck of the battleship USS *Missouri*. By one estimate, all around the world, history's greatest war took 38 million lives.

> More than 3,400 individuals have been awarded the Medal of Honor, but until 1997, no African Americans had received the award for action in World War II. On January 13, 1997, President Bill Clinton belatedly presented the medal to seven African American soldiers who fought in valorous actions. The only living recipient among the seven was former 1st Lt. Vernon Baker, 75.

During World War II, 10,400,000 soldiers served in the Army. The figure includes the Army Air Forces, which are today regarded as part of Air Force history. Total Army deaths of 305,005 (a figure that excludes non-battle deaths of Army nurses before February 1945) included 175,407 killed in action, 26,706 who died of wounds, 15,120 who died of disease, and 88,772 who died of accidental and other deaths. These figures are for the Army (including the Army Air Forces) only.

CHAPTER 8

THE COLD WAR AND THE KOREAN CONFLICT (1945–1960)

In November 1945, Gen. Dwight D. Eisenhower replaced Gen. George C. Marshall as the Army's chief of staff. In early 1946, weeks after being voted out of office, former British Prime Minister Winston Churchill told an audience in Fulton, Missouri, "An Iron Curtain has descended across the [European] continent, allowing police governments to rule Eastern Europe." The Soviet Union changed from ally to adversary. The Army began preparing for a Soviet armored assault on the plains of Western Europe and trained to wage an atomic war—as usual during peacetime, with less money and fewer soldiers than it wanted.

The Army went from 10 million soldiers to fewer than 500,000 in only 2 years. American soldiers had roles in the counterinsurgency war in Greece, the Berlin Airlift, and the early atomic weapons tests that defined the era.

National security legislation in 1947 created the Department of Defense, the secretary of defense, the Joint Chiefs of Staff (which had existed since 1942 but had no formal status), and the Central

Intelligence Agency and made the Air Force an independent service branch. It was a sweeping revision of the nation's military and intelligence apparatus, but it seemed to offer little that was new to the Army, which was reducing strength. Running for election in 1948, President Harry S. Truman may have been the very last presidential candidate to campaign on a platform calling for reducing military spending.

Also in 1948, Gen. Omar N. Bradley replaced Eisenhower as Army chief of staff. He left a year later to become the first chairman of the Joint Chiefs. Following Bradley as the Army's top officer, Gen. J. Lawton "Lightning Joe" Collins (1896–1987) became the eighteenth man to serve (since 1902) as Army chief of staff. Collins had commanded VII Corps in the Normandy invasion and (in 1948) helped to define the Army's role in the newly formed North Atlantic Treaty Organization. Bradley and Collins remained chairman and chief of staff throughout the Korean War.

Omar N. Bradley became the first chairman of the Joint Chiefs of Staff on August 16, 1950. He was also the last officer in American history to be promoted to five-star rank as a general of the Army.

Bradley's future success was predicted in the 1915 edition of the *Howitzer,* the West Point yearbook. "His most prominent characteristic is 'getting there,'" read Bradley's entry written by a classmate.

Bradley is remembered for winning the admiration of battlefield soldiers.

After missing action in the trenches of France during World War I, Bradley rose through the ranks as a protégé of Gen. George C. Marshall. In February 1941, he became first in his class to reach brigadier general, bypassing the rank of colonel, as commandant of the Infantry School at Fort Benning, Georgia, where he set up the Infantry Officer Candidate program.

Bradley added stars and performed well in North Africa in 1942 and as Gen. George S. Patton's deputy in II Corps in 1943. He took over II Corps for the Allied invasion of Sicily.

A calm, easy figure who lacked Patton's flamboyance or MacArthur's aloofness, Bradley understood how to move vast numbers of troops and move their supply lines with them. Gen. Dwight D. Eisenhower tapped him to establish the 1st Army Group and the 1st U.S. Army, which Bradley commanded during the June 6, 1944, landings at Normandy. After the invasion, Bradley took command of all U.S. ground troops in northwestern Europe.

Bradley reached four-star rank in March 1945 as head of the 12th Army Group. He headed the Veterans Administration from 1945 to 1947, became Army chief of staff from 1948 to 1949, and became the first chairman in

> 1949. In 1950, he became the last of America's World War II leaders to be conferred five-star rank. He remained chairman throughout the Korean War, frequently visiting troops in Korea, and he retired in 1953.
> Bradley died in New York on April 8, 1981. He was depicted on a U.S. postage stamp in 2001.

GERMAN CONSTABULARY

While occupying Germany in the immediate postwar years when the Cold War was still being defined, the Army found itself running a super police force, or constabulary.

In October 1945, before leaving Europe, Eisenhower created a 32,700-member constabulary in the U.S. zone of Germany.

Briefly known as the State Police, the organization became the United States Constabulary. The Constabulary was intended to be an elite force, made up of high-caliber soldiers drawn from a voluntary re-enlistment program. "They were frequently 18-, 19-, and 20-year-olds," remembered retired Master Sgt. William Tevington, 73, of Lawrence, Kansas, in an interview. "The older GIs had rotated home by then.

"We were given the power to arrest, detain, hold, and transport [people]," Tevington explained. "Those charged with offenses were tried in a court run by the military government. We in the Constabulary were a key part of the military government."

Constabulary soldiers wore a "lightning bolt" shoulder patch in yellow, blue, and red, combining the colors of the cavalry, infantry, and artillery. They wore cavalry boots with modified lace tops and the smooth face outside. Soldiers wore the Sam Browne belt, which had been discarded by most of the Army in 1937, but with shoulder straps over the left shoulder instead of the right to permit easy access to a Colt .45-caliber M1919A1 automatic pistol holstered on the right hip. (Each soldier also carried a Thompson submachine gun or an M1 Garand rifle.) On each soldier's helmet liner was a distinctive yellow circle enclosing the letter *C*. Meant to make Constabulary troops stand out, this unique attire was capped off with a golden yellow silk scarf.

Constabulary soldiers sought to achieve good relations with the German population while also enforcing the rules of the military occupation.

Germans called these soldiers *blitz polizei* (lightning police) or "circle C cowboys." Much of the soldiers' work involved displaced persons, or DPs, the refugees who were located throughout Germany after the war.

On January 10, 1946, Maj. Gen. Ernest N. Harmon, wartime commander of the 1st and 2nd Armored divisions and XXII Corps, became the first commander of the Constabulary. During the occupation of Germany and Austria, the Constabulary (which policed the civilian population) often found itself in a rivalry with the military police (which policed American soldiers). Members of the Constabulary made civil arrests and solved crimes, but they also helped resettle displaced persons and stood guard against possible trouble from the Soviet occupying forces to the east. Some of these soldiers called themselves "combat cops."

Constabulary soldiers gained a reputation for integrity. Bribery was routine and temptation was rife in a populace where wartime bombing had leveled cities and many Germans did not have enough to eat. Black marketing and corruption were widespread.

Constabulary troops were drawn largely from reconnaissance battalions (known as squadrons) equipped with M8 Gates three-quarter-ton armored vehicles, each with a 37-mm cannon and a 30-caliber machine gun. The vehicles were painted a high gloss and wore the distinctive circle with the *C* inside. Each regimental headquarters also had M24 Chaffee light tanks.

During a visit, Eisenhower said to an officer, "I thought I'd gotten rid of the last horses in the Army." The soldier replied, "We need them, sir." Horses were provided for patrolling in difficult terrain along the borders, while motorcycles policed traffic on the superhighways (*autobahnen*). The Constabulary was, in fact, also the last mounted unit in the Army.

A separate Constabulary regiment was responsible for Austria and for the U.S. zone in Berlin, which was geographically separated from the U.S. zone of Germany.

A U.S. high commission replaced the military government in the merged British- and American-occupied zones of Germany on September 21, 1949. Germany shifted to civilian rule soon afterward, with separate governments being founded in the Allied zone in the west and the Soviet zone to the east. In 1951, the Constabulary was placed under the 7th Army and the distinctive lightning bolt patches came off. The Constabulary formally ended its existence as a unique component of the U.S. Army on December 15, 1952.

KOREAN WAR

In the early hours of June 25, 1950, in darkness and driving rain, North Korean armed forces crossed the thirty-eighth parallel at half a dozen locations. Ninety thousand men and hundreds of Russian-made medium T-34 tanks launched the invasion of South Korea. North Korea also put into battle its modest air arm of 150 propeller-driven combat planes.

Korea introduced the Americans to a half-century of limited conflict. The fight for freedom in Korea was a victory, often inaccurately compared with a later conflict in Vietnam, with which it had almost nothing in common. There was virtually no insurgency in Korea, no guerrillas, and no battle for "hearts and minds." The Korean War was rarely challenged on the American home front. The war led to no protests, no riots, and no burning of draft cards. North Korea's attempt to seize South Korea was seen as an intolerable evil and was thwarted. A precedent was established when 16 countries came together under the United Nations flag, spearheaded by the United States.

North Korea's Kim Il-song was ruthless, unpredictable, and little understood in the West. In 1950, no one in the Army—indeed, not a single employee of the U.S. government and not even a single analyst at the Central Intelligence Agency on E Street in northwest Washington—was employed for the purpose of studying the North Korean leadership. Now that historical files are open in Moscow, we know that Kim sought and was granted the blessing of Russia's Josef Stalin, his mentor, before his troops plunged across the line.

Korea was divided because the U.S. allowed the Russians to enter the Pacific war (in its final days) and offered to split the task of accepting the surrender of Japanese troops on the Korean peninsula. Thus, the nation—consisting of one culture, one people, and one language—was divided in half because of a decision by the United States.

Americans were absorbed in a peacetime boom in which every middle-class citizen could hold a realistic hope of owning a house and an automobile. When Americans listened to radio news from overseas (or, in the case of a handful, watched news on early television sets), they took note principally of the looming atomic threat from the Soviet Union. If war was to come, it would come against Russia. *Collier's* magazine frightened the daylights out of everybody by devoting an issue to a fictitious "history" of World War III, which ended with American tanks rolling into Moscow.

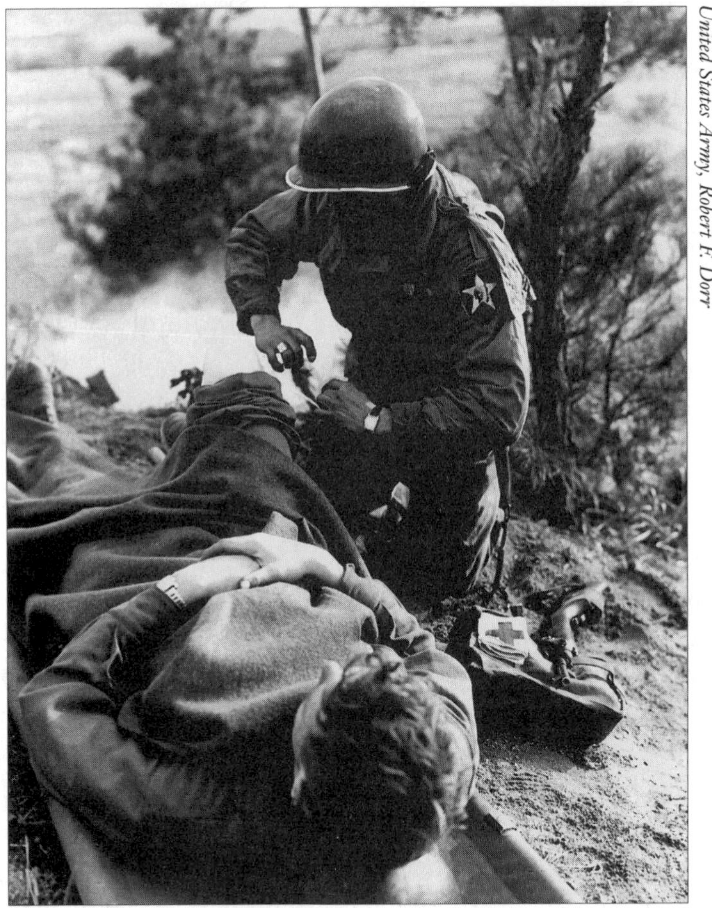

United States Army, Robert F. Dorr

Pfc. Presely J. Schmitt dresses the leg wound of a soldier wounded while on a patrol mission in Korea.

But even among military observers, many could summarize everything they knew about Korea in the unfortunate words of one American general. Before being withdrawn from Korea in 1948, U.S. forces were commanded by Lt. Gen. John R. Hodge. "Listen up, men," Hodge was fond of saying to newcomers. "You've got three things to worry about. You've got gonorrhea, you've got diarrhea, and you've got Ko-rea."

The American commander in the Far East (though not yet in Korea) was Douglas MacArthur. At 70, he was already a towering American figure of the twentieth century, widely praised for his handling of the occupation of Japan, where he was at times a king and at times a confessor, melding firmness and compassion in his one-man rule of a hobbled and humiliated enemy. MacArthur's title was Commander in Chief Far East. His jurisdiction was limited to the island nation surrounding his office on the top floor of the six-story Dai Ichi Building in Tokyo and included neither the U.S. Navy in adjacent waters nor (as of June 25, 1950) the Korean peninsula.

At 6:46 A.M. on that fateful Sunday, the U.S. Ambassador to South Korea, John J. Muccio, cabled Washington that North Korean Yak-9 fighters had strafed Seoul's Kimpo airport. Muccio had lobbied without success to have U.S. warplanes stationed in Korea. Now he pleaded for "positive and speedy action." Half a world away, President Truman left his hometown of Independence, Missouri, to return to Washington so rapidly that he left aides behind. Truman's Douglas DC-6A transport, nicknamed *Independence*, taxied out of Kansas City Municipal Airport so rapidly that navigator Capt. E. P. Christensen had to catch up and climb aboard while the plane was taxiing.

Truman acted quickly but not hastily. He initially authorized the use of force only to protect the evacuation of American citizens. On June 27, 1950, North Korean fighters swarmed over Kimpo airfield but were greeted by American fighters.

By the morning of June 28, 1950, North Koreans broke through the last organized resistance around Seoul and advanced into its suburbs. By now, Truman had placed MacArthur in charge of actions in Korea solely to evacuate Americans. In Washington, a debate raged over just how much authority to give to the general and how much of a military response to allow. Air operations were restricted to South Korean airspace. From bases in Japan and Guam, B-26s, B-29s, F-80s, and F-82s opposed the assault.

MacArthur flew to Korea on June 29 in his personal C-54, the Bataan. At his point of departure in Tokyo, the weather was deteriorating relentlessly. MacArthur reversed a decision by Gen. George E. Stratemeyer to "ground" his aircraft and then flew with Stratemeyer and several reporters to Suwon airport, 30 miles (45 km) south of the South Korean capital. MacArthur's pilot, Lt. Col. Anthony Story, touched down at Suwon in the middle of a strafing attack by North Korean fighters. After meeting with Muccio and others, MacArthur apparently made a unilateral decision to allow American warplanes to cross the thirty-eighth parallel and strike the air bases from which the North Koreans were coming.

Donald L. Ranard, a diplomat on Muccio's staff, was one of the civilians brought out of the capital with his family. "There was confusion everywhere," Ranard recalled in an interview. "Our teletype and telex facilities worked only part of the time. We had conflicting information as to whether we were going to set up a temporary embassy farther south. [This was done, first at Taegu, later at Pusan]. There were a lot of planes over Seoul and we were bussed south, over Suwon, where we were put on transports. We saw one propeller-driven fighter flying very low over Suwon with smoke pouring from its engines. We were told later that this was a reconnaissance version of one of our Mustangs."

Though some civilians flew to safety from Suwon, an American freighter, the ship *Reinholte*, was assigned evacuation duties at Inchon harbor.

At this juncture, a Washington decision gave MacArthur free rein to employ U.S. air power throughout the Korean peninsula "against air bases, depots, tank farms, troop columns, and other purely military targets such as … bridges." Within 24 hours, MacArthur also had authority to commit the first U.S. ground troops to Korean soil. The 24th Infantry Division under Maj. Gen. William F. Dean began moving from Japan to Pusan.

In the political arena, a Soviet boycott of the Security Council enabled the United Nations to pass a resolution supporting the defense of South Korea. As has been indicated, in due course, 16 nations were to supply troops to fight the Communists.

The UN action gave MacArthur an additional title. He became Commander in Chief, United Nations Command, abbreviated CINCUNC and inevitably pronounced "sink-unk." Communications continued to be a problem as the North Koreans kept coming south. Stratemeyer reported to MacArthur instances when B-26s and B-29s failed to bomb targets because medium bomber squadrons did not have clear orders. As the Navy's Task Force 77 reached Korean waters in early July and prepared to launch large-scale carrier air strikes, communication within the chain of command became a growing problem.

On the ground, the North Koreans pushed onward. Suwon fell. Six C-54 Skymaster transports from Itazuke arrived at Pusan carrying the first American ground troops to face North Korea's T-34 medium tanks—members of the ill-fated Task Force Smith, named for its commander, Lt. Col. Charles B. (Brad) Smith.

Consisting of 440 men in an infantry battalion plus a two-gun 75-mm recoilless rifle platoon, backed up by a grand total of two 4.2-inch mortars and a handful of 105-mm howitzers, Task Force Smith was ill-equipped and its men were unprepared to see their 2.36-inch bazooka rockets bouncing off the armored hull of a T-34. When Lt. Col. Smith picked a spot to make a stand a couple of miles north of Osan, 30 North Korean T-34s struck in a bold frontal attack. A 105-mm howitzer firing AT (antitank) rounds disabled two of them, but the gun was quickly knocked out. The 75-mm recoilless rifles proved to be as useless as the 2.36 bazookas. Lt. Col. Smith's soldiers fought valiantly, but without enough of anything—intelligence, food, supplies, ammunition, and, above all, antitank weapons. Task Force Smith was badly defeated, and the Communists kept coming.

United States Army, Robert F. Dorr

Members of the 40th U.S. Infantry Division going through tactical training problems.

The first Army unit to fight in Korea, Task Force Smith, will forever be remembered as a symbol of failure. Though it had excellent leaders and soldiers, Task Force Smith was sent into the crucible of combat without adequate training or equipment, and without a healthy appreciation for the prowess of North Korea's T-34 medium tanks.

On the Japanese island of Kyushu, Lt. Col. Charles B. "Brad" Smith was alerted on the night of June 30, 1950—five days after the North Korean attack—to put together a combat force of soldiers from the 24th Infantry Division's 1st Battalion, 21st Infantry Regiment. Smith assembled 440 men, many of them recent draftees. Unfortunately, this ad hoc expeditionary unit had only a handful of 75-mm recoilless rifles and 2.36-inch bazookas (rocket launchers).

C-54 Skymaster transports carried Task Force Smith to Pusan, Korea. Smith's soldiers then traveled by train to Taejon, where they arrived on July 2. By then, the North Korean invasion force had seized Seoul and was driving south, with the deadly T-34 tanks at the forefront of the assault.

Smith took up defensive positions 3 miles north of Osan. Joined by artillery reinforcements from Japan, Smith and his soldiers came face to face with the onrushing North Korean armor on the morning of July 5.

Thirty T-34 tanks plowed into the midst of the Americans, impervious to direct hits by the inadequate recoilless rifles and bazookas. The tanks approached an artillery position, and two of them were knocked out by direct fire from a 105-mm howitzer; however, additional tanks overwhelmed the gun position, and the tanks continued their advance.

Smith could not hold a defensive line and, amid the confusion, had difficulty extricating his forces. Task Force Smith scattered in disarray. When it reassembled in mid-July, more than 150 soldiers were missing in action. In time, the North Koreans were halted at Taegu. Later in the war, American units fielded the larger 3.5-inch bazooka, which was powerful enough to halt a T-34.

Everything that could be gotten into the air was dispatched to support the outnumbered American troops who were falling back.

On July 20, 1950, the important city of Taejon fell to the North Koreans. Now only a single geographic barrier—the Naktong River, which snaked around southeastern Korea and flowed north of the city of Taegu—lay between the invaders and the sea. UN troops clustered in a tiny corner of southeastern Korea known as the Pusan Perimeter. More and more men were being crammed into a smaller and smaller space, the weather was deteriorating, and air power was still struggling to cope with communications problems, equipment failures, and difficult terrain. At Taegu, a young lieutenant searched everywhere for a detailed map of the area immediately around him and could not locate one. Leaders in Washington and Tokyo worried that they now faced another Dunkirk—wherein friendly forces would be driven into the sea.

While the 24th Infantry Division fought to hold off the North Koreans in its decreasing area around Pusan, Army aviation played a role. Having given up most of its aircraft when the Air Force became an independent service (on September 18, 1947), the Army did not then have the vast fleet of helicopters and fixed-wing planes it would later enjoy.

A few Bell H-13 helicopters performed limited medical evacuation duties (soon to be joined by Air Force Sikorsky H-5s). Maj. Gen. Edward M. Almond, MacArthur's chief of staff, commuted from one battlefield location to another in a Ryan L-17 Navion airplane. Attempts to use the L-17 as a spotter for artillery and as a "forward air controller" for fighter-bombers produced mixed results. Not least of its deficiencies was a low wing, which was fine for flying characteristics but an impediment to spotting the bad guys on the ground. The Piper L-4 Cub proved more suitable for the spotting role.

For rescue, the Cub was inadequate. Equally unsuited for Korea was the Air Force's Stinson L-5 Sentinel, two of which established the service's first dedicated rescue unit at Pusan air base on July 7, 1950, but had to be withdrawn a fortnight later.

On July 13, 1950, Lt. Gen. Walton H. (Johnnie) Walker took command of the U.S. 8th Army, which meant all American ground forces in Korea, at besieged Taegu. There did not seem to be a lot of hope that Taegu—or even Pusan, at the southeastern tip of the Korean peninsula—could be held.

INCHON PAYBACK

There are conflicting versions of when MacArthur devised Operation Chromite, the "end run" amphibious landing behind the lines at the port of Inchon, a few miles west of Seoul, where portions of the harbor required a 20-foot sea wall because of rapidly shifting tides. It's likely that MacArthur was already casting his eyes toward Inchon when the first American ground troops were being overcome by the North Korean onslaught.

MacArthur lost an important commander when Maj. Gen. William F. Dean was reported missing (see following sidebar) while personally leading tank-killer teams armed with the newly arrived 3.5-inch bazookas, replacements for the useless 2.36-inch model. Dean evaded capture for 46 days while the Allies searched desperately for him. In fact, Maj. Gen. Partridge, 5th Air Force commander, flew sortie after sortie in a T-6 Texan hoping to spot Dean and bring about a rescue. Instead, General Dean was taken prisoner and was treated horribly by his captors for three years.

The highest-ranking American soldier held prisoner during the Korean War of 1950–1953, Maj. Gen. William F. Dean was awarded the Medal of Honor.

When Korean fighting began, Dean commanded the 24th Infantry Division, located at Kokura on the western Japanese island of Kyushu. On June 25, 1950, North Korean troops spearheaded by T-34 tanks invaded South Korea. Dean's troops moved to Korea and fought against heavy odds, eventually falling back to Taejon.

Dean's initial cadre of American soldiers, known as Task Force Smith, was all but annihilated by the armored assault. Rounds fired by the Army's standard antitank weapons, the 2.36-inch rocket launcher and the 75-mm recoilless rifle, bounced uselessly off the steel hull of the T-34. When Dean arrived in Taejon on July 3, 1950, the attackers seemed on the verge of seizing the entire Korean peninsula.

Gen. Walton H. Walker, commander of the U.S. 8th Army, implored Dean to hold Taejon at least until July 20, to allow time for more friendly forces to reach Korea. Dean took to the streets to fight. His troops now were equipped with newly arrived 3.5-inch rocket launchers, known as bazookas, which were somewhat effective against the T-34s.

Dean bought enough time to enable friendly forces to hold the North Korean advance farther south at Taegu. But Dean became separated from his troops and found himself behind enemy lines.

Dean spent more than a month foraging, hiding, and evading capture. He was eventually captured by the North Koreans. He was a prisoner of war from August 25, 1950, until September 4, 1953. While in captivity, he resisted enemy efforts to force him to sign a confession to war crimes.

Following his release in Korea, Dean published a memoir (*General Dean's Story*, written with William L. Worden [New York: Viking Press]) in 1954. Dean retired from the Army on October 31, 1955. He died on August 25, 1981.

Other battlefield commanders clung to the precarious foothold around Pusan. Now MacArthur created X Corps, under Almond, a joint Army-Marine-Korean force that included the Army's 7th Infantry Division and the 1st Marine Division. These were the troops who would storm ashore—or, more correctly, climb ashore, using ladders from their landing boats—at Inchon if the Pusan Perimeter could be held long enough to make the invasion possible. If it worked, Kimpo airport could be quickly seized, Seoul would follow, and the pre-war South Korean government under President Syngman Rhee could be restored to power.

The first objective of the amphibious assault was the island of Wolmi-do in Inchon harbor. About 2,200 North Korean troops were at Inchon, with 22,000 more in the Kimpo-Seoul area. Two hundred thirty ships supported the landing, mostly American, but a few from the British and other Allied navies. In the predawn darkness of September 15, 1950, the amphibious ships threaded their way up the narrow Flying Fish Channel toward Inchon. On board the amphibious flagship the USS *Mount McKinley* were MacArthur, naval commander Rear Adm. James H. Doyle, and 1st Marine Division commander Maj. Gen. Oliver P. Smith. As landing craft churned through heavy seas toward Wolmi-do, an enormous barrage of rocket projectiles was let loose by ships known as LSMRs, or Landing Ships, Medium (Rocket). F4U-4 Corsair fighters then swooped down over the Marines, attacking shore targets with 5-inch high-velocity aircraft rockets and other ordnance.

The first wave came ashore at Green Beach on Wolmi-do at 6:33 A.M. With Corsairs overhead, Marines secured the island in light fighting and in less than 30 minutes. The main assault came only 11 hours later, at 5:30 P.M., as the flood tide permitted landing boats and LSTs—Landing Ships, Tank—to carry Marines to the main Inchon sea walls identified as Red and Blue Beaches. Landing craft rammed against the sea walls, ladders went up, and Marines stormed ashore. In the deepening day, naval gunfire and new flights of Corsairs pinned down the port's North Korean defenders.

Given the difficulties with cantankerous tides and the long interval between the landings at Wolmi and Inchon, the "Chromite" invasion proceeded almost flawlessly. By the evening of the second day, September 16, 1950, more than 15,000 troops and 1,500 vehicles were ashore. General Smith assumed command of the Marines ashore and within hours the Army's 7th Infantry Division began landing behind Smith's men. By the night of September 17, Smith's Marines were able to drive inland and seize Kimpo airport. Soon the invasion force was driving toward Seoul.

The Inchon landing achieved its goal. The North Koreans, so recently on the verge of overrunning the UN Allies and winning the war, were now thrown into confusion and forced to fight on two fronts as Walker's troops began to move north from the Pusan Perimeter.

On September 27, 1950, Gen. Almond's X Corps, moving east from the Inchon beachhead, linked up with the 8th Army driving north from the Pusan Perimeter. The North Korean army, which had been so successful in the first weeks of conflict, now began to fold and retreat.

At first, it seemed that the fighting would end with the recapture of South Korea and the restoration of borders as they had existed before the fray began. South Korea's Syngman Rhee, for one, was staunchly opposed to any such resolution and wanted to use the Allies' success to reunify the divided peninsula. Truman and his advisors, while not eager to pander to Rhee, reluctantly decided that communist forces had to be destroyed. MacArthur was given authority to pursue the crumbling enemy army north of the thirty-eighth parallel.

By October 13, 1950, the North Korean port of Wonsan was in Allied hands. By October 21, American soldiers held the North Korean capital of Pyongyang. That month, Truman met with MacArthur at Wake Island for a one-day discussion of the military situation in Korea, which included planning for the coming victory and postwar situation. It has been said, in retrospect, that MacArthur was contemptuous, if not insubordinate, at this get-together. In fact, the strain between the two men developed later. The discussions were not unfriendly. MacArthur told the president that organized enemy resistance would soon end and that most troops could be withdrawn by Christmas. MacArthur saw no chance of China intervening in the war. Truman departed the meeting believing that he and MacArthur understood each other and that the general would follow orders from the White House.

On November 1, 1950, F-51 Mustangs were engaged by six swept-wing jet fighters that lashed out at them from across the Yalu River, the border between North Korea and China. The jets—introducing a new word to the lexicon, MiG—were the first hint that China might be planning to intervene.

U.S. intelligence experts knew of huge modern airfields on the Chinese side of the Yalu and had a little knowledge of the new MiG-15 fighter. But ground movements by Chinese troops somehow missed the experts, or at least MacArthur and his staff.

On November 24, 1950, UN forces launched an all-out attack. Christmas was on the minds of many Americans. MacArthur had done little to conceal the view he'd expressed to Truman, that many of his troops would be home for the holidays. One final punch into the collapsing North Korean forces, and it would be over. The UN already occupied most of North Korea. Back home, the *Washington Daily News* published a front-page photo of a wounded American soldier beneath the headline "War Almost Over." The USAF's Military Air Transport Service, which had made possible the success against the North Koreans by bringing into Korea tons of supplies and equipment, now began planning to carry troops and supplies home. There was talk of a victory parade. South Korean President Syngman Rhee, who had always wanted the Allies to do more than simply defend South Korea, saw that there *was* no North Korea anymore and was elated. A senator hailed the unification of the Korean peninsula as "the beginning of the rollback of communism."

As incredible as it seems, no one in the West had taken it seriously when Chinese Premier Chou En-lai warned two months earlier that China would send troops into Korea if the Allies advanced north of the thirty-eighth parallel. Chou was second in power only to the "great helmsman," Mao Tse-tung, but Americans had so few experts on China that no one at the Pentagon, the State Department, or the CIA raised any warning flag. Nor did anyone in the West know that the Chinese Politburo had decided to enter the war. Though unwilling to commit Russian forces on the ground (Russia's border with North Korea was only a few miles long), Stalin played to Mao's fears that the United States would use its success in Korea to unleash Chiang Kai-shek and his Kuomintang army, which had been resisting the Communists in Korea since 1945, against the mainland—exactly as conservative Republican senators were urging. By sending Russian pilots and warplanes to Manchuria in a kind of "good faith" gesture, Stalin may have tipped Mao in favor of intervening.

This was not a good deal for China, even though the Chinese were to succeed at first on the battlefield. Peking had always co-existed with its neighbors, none of whom the Chinese had ever liked very much. In effect, the blood of young Chinese soldiers was to be spilled in order to protect Russian interests. Once Mao and the Chinese Politburo made their decision, the move was accomplished with unprecedented skill. On the Allied side, no intelligence agent, no radio-intercept experts, and no reconnaissance aircraft caught the movement of hundreds of thousands of Chinese troops. MacArthur's aides insist he had no clue they were coming. The proper name for this force, incidentally, was the Chinese Peoples Volunteers.

SUDDEN ASSAULT

In a stunning move, China inserted half a million troops into North Korea. Beginning November 26, 1950, hordes of Chinese counterattacked furiously on most of the western front. It happened overnight, and it happened while Allied intelligence experts were asleep at the switch.

The Chinese came swarming into the midst of UN troops, without much heavy artillery but with no reluctance at full-scale frontal assault, using their long, thin bayonets in hand-to-hand combat before any Western official would even say that China was in the war. Now UN forces faced no fewer than 50 Chinese divisions.

Though they didn't employ bombers or fighter-bombers to support their troops, the Chinese attacked with incredible boldness on the ground. Commanded by Marshal Peng Te-huai (not, as is widely written, by Marshal Lin Piao), the Chinese Peoples Volunteers were tough battle veterans who'd seized all of mainland China from Chiang Kai-shek's armies the year before. Peng himself, with a headquarters in Mukden, 100 miles (161 km) north of the Yalu River, was a seasoned veteran of guerrilla fighting in South China, as well as of Mao Tse-tung's famous Long March (1934–1935) and the later struggles against Chiang.

In the West, the press conjured up an image of Chinese soldiers rushing into battle, shoulder to shoulder, in massed "human wave" attacks. Some reports made the Chinese infantryman an unthinking, dope-crazed fanatic bent on suicide. If only it had been so. It was true that the Chinese made little use of heavy artillery and armor, and that they launched ground attacks with enormous numbers of men—sometimes to the blare of bugles—but these were capable soldiers. When they came, they were both aggressive and smart. Peng and his lieutenants had every reason to believe that they could take the entire Korean peninsula, just as the North Koreans had almost done months earlier. As it turned out, they almost did. To both American soldiers and the American public, they inflicted a stunning defeat. Had they possessed true air power, and had the Allies not controlled the skies, their success would have been total.

On the home front, the Chinese attack was the most devastating blow to the public since Pearl Harbor. Coming at a time of festive holiday plans, the attack was doubly demoralizing. In Korea itself, the onslaught led to one of those historical comparisons that refuse to go away. Ever afterward, in the study of war, few contrasts would be as dramatic as the two very different reactions to the attack of the Army at Kunu-ri and of the Marines at the Chosin Reservoir.

OVERWHELMED

At the top of the map in northwestern Korea, soldiers of the United States Army's 2nd Infantry Division were stunned by the assault that placed them under pressure from 130,000 Chinese, or 10 times their own number. The location was an obscure hamlet called Kunu-ri, which comprised the right flank of the 8th Army. The division commander, Maj. Gen. Laurence B. "Dutch" Keiser, was charged with blocking the Chinese at Kunu-ri, thus preventing them from cutting off the remainder of the 8th Army that was located to the west and was retreating southward on the main Sinanju-Pyongyang highway. By sticking with his original plan to defend his positions as vigorously as possible and then withdraw along a route already festering with Chinese to his rear, Keiser ignored advice and missed an opportunity to withdraw eastward along the south banks of the Chongchon River. Instead of the river, he chose a gauntlet.

But the Chinese had secured roadblocks behind Keiser, held the high ground around him, and were swarming in his midst. Some American soldiers fought valiantly in the Kunu-ri battle. But many were simply slaughtered. Some American soldiers wandered about in the snow, dazed and unable to shoot back as the Chinese poured through their ranks. The

2nd Infantry Division left behind many of its dead and wounded trying to get through a 6-mile series of mountain passes separating the Americans from a more secure position held by the hard-fighting British Commonwealth Brigade. That 6-mile gauntlet became a killing ground. Keiser was relieved of his command. When bloodied, frozen survivors of the 2nd Infantry Division broke through to the British positions (on December 2, 1950), they had suffered 5,000 casualties. A small number of soldiers, led westward along the Chongchon by Col. Paul F. Freeman, escaped the carnage and lived to fight the Chinese another day, but the Kunu-ri battle lives on as a sad and shameful moment for the United States Army.

The Chosin Reservoir was different. Ever afterward, Marines would speak of it without any need to explain what reservoir they were talking about. In teeming hordes, the Chinese Peoples 3rd Field Route Army swarmed down on Maj. Gen. Oliver P. Smith's 1st Marine Division at the Chosin Reservoir. The Chinese had picked a fiendish time to strike—the coldest Korean winter in 177 years. Frostbite took a bitter toll. Blood plasma froze and was useless. Carbine stocks became brittle and cracked in men's hands. M-1 rifles could not be oiled, for the lubricant would clog the mechanism like glue. Marines tried everything from antifreeze to urine to save their water-cooled machineguns. Chinese troops suddenly occupied the high ground everywhere, looking down on the Marines. In the misery of the cruel winter, a withdrawal began.

Soon Americans saw newspaper pictures and newsreel footage (and even occasionally motion picture film on their television news) of their soldiers and Marines being overwhelmed and outfought by a strong and aggressive enemy. It was a situation no American leader could accept. More than a few people remembered that the U.S. Army and Navy commanders at Pearl Harbor had been dismissed and discredited when their forces were overwhelmed by a surprise attack. There was no place for defeat in the American tradition. Yet defeat it was. Casualties mounted.

Remarks by Truman on November 30, 1950, made it clear that the chief executive who had authorized the bombing of Hiroshima was now considering using the atomic bomb (not yet usually called a "nuclear weapon") in Korea. Ironically, MacArthur recommended using atomic bombs on several occasions; when he did so at a later date, he was opposed by Truman, who no longer felt such a drastic move necessary.

The seriousness of the turnabout in Korea was highlighted on December 16, 1950, when Truman declared a national emergency and called for an Army buildup to 3.5 million men. Truman also tapped Eisenhower, who had retired from military life, to become the Allied commander in Western Europe, where the threat of a Soviet armored assault continued to grow.

Marines at Chosin Reservoir, surrounded and outnumbered, fought their way south to the port of Hungnam while Chinese troops swarmed on the high ground above their route. "Retreat, hell. We're just attacking in another direction" was the quote affixed to this maneuver and became, in time, the title of a Hollywood film. (For more information, see the *Alpha Bravo Delta Guide to the U.S. Marines.*) But the Marines' commander, Maj. Gen. Oliver Smith, was devout and probably never uttered the word *hell.*

While the Americans scrambled to evacuate Hungnam and Hamhung under enormous pressure, farther to the west it became clear that the Chinese moved to recapture the North Korean capital of Pyongyang.

The Army was already at work developing the M41 Walker Bulldog Light tank when the Korean War began.

The brass selected the M41 because of an obvious need for an able reconnaissance vehicle that could stand up against another tank in combat, a fortuitous decision reached before June 25, 1950, when North Korea invaded its southern neighbor with a fleet of Soviet-built T-34 medium tanks.

The Army had begun testing various models of the new light tank, known variously as the T37, T37 Phase I, T41, and T41E1. The M41 production version was initially the Little Bulldog but was renamed for Gen. Walton H. Walker, killed in a vehicle mishap at Uijongbu, Korea, on December 23, 1950.

The Walker Bulldog was armed with a potent M32 76-mm gun and machine guns. The main gun's maximum range was 16,000 yards, although it was most accurate at around 2,000 yards. The Cadillac division of General Motors in Cleveland, Ohio, turned out M41 tanks powered by Lycoming and Continental air-cooled engines.

Typical of the enthusiasm that greeted the Walker Bulldog, an unnamed writer in the October 1951 issue of *Popular Mechanics* magazine called it "armor with a sprinter's speed, a deadly wallop, and a tough skin." The crew consisted of driver (who used a steering bar rather than levels), loader, gunner, and tank commander. Typically, a reconnaissance company had two Walker Bulldogs per platoon.

To go along with an assignment to the M41 tank, the Army issued a pocket-size common-sense booklet. It was a technical guide but also contained homilies such as, "If you gotta go, get in the first shot, and get back in time for dinner; you'll have to keep your Bulldog well fed, well groomed, and in good health." The booklet offered advice to any soldier who might be a little slow: "First thing to get acquainted with is the number painted on your tank." At least 2,000 Walker Bulldogs were built.

WALKER LOSS

On December 23, 1950, 8th Army commander Lt. Gen. Walker was killed in a vehicle collision at Uijongbu. A feeble attempt was made to make Walker a combat casualty and to attribute his death to a land mine. In fact, his fast-moving Jeep collided head-on with a South Korean truck. Just as untrue as the initial press release on Walker's loss is the legend, built up in the telling, that the Korean truck driver was executed on the spot. Lt. Gen. (later Gen.) Matthew B. Ridgway, another respected veteran, took command of the 8th Army.

The new year of 1951 began with half a million Chinese under Marshal Peng Teh-huai pouring southward. The Chinese lacked only air power, but modern warfare would no longer permit a belligerent to get by without controlling the sky. The air over the battlefield still belonged to the UN Allies, but the situation on the ground was grim.

The Chinese renewed their offensive on January 1, 1951. The situation was fraught with peril and chaos at Kimpo, the airfield serving Seoul, as equipment was dismantled, convoys were moved out, and aircraft began leaving. Ever afterward, it would be argued who flew the "last plane out" as the Chinese came swarming down. Kimpo came under increasing small-arms fire and was almost completely surrounded by Chinese, who, fortunately, had no heavy artillery with them. A British tank detachment and Turkish army brigade were defending the base.

Kimpo air base had to be deactivated in a hurry when it became clear that the Chinese really were coming through the wire. Fuel trucks and equipment transporters departed by road for the port of Inchon. "It was cold," remembered one soldier who helped to evacuate Kimpo. "At times it was 20 below zero Fahrenheit. F-80s had to be started on 140-octane aviation gas, not jet fuel, because jet fuel couldn't ignite in those frigid conditions."

In time, Ridgway decided to counterattack in central Korea. On March 7, 1950, the 25th Division crossed the Han River with massive air support. Unexpectedly, the communist forces abandoned Seoul on the night of March 14. Marshal Peng's Chinese army had held the capital only slightly more than two months. The steamroller Chinese assault, so shocking to American public opinion when it began, was running out of steam.

Ridgway was determined to halt the Chinese advance. He launched Operation Killer, a clever, highly mobile counterpunch aimed not at capturing turf, but at inflicting casualties. It was said throughout the Korean War that American soldiers were not natural killers. In the citizen army of the period, many were draftees, and most were reluctant to pull the trigger. A study showed that 27 percent balked, deliberately passing up a chance to aim and shoot their M1 Garand rifles when an enemy soldier presented a target. When the operation was launched, crusty top sergeants gave pep talks to the troops. "You are soldiers," one of them told members of an infantry squad. "Your job is to point that goddamned thing into the other guy's face and shoot him deader than a doornail. He won't hesitate to do the same to you."

Others chafed at the "Killer" name, so Ridgway's campaign meant to inflict casualties was renamed Operation Ripper. This, too, lacked the right tone. Soon afterward, it became Operation Courageous. By whatever name, Ridgeway's aggressive action led to the Allies seizing high ground north of the Han River on either side of Seoul and led to the Chinese pullback. It was said that Operation Killer caused the deaths of some 7,000 Chinese soldiers.

On March 23, 1951, the Allies mounted a major airdrop near Munsan-ni. C-46 Commandos and C-119 Flying Boxcars dropped the 187th Airborne Regimental Combat Team. In all, 173 aircraft dropped 3,487 troops and 483 tons of cargo. This was one of only two parachute assaults in the Korean conflict, and it was instrumental in deflating the Chinese.

As just about every soldier knew, the need for air transport was never met in a way that satisfied anybody in the Far East Air Force (FEAF). The Air Force had already employed the Douglas C-124 Globemaster to support construction of Thule air base in Greenland in the summer of 1951, but had not yet committed the C-124, with its much-needed cargo-hauling capacity, to Korean War supply missions. Lt. Gen. William H. Tunner, the

Air Force's leading expert on airlift, came to the following conclusions about the situation in Korea:

- "The ability of the 8th Army to move faster and farther [in the previous year's offensive] than any previous army in history was due in large part to air transport. Aerial resupply allowed the 8th to drive up the west coast of Korea without regard to lines of ground supply."
- "There exists a need for more than one type of combat support airlift aircraft. The C-47 was the only plane capable of routinely landing on short, rough, dirt landing strips to accommodate the wounded, but it was incapable of carrying or dropping the large cargo loads the C-119 could handle."
- "Worldwide airlift operations require a long-range, heavy-lift aircraft."

It was an almost psychic look at the future.

The Cold War was a time of new weapons and tactics, but not all of them worked. One that didn't was a vehicle to enable an infantryman to fly into battle like a comic book superhero.

Searching for a new era of aerial mobility, the Army turned to Bell Aircraft for a "flying belt," which developed into a "jet backpack." Tests were inconclusive. The jet backpack appeared in a James Bond movie, but never on a battlefield.

The Army also turned to De Lackner Aircraft for an individual helicopter, the HZ-1 Heli-Vector, on which an infantryman stood above a pair of 15-foot contrarotating rotor blades. Mounting this machine, or the similar VZ-1 Pawnee built by Hiller, the infantryman was out in the elements, helmeted and carrying a backpack, rifle, and binoculars. Though the craft flew successfully, the psychological hang-up of standing in the open above a pair of thrashing rotor blades was something no buck private was going to endure.

More conventional in approach, the American Helicopter XH-26 was an enclosed helicopter with a single seat. The Army tested five XH-26s between 1952 and 1954, but proceeded no further. A similar fate befell the Chrysler XV-6 and the Piasecki VZ-8 Sky Car, two ducted-lift aircraft that were meant to be flying Jeeps. By the end of the 1950s, the effort to provide the infantryman with personal air transportation was abandoned in favor of the traditional helicopter.

MACARTHUR DOWN

China's intervention in Korea was to prove the undoing of Douglas MacArthur, who months ago had said the boys would be home for Christmas. Early in 1951, MacArthur instructed his staff to draw up plans to regain the edge against the Chinese by dropping atomic bombs in Manchuria immediately north of the Yalu, cauterizing a narrow band of terrain along the China-Korea border that included, among other locations, the MiG-15 base at Antung. MacArthur also wanted to open a second front by unleashing Chiang Kai-shek's Chinese Nationalist troops on Formosa.

Already assured of his place in history, MacArthur wanted more. The idea of a monolithic threat was vivid in his mind, and he felt he'd been given a unique opportunity to roll back communism. MacArthur wanted to defeat his enemy and achieve quick victory. Just as he had ignored the possibility that China would intervene in the war, he now seemed impervious to the certainty that the Soviet Union would step in the instant the first mushroom cloud went up.

In an era when Washington assigned a higher priority to the Cold War than to the Korean War, using atomic bombs might establish a dangerous precedent, but *that* problem was not, so to speak, on MacArthur's turf.

ARMY HELICOPTERS

In the little-noticed world of U.S. Army aviation, in January 1951, the Army had fielded a number of Bell H-13 and Hiller H-23 light helicopters in Korea, each with a two-man crew capable of carrying one or two litters holding wounded soldiers. The Army organized helicopter ambulance detachments, with the purpose of taking over the battlefield evacuation tasks performed by the Air Force's hard-pushed H-5s. Still, during fighting at Chipyong-ni early in 1951, 6 H-6s delivered medical supplies to encircled American troops and evacuated 52 wounded. Having been denied fixed-wing aircraft by the reorganization that made the Air Force independent, the Army now wanted to employ bigger and more capable helicopters than the H-13 and H-23. But two more years would pass before the Army would have any of the larger craft known to the Air Force as the H-19 and to the Marines as the HRS-1, even though the other two service branches were already introducing this type.

The biggest event of a busy April 1951 was the downfall of MacArthur. The supreme commander was increasingly displeased with the reins placed on him by the Truman administration. He felt shackled. He seemed unaware that risk might accrue to the United States in any wider war. MacArthur made public utterances that were increasingly insubordinate, though even his superiors were too skittish to use the word "insubordination."

On April 5, 1951, minority leader Joe Martin rose in the House of Representatives to let loose a stinging attack on the Truman administration. Martin read a letter MacArthur had written a fortnight earlier insisting that there was "no substitute for victory." If MacArthur remembered the bedrock principle of the American system—military officers taking orders from elected civilians—he showed no sign of it. Leaders in Washington, among them Defense Secretary George C. Marshall, felt MacArthur had gone too far. Still, they feared he had too much support to be challenged.

According to some, a fault of Truman's was a tendency to think he knew more about military affairs than his uniformed advisors, even less controversial men like Marshall and Bradley. Where Truman stood out in comparison with MacArthur, however, was in his no-nonsense view of the American system. Though he proceeded with caution, Truman made the decision on April 6 to sack the general. Secretary of the Army Frank Pace, who had a Far East trip scheduled anyway, drew the hapless (and unwitting) task of bringing the news to MacArthur.

Pace arrived in Tokyo on April 9, not yet knowing the primary purpose of his visit. Pace had lunch with MacArthur and went on to Korea. The plan was for Pace to receive an encrypted message while in Korea and to deliver it to MacArthur in Tokyo at 10:00 A.M. on April 12, 1951. But in Washington, press leaks put real-life events well ahead of the plan. With the biggest story of the year about to come out, it became necessary for MacArthur to be informed not through a visit, but by message. Before Pace could receive word and return to Tokyo, on April 10 in Washington (April 11 in Tokyo), Bradley dispatched a message to MacArthur:

> I have been directed to relay the following message to you from President Truman:

> "I deeply regret that it becomes my duty as President and Commander in Chief of the United States military forces to replace you as Supreme Commander, Allied Powers; Commander in Chief, United Nations Command; Commander in Chief, Far East; and Commanding General, U.S. Army, Far East. You will turn over your commands effective at once to Lieutenant General Matthew B. Ridgway …."

In a separate message, Truman expressed "regret … that General of the Army Douglas MacArthur is unable to give his wholehearted support to the policies of the United States government …."

A few conservatives may have expected MacArthur to return to American soil in triumph and perhaps defeat Truman in the coming 1952 election. MacArthur received a hero's welcome in America and told a joint session of Congress, and the nation, "Old soldiers never die; they just fade away." True to his words, MacArthur enjoyed only short-lived public support.

Ridgway (who quickly received a fourth star) had been 8th Army commander since Walker's death the previous year. His job went to Lt. Gen. James A. Van Fleet, who took on the new assignment by telling the press, "The enemy is closer and in greater numbers than ever before. We can expect the attack any minute." In a week of heavy fighting in late April, Van Fleet's 8th Army gave away only tiny fragments of terrain before containing Chinese ground forces and halting a major assault.

CEASE-FIRE TALKS

An unpopular face on the growing number of American TV sets belonged to Jacob Malik, the Soviet delegate to the UN. Malik's absence from a Security Council session, and his resulting inability to cast a veto, had permitted the United Nations to intervene in the first place. On June 23, 1951, Malik stood in the UN and proposed cease-fire discussions. It's a fair guess that in Moscow, Stalin had concluded the war would progress no farther unless the Soviet Union committed its own forces.

Far from eager about doing anything to the enemy but killing him, Ridgway announced on June 30, 1951, that the UN side was willing to discuss an armistice. At the time, Ridgway's UN ground force had risen to

554,577, including 235,250 Americans, 273,266 South Koreans, and 28,061 from other nations. This was only slightly smaller than the 600,000-man force of Chinese and North Korean troops commanded by Marshal Peng.

Ridgway was acting on orders from Washington. He believed in his heart that the enemy's advantages had all been cancelled out and that there was no need to concede anything. The Republic of Korea's President Syngman Rhee was strongly opposed to any truce negotiations and was to remain so.

As the Korean War entered its second year, lines were joined on the ground. The battle line stabilized slightly north of the thirty-eighth parallel in July 1951 and remained there until the end of the war.

On July 10, 1951, the first armistice talks were held. Adm. C. Turner Joy headed the UN delegation. There were two other parties, the Chinese Peoples Volunteers and the Korean Peoples Army (KPA), the latter represented by North Korea's Marshal Nam-il, who was treated as something of a comic figure in the West with his swagger stick and blossoming cavalry trousers. The Americans had not wanted the armistice negotiations to be a three-way deal, feeling that the communist side should have one delegation, not two. The Chinese wanted to participate but retain a low profile.

The first meeting was a cosmetic exercise, with Joy and Nam-il seeking to upstage each other. The talks began at Kaesong. They were to continue for more than two years. The Allies went into the talks intending to restore the demarcation at the thirty-eighth parallel (although Rhee did not want any North Korean regime to survive). Eventually, the talks were moved to Panmunjom and focused on the return of prisoners. It must be noted that the participants in the truce talks were the armies facing each other in the field—the UN, the KPA, and the Chinese Peoples Volunteers. Not only was South Korea not represented, but no nation was.

1952–1953

The Korean War's third calendar year began far less dramatically than the second, which had seen the United Nations Allies falling back on all fronts. Now the battle line was stable. Now the terms and conditions for this first "limited war" were solidly established.

On April 17, 1952, President Truman signed Executive Order 10345, which extended military enlistments involuntarily for nine months. It was an extraordinary move for a society that depended upon a "citizen army." It reflected manpower problems that continued to plague all five American service branches. Although Truman has been regarded, before and since, as one of the most courageous of chief executives, the White House was reporting a real drop in the president's support in the American hinterlands. As the year unfolded, it was not to be the incumbent Truman but an Illinois democrat, Gov. Adlai Stevenson, who sought voter approval for the nation's top job.

Three days after Truman's unpopular announcement, on April 20, 1952, the UN Command announced that only 70,000 of 134,000 Chinese and North Korean prisoners of war (POWs) wanted to return home. The question of what to do about POWs was rapidly becoming the biggest hang-up in the Panmunjom truce negotiations, which lurched ahead in on-again, off-again fashion. The Allies wanted to get all of their prisoners back, but also wanted to offer asylum to enemy POWs who genuinely did not want repatriation. In the end, 30-odd American "turncoats" chose not to return, but the handling of communist POWs in the south had larger dimensions and presented no ready solution.

It didn't help matters that communist POWs being held on the South Korean island of Koje-do—those who remained loyal—rioted and managed to make the camp commandant, Army Brig. Gen. Francis T. Dodd, a prisoner in his own prison camp. Dodd's humiliation led to concessions on treatment for the communist POWs and further confused discussions at Panmunjom about how to resolve the POW issue if a cease-fire were achieved.

In May 1952, Gen. Mark Clark replaced Ridgway as commander in chief of UN forces and commander of U.S. forces in Korea. Clark was a serious, no-nonsense soldier who had commanded the 5th Army in Italy during World War II. He remained in charge through the end of the Korean fighting.

In the 1950s, the Army developed the heaviest road-portable field gun ever built. The Atomic Cannon equipped a battalion in Western Europe at the height of the Cold War.

The T131 Atomic Cannon fired a 280-mm shell. In 1952, the Army began testing nuclear artillery projectiles at Fort Sill, Oklahoma. Said one officer, "The next time hordes of enemy troops come swarming in our direction, as the Chinese did in Korea, we'll have a surprise for them."

Nuclear weapons were being tested in the atmosphere. On May 25, 1953, the Atomic Cannon fired a live atomic round at Frenchman Flat, Nevada. Known as the "Gable Shot' in a test series called Upshot-Knothole, the firing sent a Mark 9 nuclear round to a distance of 7 miles, where it detonated 524 feet above the desert, releasing 15 kilotons of force, or about the power of the bomb dropped on Hiroshima in 1945.

The Army assigned most of its 20 Atomic Cannons to its sole battalion, the 216th Field Artillery Battalion, at Grafenwoehr, West Germany, between 1957 and 1963.

The lighter Mark 19 shell, which had a range of 18.6 miles, replaced the Mark 9. Troops were constantly told they would be in no danger from their own atomic explosion. They would wear protective goggles, stare right in the direction of oncoming Soviet tanks, and fire away.

Ultimately, the heavy Atomic Cannon was replaced in the Army's inventory, not because of sudden insights about the danger of nuclear weapons on the battlefield, but because smaller, cheaper weapons became available to do the same job. In 1956, the Army developed its first Mark 33 nuclear rounds, which could be accommodated by existing, more mobile 8-inch howitzers. The Atomic Cannon was no longer needed.

ARMY AIR

U.S. Army aviation was just getting on its feet during the conflict in Korea. In early days, Army helicopter companies came under the control of the Ordnance Corps and later of Transportation Truck Companies. There were only four helicopter companies in the entire Army, not including the small Medical Evacuation detachment assigned to MASH (Mobile Army Surgical Hospital) units. Two were in the United States and two more, the 6th and the 13th, were in Korea.

The Army began to fly its first practical transport helicopter in the Sikorsky H-19C with the arrival in Korea in January 1953 of the 6th Transportation Company. The 6th had been formed at Fort Sill, Oklahoma, originally with just a handful of Bell H-13s and Boeing L-15s. It was moved to Fort Bragg, North Carolina, for early H-19 flying and then went to Chunchon, Korea, where it was mated with a new batch of 21 factory-fresh H-19Cs.

The warrant officers who flew Army helicopters in those days were seldom young, seldom new, and mostly World War II veterans. Many had been pilots as sergeants during the "big" war and, had they remained in service after the war, probably would have become Air Force commissioned officers. One of them had flown P-38 Lightnings.

First Lt. Harry Black went to Uijongbu, a few miles north of Seoul, with the second Army H-19 outfit, the 13th Transportation Company. Black's fellow soldiers were making effective use of the H-19C and were soon tasked to support armistice negotiations at Panmunjom, flying helicopters with yellow bands encircling their fuselages.

On January 20, 1953, Gen. of the Army Dwight D. Eisenhower took office as the thirty-fourth president. With a shift of administration and party, many changes in Washington affected the fighting in Korea. Eisenhower gained the White House partly on a pledge to go to Korea, and he did so before his inauguration.

Charles Wilson became secretary of defense, while the new executive continued the practice of turning for military advice to the Joint Chiefs' chairman, Gen. of the Army Omar N. Bradley. John Foster Dulles replaced Acheson as secretary of state and began a crusade against communism that occupied him more than the war in Korea.

On April 11, 1953, truce negotiators at Panmunjom followed through on Mark Clark's proposal for the two sides to exchange seriously ill and wounded prisoners of war. Operation Little Switch began two weeks later; 149 American, 64 other UN, and 471 South Korean prisoners were freed. In exchange, 6,679 communist prisoners were let go. U.S. Army and Marine Corps helicopters played an important role in transportation.

Despite evidence that bomb damage assessments were inflated, it was an American prisoner of war, ironically enough, who was later able to confirm that the aerial campaign over North Korea was taking a heavy toll and that the bleak conditions in the aftermath of heavy bombing were a factor at the truce table. As Dr. Robert F. Futrell recalls …

> What North Korea looked like after [sustained] air attacks was well described by Maj. Gen. William F. Dean, whose communist captors moved him about to various places of imprisonment in the spring of 1953.

> "The town of Huichon amazed me," wrote Maj. Gen. Dean. "The city I'd seen before—two-storied buildings, a prominent main street—wasn't there anymore. I think no important bridge between Pyongyang and Kanggye had been missed, and most of the towns were just rubble or snowy open spaces where buildings had been.
>
> "The little towns, once full of people, were unoccupied shells. The villagers lived in entirely new temporary villages, hidden in canyons or in such positions that only a major bombing effort could reach them."
>
> Dean was also impressed with communist countermeasures to air attack. Duplicate bypass bridges had been built, and bridge spans were stored, ready to be slipped into place when needed. Sacks and boxes of military supplies were stored in the remnants of villages. Maj. Gen. Dean thought that the enemy's countermeasures were improving faster than the United Nations command's means of destruction, but he failed to recognize that the Reds could have no really effective countermeasures to positive aerial destruction, which was making their cause both hopeless and extremely costly. Each day the war continued, the Reds lost more and more economic wealth.

It should not be understood that Dean was being taken on a holiday tour. American and Allied POWs were brutally treated by their captors. Most were inadequately fed and denied medical care and shelter from Korea's harsh elements. Some were physically tortured. Others were subjected to the sustained mental assault that came to be known as brainwashing. Maj. Gen. Dean, as the highest-ranking American in captivity, was treated worse than most. While truce talks over the fate of POWs began to show some movement, the communist side continued to refuse Red Cross visits, mail, and other amenities.

While "Little Switch" was being worked out but before the POW exchange actually took place, Lt. Gen. Otto Weyland argued that FEAF must "lean over backward" and "accept temporary loss of effectiveness" in order to ensure the safety of the sick and wounded POWs who were being transferred southward. In order to continue air pressure attacks, Weyland asked for authority to mount a major B-29 Superfortress attack against a complex of buildings, barracks, and warehouses at Yangsi, 12 miles (19 km) southeast of Sinuiju on the night of April 15, 1953 (which, although the

Americans almost certainly did not know, was Kim Il-song's birthday). General Clark approved this attack against a "sensitive" target, but the Pentagon pointed out that the Yangsi complex was too close to the route to be followed by one of the POW convoys. To give the enemy no excuse to renege on the prisoner exchange—which, in due course, went off as described—Clark asked Weyland to defer the B-29 attack.

Armistice negotiations at Panmunjom were doing better—if not exactly going well—after a troubled history of false starts and frequent interruptions. By early April, UN officers believed there was a genuine possibility not just of progress on prisoners who weren't wounded, but of bringing about a cease-fire soon. The good news of an impending settlement was also bad news, however: It invited the Chinese to attack. On the map, battle lines had been unchanged for two years, but there was now a strong incentive to seize more ground and hold it. Both sides expected any cease-fire to draw a line where opposing armies faced each other. If the Chinese could gain more ground, they'd keep it when the shooting stopped.

LITTLE SWITCH

Even as the first wounded prisoners were readied for release, the Communists showed that they were almost as intractable as ever. When the actual "Little Switch" exchange went down on April 20, 1953, the Communist side was reluctant to disclose the locations of its prisoner convoys. Moreover, Communist returnees seized every opportunity to create nuisances and express defiance. When truce talks resumed on April 26, the Communist side demanded to be given unlimited access to prisoners who were unwilling to be repatriated. What to do about "turncoats"—those who did not want to come home—was now the biggest impediment to ending the fighting.

When the cease-fire was signed at 10:00 A.M. on July 27, 1953, by generals Harrison and Nam Il, it was to become effective 12 hours later, at 10:00 P.M. As the day progressed, at Munsan-ni, flanked by generals Taylor, Weyland, and Anderson and by admirals Robert P. Briscoe and Joseph J. Clark, Gen. Mark Clark signed the truce as chief representative of the United Nations Command. Kim Il-song and Peng Te-huai, who had refused to meet with Clark unless representatives of the Republic of Korea were barred, signed at their own headquarters.

It should be noted that of the three principal signatories—Clark, Peng, and Kim—only the North Korean, Kim Il-song, was *both* the commander of an army in the field (the capacity in which he signed) and a chief of state. Mark Clark and Peng Te-huai, of course, commanded armies in the field but did not head any government. As for the Republic of Korea, with its leader, Syngman Rhee, still opposed to a settlement, it had no signer of the armistice.

James A. Van Fleet lived to the age of 100, but his most important memory—a far from happy one—was commanding U.S. troops in Korea.

To the editors of the 1915 *Howitzer,* the West Point yearbook, Van Fleet was "a brusque, outspoken individual and not much of a mixer ... [whose] reticent attitude kept some of us from knowing him as well as we should ...."

He served with Gen. John Pershing in the Army's expedition against Pancho Villa. He commanded a machine gun battalion during World War I. In 1944, Van Fleet's 8th Infantry Regiment spearheaded the D-Day landing at Normandy's Utah Beach. He commanded the 90th Infantry Division, the "Tough 'Ombres," in the Battle of the Bulge.

On April 11, 1951, Van Fleet became commander of the 8th Army. He staved off the final attempt by Chinese forces to stay on the offensive.

President Harry S. Truman pronounced Van Fleet "the greatest general we ever had." His son, James A. Van Fleet Jr., was lost on a night mission in a B-26 bomber, and was later presumed dead by the U.S. government.

Although the Allied effort in Korea ultimately achieved its purpose, Van Fleet was embittered by limitations on his ability to wage an aggressive fight. He decided to retire and was replaced in Korea in February 1953 by Gen. Maxwell D. Taylor. On his return to the United States, Van Fleet said publicly that the U.S. should have achieved total victory in Korea, but "we could not have done so with our hands tied." He left active duty on April 30, 1953, at four-star rank.

When Van Fleet died in 1992, he was the only known grandson of a veteran of the American Revolutionary War.

KOREA RESULTS

Thus, the war in Korea ended, replaced by an armistice agreement signed by the opposing armies but never by any government. The POW issue was finally resolved.

Many statistics emerged from the Korean conflict, some more valuable than others. To Americans, the most important number is 54,246, the total number who lost their lives in the 1950–1953 fighting. This is almost as high as the 57,690 figure for the Vietnam War, which lasted five times as long. The Korean total includes 33,629 battle deaths (compared with 292,131 in World War II and 47,244 in Vietnam). It also includes 20,617 deaths from other causes (compared with 115,185 in World War II and 10,446 in Vietnam). Americans listed as wounded in action totaled 103,284. There has been little recognition of those who paid the highest price. A memorial for Korean War veterans was opened in Washington, D.C., only in the mid-1990s.

The Army, which began the Korean conflict as a hollow force of 591,487 soldiers in just 10 divisions (and suffered terribly for being unprepared), reached a peak strength of 2,834,000. There was some draw-down after the armistice, but the shape of the Army for the Cold War era was now established.

Following the tradition of moving from a wartime command to the Army's top officer position, Ridgway became the Army's nineteenth chief of staff on August 16, 1953, a position he held for just under two years. While serving as top soldier, Ridgway helped dissuade President Eisenhower from committing U.S. troops to Indochina.

Ultimately, Ridgway encountered huge frustrations in a sea of interservice rivalry and eventually resigned in disgust. Another well-known World War II airborne commander, Gen. Maxwell D. Taylor, succeeded him as chief of staff on June 30, 1955.

> In 1963–1964, two Army officers spent a year in captivity in North Korea after they flew an OH-23 Raven helicopter into North Korea and were shot down. Capts. Ben W. Stutts and Charleton Voltz were piloting an OH-23 on May 17, 1963.
>
> Their two-seat, bubble-nosed observation helicopter, which carried no photographic or surveillance equipment, was on a routine mission checking boundary markers on the southern side of the demarcation line. A North Korean gun battery fired on the helicopter and brought it down. American soldiers at an observation post observed both pilots being seized by North Korean troops. The North Koreans detained Stutts and Voltz in sparse facilities, interrogated them frequently, and refused to allow them outside contact.

The sighting of the pair was for months the only evidence on the U.S. side that they were still alive. Maj. Gen. George H. Cloud, the senior U.S. official in the Military Armistice Commission, haggled for months with his North Korean counterpart, demanding their release.

Maj. Gen. Robert Seedlock, Cloud's replacement, made an attempt to hand over letters from the men's wives, only to have them handed back by the North Korean delegate.

On March 5, 1964, Air Force Maj. Gen. Cecil Combs, Seedlock's replacement, issued an apology that included an "admission" of "espionage activities" by the OH-23 pilots. The North Koreans released Stutts and Voltz at Panmunjom on May 16 after the pair had been imprisoned for exactly one year.

The North Koreans brought Stutts and Voltz to Panmunjom in prison attire. The captains met with Army Lt. Gen. Thomas W. Dunn, acting commander in chief of the UN Command, and made telephone calls to their wives. Stutts later said that the two pilots were "very sorry" for "all of the trouble [they had] caused."

Combs, meanwhile, issued a statement saying that he had signed a "receipt" for the two pilots because it was the only way to get them released. He said that the U.S. side had not been engaged in espionage.

POST-KOREA

In 1954, the Army faced a new enemy, Sen. Joseph McCarthy (1909–1957), who claimed communists had infiltrated the Pentagon and other Washington agencies. McCarthy identified individual soldiers as communists but showed no evidence. Ultimately, a televised hearing with Army Secretary Joseph Welch (1890–1960) ended McCarthy's ascendancy when Welch pleaded, "Have you no decency, sir? At long last, have you no sense of decency?"

The expected nuclear war with the Soviet Union was on everyone's minds in the 1950s, but so, too, was the civil rights movement. In September 1957, the grim prospect arose that Army National Guard soldiers and 101st Airborne Division paratroopers might fight on opposite sides, not against Soviet tanks rolling into Germany, but on the streets of Little Rock, Arkansas.

Three years earlier, the Supreme Court had ruled that racial segregation in public schools was unconstitutional. Arkansas was moderate by the standards of the era and moved quickly to implement the ruling, which would assign black students to previously all-white schools. But Gov. Orval Faubus was an arch-segregationist. He proclaimed, "Negroes will attend [Little Rock's] Central High School over my dead body."

Faubus called out the state's National Guard to surround the school and prevent black students from entering. He claimed that he was protecting citizens from violence. On September 2, 1957, Guardsmen blocked Negro students at the school entrance, a scene that appeared on newspaper front pages around the nation.

President Eisenhower was prepared to use the Army to enforce the law. Ike chose the elite 101st Airborne Division—known for its heroic actions in World War II. Had events unfolded differently, most soldiers, in both the Guard and the 101st, would have had no strong opinion about the issue that seemed to be leading them toward a collision.

On September 20, 1957, a federal judge headed off any collision by granting an injunction against Faubus's using Guard troops to prevent integration.

Nevertheless, the administration federalized Arkansas National Guardsmen—taking the soldiers out of Faubus's hands. Secretary of the Army Wilber M. Brucker sent a telegram to Faubus, explaining that Eisenhower "[desired] the personnel of the Arkansas National Guard organizations to proceed forthwith" to points of assembly. The Eisenhower Administration rushed 1,000 members of the 101st into Little Rock to preserve order. Eisenhower said the moves were necessary to "avoid anarchy."

Guardsmen and paratroopers, now on the same side, were placed under Maj. Gen. Edwin Walker, a combat veteran of World War II and Korea. Jack Raymond of *The New York Times* reported, "Walker's mission is to make sure that no one frustrates Federal Court orders that nine Negro pupils be admitted to Central High School."

On September 25, 1957, an Army station wagon carried 9 black students to the front entrance of the school while an Army helicopter circled overhead and 350 armed paratroopers stood at parade rest around the building. There was verbal and physical abuse as "The Little Rock Nine" nervously entered Central High School. Halls were quiet within the school as the students proceeded to prearranged classes. Schoolwork proceeded normally. Two dozen soldiers without bayonets patrolled the halls.

The world watched Little Rock Central High School throughout the school year, which ended on May 27, 1958, with commencement ceremonies for 601 seniors, including Ernest Green, the school's first black graduate.

TECHNICAL WAR

The Cold War took a dramatic turn on October 4, 1957, when the Soviet Union launched the volleyball-size unmanned satellite called Sputnik into orbit. The metal sphere passed over Americans' heads every 90 minutes, traveling at 18,000 miles per hour. The U.S. space program was in disarray, partly because of the decision to put it in civilian hands. The Army was, in fact, close to matching the Soviet feat with a satellite mounted on a Jupiter rocket, but the psychological impact of Sputnik was incredible. Americans, accustomed to leading the world in science and technology, suddenly believed they were trailing.

CHAPTER 9

VIETNAM (1959–1975)

In the new era opened up by Sputnik, John F. Kennedy (1917–1963) used the "missile gap" and the space program in the campaign that enabled him to win narrowly against Richard M. Nixon (1913–1994) and to become, on January 20, 1961, the thirty-fifth U.S. president. Kennedy's first military foray—the doomed Bay of Pigs operation in Cuba in April 1961—was a disaster, but he quickly endeared himself to the Army by demonstrating his admiration for the Special Forces and putting his imprint on the decision already made to have them wear the green beret. Early in his administration, he authorized sending Special Forces advisors to a country few Americans knew about: Vietnam.

American troops were involved in Vietnam as far back as 1954, when some assisted the French when they suffered a defeat at Dien Bien Phu and withdrew. U.S. advisors began helping the South Vietnamese as early as 1959 when a few hundred Americans were on the scene. On July 8 of that year, guerrillas killed Maj. Dale Buis and Master Sgt. Chester Ovnard, usually considered the first Americans to lose their lives in the Vietnam War. By the end of 1961, more than 3,000 U.S. military personnel were in South Vietnam. On February 6, 1962, the Army stood up the Military Assistance Command Vietnam (MACV) in Saigon.

One of Kennedy's key advisors was Gen. Maxwell Taylor, who came out of retirement to serve as chairman of the Joint Chiefs from 1962 to 1964. Taylor later became the U.S. ambassador to Vietnam.

Kennedy was the key figure in the October 1962 Cuban Missile Crisis, when the Soviet Union was forced to withdraw operational missiles from the island nation 95 miles from U.S. soil. The Bay of Pigs was largely run by the Central Intelligence Agency and the Missile Crisis was handled by the Navy and Air Force, but, of course, some soldiers had roles in both.

Kennedy's regime was "Camelot" to some, but it was also brief. On November 22, 1963, an assassin shot and killed Kennedy on a visit to Dallas, Texas. Vice President Lyndon B. Johnson became the thirty-sixth president of the United States. Johnson was almost immediately presented with plans to enlarge the U.S. role in Southeast Asia.

The Army's U-1 Otter served in the Cold War and in Vietnam. For years the backbone of the fixed-wing aviation fleet, it was the heaviest single-engine utility aircraft in the world. It seemed equally at home in the frozen Arctic and the tropical climes of Vietnam.

The plane maker specialized in aircraft for bush flying. Some wondered if the plane could operate in Canada's harsh climate and sparsely populated hinterlands on just one engine. But the Otter achieved good reliability, as it turned out, with its 600-horsepower Pratt & Whitney R-1430 Wasp Major engine. Moreover, it hauled 14 passengers or a freight load of up to 2,240 pounds.

In 1953, the Army tested a prototype at Fort Bragg, North Carolina. The Army's version was briefly known as the C-137, but in Washington, a decision was made to create a "U" for utility category in order to shroud the real purpose of a spy plane then being developed in great secrecy. The Otter was renamed the U-1 and the spy plane became the U-2. The Army purchased 223 U-1A Otters and used them around the world.

The Army was pleased with the U-1A Otter, and in February 1962, it became one of the first Army planes deployed to Vietnam. Most performed utility and transport duties. A few were modified for electronic warfare duty and were redesignated RU-1A. In Vietnam, Otters were used for utility work, surveillance, and occasionally direct fire support. They soldiered on well after the time when other fixed-wing aircraft were being replaced by helicopters. The Army couldn't have asked for a better single-engine transport.

The last U-1A Otter remained in Army service until 1974. A small number stayed in Reserve and Army National Guard units for several more years.

ARMY CHANGES

The Army went through a succession of chiefs of staff who favored a commitment to Vietnam. Gen. Lyman H. Lemnitzer (1899–1988) served as the twenty-first chief of staff from July 1959 to September 1960, and then moved up to become chairman of the Joint Chiefs of Staff from 1960 to 1962. Lemnitzer graduated from West Point in 1920 and was a lieutenant for 15 years before serving in two wars and rising in the ranks. Even after being chairman, Lemnitzer would serve as Allied commander in Europe until 1969. He wore four stars for almost as long as he wore lieutenant's bars. Throughout his time in the leadership of the Army, Lemnitzer believed the U.S. could win in Vietnam and prevail in the Cold War.

When Lemnitzer was promoted to the top military job, Gen. George Decker (1902–1980) became Army chief of staff. Decker expanded the Army to 16 divisions, oversaw crises in Berlin, and increased special warfare forces. He, too, believed that special forces could achieve U.S. policy goals in Vietnam.

In that faraway country, still little-noticed by most Americans, the number of advisors grew modestly during the Kennedy administration when the Army's Special Forces, or Green Berets, were viewed as the antidote to what the other side called a war of national liberation. At the start of 1964, nearly 15,000 U.S. "advisors" were in South Vietnam, many of them participating in combat while ostensibly serving only to give advice.

In January 1964, Lt. Gen. (later Gen.) William Westmoreland replaced Gen. Paul Harkins as MACV commander. American soldiers were now becoming a familiar sight in Saigon's streets, and the sound of helicopters overhead was growing ubiquitous. Also in 1964, Harold K. Johnson became the twenty-third Army chief of staff, a job he would hold for four years. Johnson was a pivotal figure in increasing the role of U.S. advisors in Southeast Asia and in arguing for greater use of conventional military forces.

Army advisors were, of course, very much in the thick of the fight. One symbol of their courage was Capt. Roger H. C. Donlon, who commanded Special Forces Detachment A-726 at Camp Nam Dong, in the Vietnamese mountains near the Laotian border. On July 6, 1964, while Americans still largely had not yet noticed Vietnam, Donlon's camp—manned by

12 Americans, 60 Nungs, and 100 loyal Vietnamese—came under assault from a reinforced Viet Cong battalion.

"I remember the burning buildings, the intensity of a protracted night battle," Donlon said later of the five-hour action. "I remember the dead and wounded … mortars, grenades, withering gunfire …."

Donlon emphasized the contribution of those who fought with him—including Master Sgt. Gabriel Alamo, who died in a mortar pit firing a 57-mm recoilless rifle, and Sgt. John Houston, who was cut down returning Viet Cong fire. The defense of Nam Dong was a point-blank battle. Donlon directed the defense in the midst of a barrage of Viet Cong mortar shells, falling grenades, and heavy gunfire.

When the fight began, he marshaled his troops and ordered the removal of needed ammunition from a burning building. Donlon then ran through a hail of small-arms fire and exploding grenades toward the camp's main gate, where Viet Cong troops were attempting to break through. Donlon used his AR-15 rifle—forerunner of the M16—to kill several at point-blank range.

The counterfire resulted in Donlon being severely wounded in the stomach. This did not prevent him from joining some of the defenders—also wounded—in a 60-mm mortar pit. With rifle fire, he covered the men's withdrawal to a safer point 30 yards away. He was dragging a wounded soldier out of the besieged gun pit when an enemy mortar shell exploded and inflicted a new wound in his left shoulder. Still, Donlon got his men and their mortar to the new location where they could use the mortar to return fire.

He then ran under heavy fire to a new position and retrieved a 57-mm recoilless rifle. He returned to the abandoned gun pit and evacuated ammunition for the two weapons. An enemy hand grenade went off near him and inflicted a third wound to his leg.

Donlon continued to ignore his own wounds and scrambled to a different 60-mm mortar position to rally troops; then he returned to the original mortar and helped wounded men continue to use it to fight back. He was continuing to direct the ongoing battle when an exploding enemy mortar shell inflicted further wounds to his face and body.

Daylight brought reinforcements. An Army CV-2 Caribou aircraft arrived to drop supplies. The enemy troops retreated into the jungle, leaving behind 62 dead and many weapons and grenades. At Nam Dong, 55 defenders lost their lives, among them Warrant Officer Kevin Conway, the first Australian soldier to die in Vietnam.

Because the Viet Cong had failed to dislodge friendlies from Nam Dong, it was a clear victory in a war that was still being defined.

On December 5, 1964, Donlon was summoned to the White House, where President Lyndon Johnson awarded him the first Medal of Honor given to an American in Vietnam, and the three thousand, one hundred seventy-ninth since the nation's highest award had been established exactly a century earlier. Donlon's 27-year Army career included additional duty in Vietnam and a tour in Korea. He retired as a colonel.

Major Ed W. "Too Tall" Freeman had the Medal of Honor draped around his neck by President George W. Bush on July 16, 2001.

On November 14, 1965, Freeman was the pilot of a UH-1 Huey helicopter in the 229th Assault Helicopter Battalion, 1st Cavalry Division, in the Battle of Ia Drang Valley. Said the Army:

"The unit was almost out of ammunition after taking some of the heaviest casualties of the war, fighting off a relentless attack from a highly motivated, heavily armed enemy force.

"When the infantry commander closed the helicopter landing zone due to intense direct enemy fire, Captain Freeman risked his own life by flying his unarmed helicopter through a gauntlet of enemy fire time after time, delivering critically needed ammunition, water, and medical supplies to the besieged battalion.

"His flights had a direct impact on the battle's outcome by providing the engaged units with timely supplies of ammunition critical to their survival, without which they would almost surely have gone down, with much greater loss of life."

The Army account continued: "After medical evacuation helicopters refused to fly into the area due to intense enemy fire, Captain Freeman flew 14 separate rescue missions, providing life-saving evacuation of an estimated 30 seriously wounded soldiers—some of whom would not have survived had he not acted. All flights were made into a small emergency landing zone within 100 to 200 meters of the defensive perimeter where heavily committed units were perilously holding off the attacking elements."

Freeman later told Gayle Alvarez of the *Idaho Statesman* newspaper that he was afraid during the relentless helicopter missions. Alvarez wrote, "He remembers nervously eating franks and beans and chain-smoking Vantage cigarettes. 'God knows how many I smoked. Till I had a blister on my tongue.'"

Born in 1927 in Mississippi, Freeman decided at age 13 to become a soldier. He served in the Navy before joining the Army in 1948. During the Korean War, he won a battlefield promotion to first sergeant and later received a battlefield commission.

GULF OF TONKIN

The Gulf of Tonkin incident of August 1964 was an encounter between at least one U.S. warship and at least three North Vietnamese patrol boats. Because of what was described in public as an unprovoked attack on U.S. ships, President Lyndon B. Johnson was able to persuade Congress to pass the Gulf of Tonkin Resolution, a rubber stamp for wider and deeper U.S. involvement. At the end of 1964, U.S. troop strength in Vietnam reached almost 2,400.

On February 7, 1965, a Viet Cong attack on a U.S. base at Pleiku killed eight Americans and prompted Johnson to order prolonged air strikes over North Vietnam. A few weeks later, the air campaign over the north was named Operation Rolling Thunder.

On June 27, 1965, the Army's 173rd Airborne Brigade launched a major offensive northeast of Saigon. Some 50,000 soldiers and Marines fought in the action.

When the 1st Cavalry Division set up shop at Anh Khe, South Vietnam, a flat, highland base that troops dubbed "the Golf Course," the Army's most seasoned soldiers were at work. Led by Maj. Gen. (later Lt. Gen.) Harry W. O. Kinnard, who had been a junior 2nd lieutenant at Pearl Harbor, the 1st Cav had trained for more than two years to perfect airmobile tactics that enabled troops to go to war aboard helicopters, in much the way they had used horses in the past. In November 1965, the 1st Cav took on North Vietnamese regular troops in the Battle of Ia Drang Valley and fought them to a standstill.

United States Army, Robert F. Dorr

Bell UH-1 Huey helicopters prepare to move out.

The Army bought 9,440 UH-1 Huey helicopters between 1958 and 1980.

Making up for being late to field practical helicopters during the Korean War, the Army introduced new helicopters in the 1950s and developed methods for using them effectively. In the design of the Huey, the Army took full advantage of the small gas turbine engine.

Dr. Anselm Franz developed the first practical small gas turbine in 1953 as the Avco Lycoming T53. It weighed 3,000 pounds less than other engines then in use without sacrificing power. It was the perfect match for a new helicopter being developed by Bell Aircraft.

The Army called it the XH-40, and it went aloft for its first flight on October 22, 1956. Two years later, as the Army introduced a new system for naming its aircraft, this helicopter became the HU-1. In 1962, another name change made it the UH-1.

Once the Army began flying the Huey, it devoted a major effort to helicopter doctrine. In April 1962, the Howze Board, named for Lt. Gen. Hamilton Howze (1908–1990), was formed to study Army aviation requirements. The board's report, submitted in August 1962, led to the creation of the air assault division. Defense Secretary Robert McNamara authorized extensive testing of the air assault concept, and in 1963, the 11th Air Assault Division was formed to continue tests on a larger and more realistic scale.

The first fighting force to use large numbers of Hueys for major ground combat operations was the 1st Cavalry Division.

In Vietnam, some Hueys were "slicks," plain transport ships lacking external armament except for an M-60 machine gun mounted in the door of each side that shuttled troops from one place to another. Others were gunships, armed with guns and rockets to support men and machines arriving at a landing zone. Fewer in number, but never to be forgotten, were the "dustoffs"—the medical evacuation Hueys that gave many American soldiers their lives. More wounded men survived in Vietnam than in any previous war because of the quick response and flexibility of the Huey.

Army officers understood what had happened. A well-trained outfit had done a good job. But civilian leaders misunderstood and made a horrendous miscalculation. They figured that if one Army division could perform well against a seasoned foe, any Army division could do so. This reasoning overlooked the fact that the men of the First Cav had spent two years together, knew each other, and knew how to fight. Soon draftees who didn't know each other were arriving in droves, and soon afterward, the Army in Vietnam began to have problems with discipline, drinking, and drugs. Some may even have "fragged" their own officers, killing them on the battlefield with grenades or rifle bullets. These problems never reached more than a few units in Vietnam and were later exaggerated in film and legend, but the competence of the average American soldier in combat went down dramatically as the numbers increased.

GROWING WAR

On September 23, 1966, MACV announced what had been publicly known for several years—that the United States was using chemical defoliants, including Agent Orange, to destroy jungle canopy in Vietnam. The following month, President Johnson met with heads of six Asian nations in the Philippines but was able to persuade only South Korea to send a meaningful number of troops to support the U.S. effort.

By the end of 1966, U.S. troop strength in Vietnam was 385,000, or about 100,000 more than Defense Secretary Robert S. McNamara had promised a few months earlier. By 1967, the brass was giving names to military operations that neither press nor public could absorb, examples being Operation Cedar Falls in January and Junction City in February, when 25,000 troops battled Viet Cong and North Vietnamese regulars.

The Huey gunship was one thing, but when the Army decided to transform the big CH-47 Chinook cargo helicopter into a battlefield weapon, some soldiers scratched their heads.

In June 1965, the Army invested in four modified CH-47As. The first of these gun-toting, twin-rotor helicopters made its initial flight on November 6, 1965.

Designing the helicopters, engineers deleted all cargo-handling equipment, all soundproofing, and all but five troop seats, and then added 2,000 pounds of armor plating and weapons pylons on each side of the helicopter outboard of the front wheels. This was capped off with a nose gun installation.

The discotheque was a new ingredient in American life, so the helicopters were nicknamed "Guns A Go-Go." Each carried two 20-mm fixed forward-firing, pylon-mounted cannons, and two pylon-mounted XM-128 units, each carrying nineteen 2.75-inch rocket projectiles. Also aboard the armed Chinook was a single chin-mounted M5 40-mm automatic grenade launcher providing two minutes of fire at 500 rounds per minute. The pilot controlled the grenade launcher, which was able to cover an extensive area on either side of the helicopter's flight path. The weapons systems for the ACH-47A typically weighed 3,595 pounds, significantly degrading the Chinook's flying characteristics.

The 1st Air Cavalry Division took three of the four ACH-47A gunships to Vietnam in June 1966.

The Vietnam detachment of "Guns A Go-Go" was the 228th Aviation Battalion of the 1st Cav and was made up of spirited soldiers who felt they were bringing a new form of warfare to the battlefield. The unit flew numerous sorties providing direct support to American and Australian ground combat troops. The guns aboard the Chinook had considerable reach and power. They also made plenty of noise, adding to their psychological impact. One of the ACH-47As was destroyed and one was seriously damaged in combat.

Eventually, the development of the smaller, more nimble AH-1 Cobra made the Chinook gunship seem unnecessary. Commander Gen. William C. Westmoreland wanted up to 24 additional "Go-Gos." The Army, committed to the Cobra, was unwilling to develop the Chinook further.

At the start of 1968, the U.S. had completed much of the buildup that would bring troop strength in South Vietnam to over half a million soldiers. In January 1968, the Viet Cong and U.S. leaders were both increasingly optimistic about the course of the war. Intelligence estimates routinely understated the size of Viet Cong and North Vietnamese forces. At the very time protests were increasing on the home front, Americans were being told they were winning. Statements from Washington and the daily MACV press briefing in Saigon were soon dubbed the "Five O'clock Follies" by war detractors.

United States Army, Robert F. Dorr

From behind his Browning .30-caliber machine gun, Specialist Roland I. Williams watches for Viet Cong gunfire from the door of an H-21 helicopter while flying near Ap Trach, southwest of Saigon.

The Tet Offensive changed all that. Launched at the end of January 1968 and named for the lunar new year, this large attack by scattered units was orchestrated by North Vietnam's Gen. Vo Nguyen Giap.

Fighting took place inside cities, including at the American Embassy in Saigon, where Viet Cong fighters got inside the building and inflicted minor damage. U.S. and South Vietnamese troops won virtually all of the battles that followed, but the American news media reported Tet as a defeat and the American public understood it as one. For the Army, it was a vivid reminder that urban fighting, with its attendant risk for civilians and terrible perception from the media, should be avoided at all costs.

Master Sgt. Roy Benavidez (1935–1998) received the Medal of Honor from President Ronald Reagan at the White House in 1981. Soon afterward, the Navy christened the transport ship T-AKR 306, a Bob Hope–class LMSR vessel (Large, Medium-Speed Roll-On/Roll-Off ship), in honor of the Army sergeant.

Benavidez was born in 1935 and joined the Army at age 20. On May 2, 1968, serving with Detachment B56, 5th Special Forces Group (Airborne), 1st Special Forces, Benavidez was at a forward operating base monitoring by radio when a 12-man reconnaissance team in a dense jungle area west of Loc Ninh, Vietnam, came under assault from large numbers of North Vietnamese regular troops.

Helicopters attempted to extract the embattled Americans but were unable to land due to intense enemy small arms and antiaircraft fire. When these helicopters returned to off-load wounded crew members and to assess aircraft damage, Benavidez voluntarily boarded a returning aircraft to assist in another extraction attempt.

Benavidez returned to ground fighting, exposed himself to enemy fire, and was critically wounded. Still, he continued carrying wounded soldiers to helicopters. Benavidez continued to direct the rescue while gathering the survivors into a defensive perimeter. He distributed water and ammunition, cared for the wounded, safeguarded classified documents, and provided covering fire for the team. Benavidez, who was wounded more than 40 times during the action, is credited with saving the lives of 8 men.

Gen. William C. Westmoreland awarded the Distinguished Service Cross to Benavidez. His Medal of Honor award was approved subsequently. Benavidez was the author or co-author of at least three books about his life. In *The Three Wars of Roy Benavidez,* he wrote of the challenges of a Hispanic American growing up in DeWitt County, Cuero, Texas; of his religious faith; and of combat in Vietnam. He died in 1998.

On March 16, 1968, soldiers under 1st Lt. William Calley of Charlie Company, 1st Battalion, 20th Infantry, 11th Infantry Brigade of the 24th American Infantry Division massacred innocent women and children. Other U.S. soldiers tried to prevent the My Lai Massacre or helped to expose it later. The Army's final estimate was 347 civilians killed, none of them armed. Calley was prosecuted and served brief time in prison, viewed by some as a scapegoat for Army excesses and by others as a war criminal who got off too easily. This kind of misconduct by American soldiers in

Vietnam was not widespread, despite the attention given to it by the media and by Hollywood; most soldiers never attacked civilians.

On March 31, 1968, President Johnson announced a partial bombing halt, called for cease-fire negotiations, and surprised Americans by announcing that he would not campaign for re-election. The nation was in turmoil, with the civil rights movement, the antiwar movement, and the sexual revolution unfolding against a background of violence, including the killings of Martin Luther King (April 4) and Sen. Robert F. Kennedy (D.-New York, June 6). It was also the year of a presidential election race between Hubert Humphrey and Richard M. Nixon.

During 1968, Gen. Creighton Abrams replaced Westmoreland in Vietnam, and Westmoreland moved to the Pentagon to become the Army's twenty-fifth chief of staff.

On January 20, 1969, Richard M. Nixon became the thirty-seventh president of the United States. In August in a speech on Guam, he enunciated what became known as the Nixon Doctrine, billed as a plan to look to U.S. allies in Asia to supply the manpower for their own defense. It was, in fact, a plan to withdraw from Vietnam and to reduce the U.S. presence in Korea. By then, Nixon had announced that he was pulling out 25,000 of the 535,000 U.S. troops in Vietnam.

On July 1, 1969, Social Security numbers began to replace the previously assigned service numbers to identify all active-duty Army members, reservists, and retirees.

During the Tet Offensive on January 31, 1968, American soldiers in a UH-1 Huey helicopter were downed at a South Vietnamese compound in Hue. Once on the ground, they found themselves in a friendly enclave with South Vietnamese troops, but surrounded by attacking North Vietnamese. Pilots of several aircraft tried to help the embattled Huey crew but were warned by higher headquarters to stay clear of Hue.

Warrant Officer Frederick E. Ferguson was flying a logistical mission nearby and joined a flight of gunships near Hue. He briefed his crew, chose a flight path, and alerted his company commander via radio that he was going to attempt a rescue. He was advised, but not ordered, not to try.

The compound was under automatic weapons fire. Within the compound, two Americans suffered wounds. Mortar shells exploded around them. With three gunships helping, Ferguson lowered his helicopter, oblivious to the gunfire, to within inches of the railroad tracks heading into the compound. He saw enemy gunners on rooftops, in doorways, and in the streets.

Ferguson crossed the compound wall and used every ounce of power available to slow his helicopter for a landing in the only clear area within the fire-raked walls. His skids had scarcely touched the ground when the wounded were loaded aboard—now four Americans plus a South Vietnamese who had taken a 12.7-mm round near his left ear.

The Huey vaulted skyward just as three mortar rounds exploded where the helicopter had been seconds earlier. The blasts lifted the tail boom and spun the Huey to the left. Ferguson adjusted his escape plan and continued a left turn, departing now on the same bullet-strewn route he had used to approach.

Ferguson's Huey was hit again and again as he streaked for safety. An escorting gunship had its fuel tank shot away, and the pilot reported that he was going down.

Despite mortal damage (the Huey would never fly again), Ferguson successfully delivered his wounded passengers to a clinic at Phu Bai.

Ferguson was awarded the Medal of Honor. He later became the deputy director of the Arizona Department of Veterans' Services.

United States Army, Robert F. Dorr

Members of "B" Company, 1st Battalion, 12th Infantry, 1st Air Cavalry Division on patrol during "Operation Lincoln" being carried out in the Chu Pong Mountain Range near the Cambodian border.

FIGHTING IN 1969

One of the heroes of Vietnam fighting in 1969 was Michael J. Novosel, an "old man" at 42 in a conflict in which the average soldier was about 20. Novosel had piloted B-29 Superfortress bombers over Japan in World War II, but when Vietnam came along, the Air Force said it had no place for him. Novosel became an Army warrant officer and helicopter pilot, and accumulated flying hours in the UH-1 Iroquois, the famous "Huey" helicopter. His son Mike followed; for a time, the father-and-son team, both named Mike Novosel, were flying Hueys in combat with the 283rd Medical Detachment (Helicopter Ambulance).

On October 2, 1969, already in combat for nearly eight hours that day, UH-1 pilot Novosel was directed to a pick-up on the Cambodian border. South Vietnamese troops were surrounded and outgunned in a field of high elephant grass.

A circling spotter plane told Novosel and his crew that the situation was hopeless. Automatic weapons fire swirled around his Huey. Novosel went into this firestorm searching for a lone friendly soldier hidden in the elephant grass. He made three attempts to locate and rescue the man, taking hits each time.

Crewmembers Specialists Four Herbert Heinold and Joe Horvath rescued the soldier. Then more South Vietnamese materialized amid the swaying grass. Novosel had to climb above the enemy's gunfire several times and then descend again to search and pluck friendlies to safety. Over agonizing minutes, he filled his Huey with 10 South Vietnamese soldiers who had no other way out of their trap.

Novosel took these troops to a nearby Special Forces camp where he refueled; then he returned to the battle scene. Again he attempted to locate and rescue South Vietnamese troops nearly submerged in the high grass. On his third journey into the "hot" zone, he received help from Army AH-1 Cobra gunships and Air Force fighter-bombers. Under heavy fire, he picked up nine more friendlies. But now a tenth survivor stood. Novosel was still under fire and was running out of daylight.

Novosel hovered at low level, and Horvath hauled the man aboard. At that instant, a Viet Cong soldier stood about 30 feet in front of the helicopter and emptied the clip of his AK-47 automatic rifle straight at the pilot in the right seat. The helicopter went out of control momentarily until co-pilot Tyrone Chamberlain could gain control. Neither pilot had been hit by the spray of 7.62-mm rounds, but metal fragments had pulverized Novosel's legs.

In a June 1971 White House ceremony, Nixon awarded Novosel the Medal of Honor.

> First Lt. Sharon A. Lane was the only American woman killed by enemy fire in Vietnam. An Army nurse, she is remembered for handling a difficult workload calmly and quietly.
>
> Lane was born in 1943 and grew up in Ohio. She joined the Army Nurse Corps Reserve in 1968, the year U.S. military strength in Vietnam peaked at 536,100.
>
> The Army assigned her to Fitzsimons General Hospital in Denver, Colorado, where she worked in three outlying tuberculosis wards. There, Lane worked in the cardiac division's intensive care unit and recovery room. In early 1969, the Army assigned her to Vietnam.
>
> Now a first lieutenant, she arrived at the 312th Evacuation Hospital at Chu Lai on April 29, 1969, and went to work in the intensive care ward for a few days before being assigned to the Vietnamese ward. Fellow nurses remember that she worked 5 days a week, 12 hours a day, in this ward, plus an additional day each week in intensive care.
>
> On June 8, 1969, just as Lane was completing an overnight shift in the Vietnamese ward, the hospital came under Viet Cong mortar and rocket fire. The procedure was to get ambulatory patients under their beds and to cover those unable to move with a mattress. Lane was busily attempting to secure patients when a Soviet-built 122-mm rocket fired by the Viet Cong struck the ward. A piece of shrapnel struck Lane in the throat. She was killed instantly. She was 25 years old.
>
> Eight American military women died in Vietnam. All were nurses. Seven were in the Army; one was in the Air Force. Two Army nurses who were men also died in the conflict. Lane was the only American servicewoman to be awarded a bronze star with the *V* decoration on the ribbon, for valor. She also posthumously received the Purple Heart medal and other awards.

In April 1970, U.S. troops invaded Cambodia to root out North Vietnamese sanctuaries. During protests at Kent State University, Ohio, National Guardsmen fired on and killed four demonstrators.

In 1972, Nixon resumed daily bombing of North Vietnam. Also in 1972, Gen. Bruce Palmer became the Army's twenty-sixth chief of staff, although he served only a few months. Abrams returned from Vietnam to become the twenty-seventh chief late that year.

The U.S. combat role officially ended in Vietnam on January 23, 1973, and in Cambodia in August 15.

On August 9, 1974, the day Nixon became the only American president ever to resign, Gerald Ford became the thirty-eighth U.S. president. Also in 1974, Gen. Frederick C. Weyand became the Army's twenty-eighth chief of staff.

"I'm supposed to be the best tank commander in the Army," Lt. Gen. George S. Patton is supposed to have said, "but I have one peer, Abe Abrams." Army Gen. Creighton Abrams, who became the top commander in Vietnam and, later, chief of staff, cultivated a rough, gruff style much like Patton's.

Abrams' 37th Tank Battalion, 4th Armored Division, led the advance by Patton's Third Army across France and into Germany, launching a counter-attack in France in September 1944, Abrams drove his tanks into German territory. In just 1 day, he took 354 prisoners and captured 12 tanks, 85 vehicles, and 5 heavy guns. He lost just 12 soldiers and no tanks.

Abrams led the U.S. breakout from the German siege of Bastogne, Belgium, during the Battle of the Bulge. At that battle, Abrams is reported to have told his troops, "They've got us surrounded again, the poor bastards!"

As commander of the 3rd Armored Division, Abrams had his portrait on the cover of *Time* magazine in 1961. He became deputy commander of the U.S. Military Assistance Command in Saigon in 1967. He replaced Gen. William C. Westmoreland as the top U.S. officer in the war zone in 1968.

Abrams departed Vietnam to become chief of staff of the Army in 1972. Abrams supervised the Army in the closing stages of the Vietnam War, including withdrawal of American troops from the war zone, reductions in Army strength, elimination of the draft, transition to all-volunteer status, and completion of a major reorganization.

Abrams died in 1974. The Army's famous M1 Abrams main battle tank is named after the general.

On April 30, 1975, Saigon fell to advancing North Vietnamese troops. The watching world saw a T-54 main battle tank break through the iron gate of President Nguyen Van Thieu's Independence Palace. North Vietnamese infantry swarmed over Tan Son Nhut airfield. The United States ordered a final helicopter evacuation of Americans, their families, and some loyal South Vietnamese. During the evacuation, dubbed Operation Frequent Wind, two U.S. troops were killed.

United States Army, Robert F. Dorr

A crewman loads rockets onto a UH-1 Huey helicopter.

The average age of the 58,148 killed in Vietnam was 23.11 years. (Although 58,169 names are in the November 1993 database, only 58,148 have both event date and birth date. Event date is used instead of declared dead date for some of those who were listed as missing in action [Combat Area Casualty File (CACF)].)

Deaths	Average Age
Total 58,148	23.11 years
Enlisted 50,274	22.37 years

Deaths	Average Age
Officers 6,598	28.43 years
Warrants 1,276	24.73 years
E1 525	20.34 years
11B MOS 18,465	22.55 years

Five men killed in Vietnam were only 16 years old. [CACF]

The oldest man killed was 62 years old. [CACF]

A total of 11,465 KIAs were less than 20 years old. [CACF]

CHAPTER 10

THE ARMY IN THE MODERN ERA (1976–2002)

Jimmy Carter became the thirty-ninth U.S. president on January 20, 1977. Vietnam lay behind, but the beginnings of an all-volunteer Army were not encouraging. The new Army chief of staff (the twenty-ninth) was Gen. Bernard Rogers, who held the post until 1979, when he went to become the Allied commander in Europe. Gen. Edward C. "Shy" Meyer followed, serving as the thirtieth Army chief of staff from 1979 to 1983. Both men faced unparalleled challenges within the Army.

In the late 1970s, the Army, like the American civilian sector, was plagued by racial strife and drug problems. The latter were eventually solved with a "zero tolerance" testing policy, but the Carter years were not a happy time for the military. A harbinger was the November 4, 1979, seizure of the American Embassy in Tehran, Iran, by revolutionary followers of the Ayatollah Ruhollah Khomeni (1900–1989). Headlines and magazine cover photos of American diplomats being held hostage tarnished the final part of the Carter years. Among the 53 hostages were several military members who had been serving at the embassy. Under Carter, an April 1980 attempt to rescue the hostages failed, pointing to the need to provide better funding to special operations forces. The failure at "Desert One" ultimately led to the Goldwater-Nichols legislation that reformed the military a few years after the Carter era.

After defeating incumbent Carter in the 1980 campaign, Ronald Reagan became the fortieth U.S. president on January 20, 1981. Reagan pledged to rebuild the armed forces and to confront the Soviet Union, which he dubbed the "Evil Empire." On March 23, 1983, Reagan delivered a speech known today primarily because it proposed the "Star Wars" program of missile defense, officially dubbed the Strategic Defense Initiative (SDI) and forerunner of today's National Missile Defense (NMD) program.

Reagan's team included Secretary of Defense Caspar Weinberger, Secretary of the Army John O. Marsh (an infantry veteran), Chairman of the Joint Chiefs Gen. John W. Vessey Jr., and (initially) Army Chief of Staff Gen. Edward C. "Shy" Meyer. In 1983, Meyer was replaced by Gen. John A. Wickham Jr., the thirty-first officer to serve as top soldier. Gen. Carl E. Vuono, in turn, replaced Wickham, as chief of staff in 1987.

United States Army, Robert F. Dorr

The M60 machine gun crew of the Combat Support Company, 1st Battalion, 25th Infantry Division lay down a field of fire to restore the forward battle zone during the joint training exercise Team Spirit in Korea in 1982.

Soldiers accustomed to riding rather than walking over rough terrain know that it can be bumpy when the ride is the Army's M-998 HMMWV, otherwise known as the Humvee or Hummer.

The Humvee (High-Mobility, Multipurpose Wheeled Vehicle) entered service in 1985. A military news release summarizes the contribution made by the Humvee since then:

"In the 1980s, the Humvee replaced the famed Jeep as the Army's basic utility vehicle. Generally, it is the workhorse of the wheeled-vehicle fleet. It is used as a weapons carrier to tow light howitzers or carry mortars for the Army.

"Variants of the Humvee are also used as ambulances, military police tactical vehicles, and for battlefield reconnaissance. The Humvee has a cargo capacity of 1 to 2 tons, depending on the configuration. It is a highly mobile tactical vehicle with a common chassis for various configurations, including cargo/troop carrier, armament carrier, Tow missile carrier, ambulance, and shelter carrier."

The Humvee has a maximum speed of 65 miles per hour and a range of 300 miles. The Humvee is 15 feet in length and weighs 5,200 pounds.

The prototype Humvee entered tests in 1980, and has since been described as the Army's third-generation utility vehicle, following the Willy's Jeep of World War II and the M151 Jeep introduced in the post-Korea 1950s.

The Army's first order in 1985 was for 55,000 Humvees. About 160,000 have been built for the U.S. military and international military users.

In a June 14, 2000, event at New York's Times Square, Secretary of the Army Louis Caldera wielded a saber to cut a birthday cake shaped in the form of a full-size Humvee.

URGENT FURY

Operation Urgent Fury was the invasion of the Caribbean island of Grenada between October 23 and November 21, 1983. President Reagan ordered U.S. forces to invade Grenada, which he warned had been taken over by "a brutal group of leftist thugs." The job given to U.S. troops was to uproot Cuban troops who were using the former British colony as a holding place for military arms. U.S. forces also were to evacuate U.S. citizens, neutralize resistance, and stabilize the situation. It was a "combined arms" operation, meaning that the service branches were to work together. The commander of the operation was the Navy's Vice Adm. Joseph Metcalf III, who reported to Adm. Wesley L. McDonald, commander in chief of the U.S. Atlantic Command.

The Grenada invasion took place only a few days after a terrorist bombing in Lebanon that killed 241 U.S. Marines and just a decade after the United States ended its combat role in Vietnam. To *Newsweek*, Grenada warranted a cover story, "Americans at War," while *Time* combined the Beirut and Grenada events on its cover. A British publication called the struggle on this tropical island "War in Paradise."

Metcalf launched Urgent Fury from his flagship, the USS *Guam* (LPH-9), one of numerous ships that launched helicopter-borne Marines, Army Rangers, and 82nd Airborne Division paratroopers. Marines carried out a predrawn helicopter assault on Pearls Airport at 5:00 A.M. on October 25. There, Marines stormed gun positions manned by the Peoples Revolutionary Army (PRA) and overwhelmed them.

To secure objectives in Grenada, the island was operationally split in half. The Marines covered the northern half. To the south, Salines airfield had been "prepped" by an attack by 12 members of Navy Seal Team 6 the previous night, but resistance lingered. Army Rangers, arriving at the airfield at Point Salines at dawn in C-130 Hercules aircraft, met stiffer opposition than the Marines at Pearls. To avoid the antiaircraft fire, the Rangers jumped from very low altitude, just 500 feet.

From the beginning, horrendous command, control, and communications plagued this "combined arms" effort. The military had not yet decided on a policy to encourage "jointness" among service branches, and there was little. Navy and Army communications systems were not compatible in many cases. The legend was created that a team of soldiers used a pay phone to call the United States in order to be patched in to a Navy fire controller. There were several "friendly fire" incidents. The strafing of American paratroopers by a Navy A-7 Corsair II was described in the November 14, 1983, issue of *Time* magazine:

> The airborne unit was trying to rout Cuban soldiers in their well-fortified Calivigny barracks when it called for Navy air help. Their location was close to an abandoned Cuban antiaircraft gun that still pointed toward the sky. "All of a sudden the world blew up," said Lt. Scott Schafer, who was hit by shrapnel when the Corsair fired. Twelve paratroopers were wounded. As the plane banked for another strike, a ground officer reached the pilot by radio to warn it away.

After an initial day of serious fighting, Operation Urgent Fury became a series of skirmishes. Within three days, all main objectives had been accomplished. A formal cease-fire came on November 2. Operation Urgent Fury cost U.S. forces 18 dead and 113 wounded, compared with 60 Grenadians and Cubans killed and 200 wounded.

In total, the invasion force consisted of 1,900 U.S. troops, which grew to 5,000 within 5 days. Americans were helped by 300 troops from neighboring islands. Their opposition comprised 1,200 Grenadians, 780 Cubans, and a few dozen Soviets, North Koreans, East Germans, Bulgarians, and Libyans.

The Reagan Administration was a time of flexing muscle and showing force around the world, often in operations that involved few, if any, of the Army's soldiers. In Lebanon, efforts to free Americans held hostage were largely stymied. A one-day air strike in the Bekaa Valley in December 1983—carried out in part by the carrier the USS *Independence*, which had just arrived from Grenada, thus involving itself in combat in two locations on one cruise—was an inconclusive and unfocused effort against pro-Iranian terror groups in Lebanon. Long-range air strikes against Libya in April 1986 were more successful but were undercut by the administration's secret "arms for hostages" dealings with Iran.

George Bush became the forty-first president of the United States on January 20, 1989, after many years in various government postings, including eight as Reagan's vice president.

> Before becoming secretary of state in 2001, Colin Powell was an Army officer who rose through the ranks to become chairman of the Joint Chiefs of Staff.
>
> Powell's early experience in Vietnam shaped his views about war. In his 1995 book, *My American Journey,* he urged that politics not interfere with soldiers.
>
> "Many of my generation," Powell wrote, "vowed that when our turn came to call the shots, we would not quietly acquiesce in halfhearted warfare for half-baked reasons that the American people could not understand."
>
> As Powell sees it, American troops should be sent into battle only when there are clear political objectives and there is a clear exit strategy and a timetable. Congress and the administration must be committed to giving troops the resources to achieve superiority.

Powell was born in Harlem, New York, in 1937 and became an Army 2nd lieutenant in 1958. Powell married Alma Johnson and soon afterward arrived in Vietnam as a captain in 1962. In *My American Journey,* he describes living and working in a thatched hut with a dirt floor and sleeping on a bamboo cot. He spent mornings on patrol for Viet Cong guerrillas. Powell "had no qualms about what we were doing."

Powell was wounded during this early combat tour in Vietnam. His belief in properly equipping and supplying the American soldier was solidified during his second tour.

He became chairman of the Joint Chiefs of Staff from 1989 to 1993, under the first President Bush and President Bill Clinton.

Many in the media, including the British Broadcasting Corporation's web page, reported Powell's most famous quote during the 1991 Persian Gulf war, when he described his plan for dealing with the Iraqi ground force: "Our strategy for going after this army is very, very simple. First we are going to cut it off; then we are going to kill it."

JUST CAUSE

In the late 1980s, the Army was in healthier shape than in the late 1970s—random testing had all but eliminated drug use, and race problems were less pronounced—but the armed forces were living in a frustrating time. Bush, who at 18 years old had been the youngest naval aviator during World War II, understood the military but lacked the natural "Aw, shucks" way of relating to soldiers that had been a gift for Reagan. The Army and the military generally had been battered by a decade of dismal failure (Desert One), ambiguous and inconclusive military operations (in Lebanon, Nicaragua, and Libya), and only one small success (Grenada). Although the Soviet Union was beginning to unravel, the Cold War was winding down, and there was talk of a "New World Order." New military challenges seemed to pop up everywhere on the map. To the Bush administration, one of these was in Panama, where dictator Manuel Noriega had been indicted by a U.S. court on narcotics charges.

Bush had a formidable military team with Defense Secretary Dick Cheney, Joint Chiefs Chairman Colin Powell, Army Chief General Carl Vuono, and the boss of U.S. Southern Command, Gen. Maxwell R. Thurman.

As Pentagon experts began putting together a plan for action against Noriega, they at first dubbed it Operation Blue Spoon. Cheney is reported to have said, "The American people need a better name to rally behind." A long history of giving military operations names that lacked context or meaning came to an end. At Cheney's order, the Panama effort became Operation Just Cause.

It began with the largest airborne assault since World War II, spearhead of the effort to oust Noriega and protect U.S. citizens. On December 20, 1989, 82nd Airborne Division paratroopers under Lt. Gen. Carl Stiner made a night drop on Omar Torrijos Airport, near Panama City. They fanned out and engaged Panama Defense Forces (PDF) troops in scattered skirmishes, supported by AC-130 Spectre gunships.

The airborne soldiers linked up with the 3rd Battalion, 504th Parachute Infantry Regiment that was already in Panama. After the seizure of the airfield—which reverted to its original name, Tocumen Airport—the 82nd pursued the PDF in new assault missions in Panama City and the surrounding areas.

In a pitched battle at Tocumen airfield, paratroopers trapped three PDF troops inside a men's restroom at the terminal. When the Panamanians refused to surrender, the U.S. soldiers tossed grenades into the room and sprayed it with gunfire, killing the trio.

The airdrop included M551 Sheridan reconnaissance vehicles. The Sheridan was a kind of mini-tank that had enjoyed some success in Vietnam and was the only combat vehicle capable of being dropped by parachute. Within a few years, it would be gone from inventory, its capability never replaced.

In the first days of fighting, Army Capt. Linda L. Bray led the 988th Military Police Company in an effort to neutralize a PDF attack-dog kennel at the edge of Panama City. In a three-hour battle with heavily armed PDF troops, Bray's soldiers killed three and seized the objective. Press reports called Bray the first female officer to lead combat troops in a battle.

A week after the assault was launched, U.S. troops had captured or detained about 80 percent of the 3,500 troops that made up the military contingent of the 16,000-member PDF.

The Army fielded 167 helicopters in Panama, including the AH-64 Apache battlefield helicopter in its combat debut, firing AGM-114 Hellfire missiles, 2.75-inch rocket projectiles, and 30-mm cannon shells. When called in for air support, the entire fleet took damage on 41 and lost 4, including 3 special-operations MH-6 "Little Birds" from the 160th Special Operations Aviation Group at Fort Campbell, Kentucky.

After hiding out in the nunciature (papal embassy), on January 3, 1990, Noriega surrendered to U.S. troops and was flown in an Army UH-60 Blackhawk helicopter to Howard Air Force Base, Panama, where he was turned over to federal agents and flown to the United States.

The fight for Panama cost 23 Americans killed and 300 wounded. About 600 PDF defenders died. Operation Just Cause continued until January 12, 1990, although some troops began returning stateside on January 8. The Army gave an unprecedented number of awards for the action—roughly 1.8 for each soldier.

As a test of the new concept of "jointness" being promoted within the armed forces, Just Cause was a diverse mix of military units, including the Army's 2nd Airborne, 7th Infantry Division, 75th Ranger Regiment, a Joint Special Operations Task Force, and, of course, the 82nd. There were 22,500 U.S. troops in all. Because the mission could be launched at a time of U.S. choosing, a report later faulted the brass for not being fully prepared for the tenacity of the Panamanian defenders, and there was also criticism for not doing a good job of keeping the invasion secret. Still, Just Cause was generally viewed as a success, not least because it made Noriega a prisoner of war in Florida. There were few of the command and control problems that had plagued the invasion of Grenada six years earlier. One unforeseen complication was the bitter cold snap that swept the United States before Christmas. Ice delayed C-5 Galaxy and C-141B Starlifter takeoffs from Fort Polk, Louisiana, and Pope Air Force Base, North Carolina, including 20 Pope-based flights carrying paratroopers. In just three hours of flying time, American soldiers traversed from freezing temperatures to a balmy, tropical setting—a disorienting experience.

DESERT STORM

When Iraq's Saddam Hussein invaded Kuwait on August 2, 1990, the United States responded with Operation Desert Shield, a massive buildup of military strength in the Persian Gulf region. Among the first on the scene were paratroopers of the 82nd Airborne Division, who took up station in Saudi Arabia to serve as a tripwire if the Iraqis kept coming. Saddam did not extend his reach beyond Saudi Arabia, but the buildup went on and eventually exceeded half a million U.S. troops.

For the Army, the buildup took place in two stages, the second beginning in mid-November when a decision was made to increase the stakes by bringing in heavy armor units from Europe. Gen. H. Norman Schwarzkopf, commander in chief of U.S. Central Command, made the point that he needed robust forces, including the beefy M1A1 Abrams main battle tank. While forces poured in, the events in the Persian Gulf were covered in real time on television, and the world became familiar with desert camouflage, the M16A1 infantry rifle, and those ever-present rations, the Meals Ready to Eat (MRE). Soon the average American on the street was tossing off new words like *Humvee* (the tactical vehicle that had replaced the Jeep) and *Patriot* (the Army's air defense missile).

The first round of fighting came when Army AH-64 Apache helicopters knocked out Iraqi air defense radar installations in Operation Normandy. That happened on the night of January 17, 1991, after Saddam Hussein ignored an ultimatum. That night, warplanes of the Allied Coalition flew more than 750 sorties. Targets throughout Iraq and Kuwait included military emplacements, air defense assets, and command and control facilities. The air campaign deprived Saddam Hussein of the initiative and prepared the theater for a coalition ground assault that would complete the destruction of Iraqi forces in Kuwait with minimal losses.

> In 1991, Army Gen. H. Norman Schwarzkopf was one of the most famous people in the world. Schwarzkopf says he learned much about Army life from his dad.
>
> The elder Schwarzkopf (1896–1958) was a West Pointer, military policeman, and New Jersey state policemen who became a key figure in the investigation of the Lindbergh baby kidnapping in 1932. The elder Schwarzkopf returned to military service in 1940, reaching the rank of brigadier general.
>
> Before heading U.S. Central Command in Operation Desert Storm, the younger Schwarzkopf served two combat tours in Vietnam and was deputy commander of U.S. forces participating in the Grenada invasion in 1983.
>
> Schwarzkopf was born in 1934 in Trenton, New Jersey. He graduated from West Point in 1956 and was commissioned a second lieutenant of infantry.

Schwarzkopf then obtained a graduate degree in mechanical engineering from the University of Southern California in 1964 and was assigned as an airborne advisor in Vietnam in 1965–1966.

During his second tour in Vietnam, Schwarzkopf was assigned to the Headquarters, U.S. Army Vietnam, and was commander of the 1/6 Infantry, 23rd Infantry Division in 1969–1970.

Under Schwarzkopf, the Desert Storm conflict began on January 17, 1991, with an air campaign against Iraqi forces.

Kuwait was liberated on February 27, 1991. Since retiring in August 1991, Schwarzkopf has been a sought-after speaker. His best-selling biography is *It Takes a Hero.*

United States Army, Robert F. Dorr

General Colin L. Powell, Chairman, Joint Chiefs of Staff, U.S. Army, points out areas in Iraq and Kuwait, indicated by red circles, which contain the highest concentration of air defenses, including radar, artillery, and surface-to-air missiles, at a press briefing to give an assessment of Operation Desert Storm at the conclusion of the first week of hostilities.

The air campaign began with 15,000 sorties in the first week, and the Iraqis responded by firing 43 Scud medium-range ballistic missiles. The 1st Cavalry Division began combat operations as part of a plan to deceive the Iraqis about the intentions of the Allied Coalition. Army Special Forces soldiers were among the special operators carrying out clandestine missions behind the lines, including secret raids aimed at disabling Scud launchers.

Although Schwarzkopf held off launching a major ground offensive, U.S. troops battled Iraqis at the small town of Khafji on the Saudi-Iraqi border. Marines and soldiers backed up by air support were able to secure a blocking position and halt the Iraqi troops.

After more than five weeks of air strikes, ground operations commenced on February 24. After arranging a Marine Corps amphibious feint along the coast of Kuwait that focused the attention of Iraqi forces to the east and south, and launching secondary attacks along the border between Kuwait and Saudi Arabia, Schwarzkopf attacked on a sweep from the west northward deep into Iraqi territory. Coalition ground troops then approached Kuwait eastward from an unexpected direction—from inside Iraq. This cut off enemy supply lines and avenues of retreat. Some called it the "left hook"; Schwarzkopf dubbed it the "Hail Mary" play. The main attack force consisted of U.S. Army, French, and British forces.

Coalition forces liberated Kuwait on February 27, 1991, and negotiated a halt to the fighting the following day, just 100 hours after full-scale ground fighting began. On March 3, a cease-fire conference was held at Safwan. The Iraqis agreed to Coalition demands, and their forces disengaged near Basra. By the time Gen. Schwarzkopf returned from Riyadh to his MacDill Air Force Base, Florida, headquarters in April, he had become an international figure.

DEVELOPMENTS IN THE EARLY 1990s

In June 1991, Gen. Gordon R. Sullivan became the Army's thirty-third chief of staff. Sullivan was a powerful booster of a concept called Force XXI, a theoretical plan for the Army of the twenty-first century. This included slimming down and modernizing the typical Army division. The most significant change was to be the command-and-control apparatus in the new division—a near-paperless operation in which most information would pass back and forth at the speed of computers.

A Bronze Star holder for service in Vietnam, Army National Guard Col. Margarethe Cammemeyer won a 1994 federal court case that allowed her to remain with her unit after revealing that she is a lesbian, notwithstanding the "Don't ask, don't tell" policy then taking effect in the Clinton administration. Cammemeyer completed her military career, retired, and went on to work in public service.

Bill Clinton became the forty-second U.S. president on January 20, 1993, and, in an immediate and controversial move, began the process that produced the Pentagon's "Don't ask, don't tell" policy toward gays. The Army was in the midst of a downsizing process and was caught unprepared for heavy fighting in Somalia in 1993 that resulted in high casualties during a flawed, fruitless attempt to flush out a local warlord. Plans for the future remained on the front burner when Gen. Dennis Reimer replaced Sullivan to become chief of staff number 34 in July 1995. Reimer refined plans for a new kind of Army division. Still evolving today, the plan includes changes such as these:

- Equipping individual soldiers to plug into digital communications systems.
- Providing Army XXI division with three maneuver brigades—one armored and two mechanized infantry. The armored brigade would have two armored battalions and one mechanized battalion. Mechanized brigades would consist of two mechanized battalions and one armored battalion.
- Streamlining battalions to include three companies rather than four.
- Equipping each armored battalion with 45 modernized M1A2 Abrams tanks, and mechanized battalions with 45 new M2A3 Bradley fighting vehicles.

In 1995, battalions had 58 M1A1 Abrams and 58 M2A2 Bradleys, respectively.

The way the Army views it, tactical command and control of soldiers in battle can be just as much a weapon as any gun, tank, or helicopter. That's why the Army is working to integrate the communications used by warfighters in the heat of combat.

The Department of Defense is tweaking "network-centric warfare"—otherwise known in geek-speak as "linking multiservice combat assets across a seamless communications array." That means, among other things, the Army being able to talk to the Navy and Air Force.

In 2002, Lt. Gen. Harry Raduege, director of the Defense Information Systems Agency, acknowledged that in Afghanistan, the military service branches were relying on a hodgepodge of "service-centric" communications systems that weren't all connected to each other. Raduege told a conference that soldiers are still having difficulty communicating: "We have a myriad of stove-piped systems that can find, fix, and track targets and engage, assess, and exercise operational command and control, but most of these systems don't talk to each other."

Possibly having in mind Special Forces operations aimed at rooting al-Qaeda terrorists from the Tora Bora region of Afghanistan, Raduege said that small groups of highly specialized soldiers can access many current systems that lack the necessary bandwidth and flexibility to make them accessible to all the armed forces.

The general's agency is working on the Network Centric Enterprise Services program. Pilot tests of the system scheduled for 2005 will bring "jointness" to the military at new levels.

With this system, even a lone soldier out front on patrol would be able to log into the network, receive intelligence information, and learn about threats around him. That soldier's understanding of the battlefield situation could then be shared with others throughout the system, making it easier, for example, to call in air strikes or to direct forces in reserve.

Pentagon officials see a future in which every soldier will have the means to communicate with everyone up and down the chain of command, using digital technology that didn't exist even a decade ago.

ALLIED FORCE

On the night of March 24, 1999, forces under the U.S. and Allied European commander Army Gen. Wesley Clark began Operation Allied Force. Pentagon spokesman Kenneth Bacon called the operation "a serious effort" against the military forces of Yugoslavia's president Slobodan Milosevic. Diplomatic efforts to restrain Yugoslav violence against the ethnic Albanian populace of rebellious Kosovo province had broken down; after months of threatening to take military action, the North Atlantic Treaty Organization did. Kosovo was primarily an air campaign, with thousands of sorties being flown—but the Army pulled difficult duty and made many sacrifices.

Kosovo was not without controversy for the Army. Most of it swirled around Task Force Hawk—an expedition into Albania that ultimately produced no visible military result.

On April 5, 1999, Clark announced plans to deploy 24 AH-64A Apache helicopters (1 battalion, consisting of 3 companies of 8 aircraft each) to Tirana, Albania. It was noted that 3,000 people would be needed to support the Apaches in Kosovo, with nearly 200 military flights. The helicopters were expected to come from the 11th Aviation Regiment, Illesheim, Ansbach, Germany: the "Killer Bees." The Apache was famed for its lethal performance on the battlefield, but it also suffered from reliability problems. It was initially reported that Task Force Hawk's Apaches would be in place in Albania within five to seven days; later estimates stretched this to weeks.

On April 13, 1999, Clark made it known that he was requesting 300 additional aircraft, a considerable boost that would strain available U.S. resources. It was reported that of 5,000 sorties flown so far, about 2,000 had been strikes on Yugoslav targets—but more than 50 percent of Clark's warplanes brought their bombs home because of the weather.

The long-delayed arrival of Task Force Hawk in Tirana began on April 24, 1999, after Army officers picked a new landing site after heavy rains turned their preferred spot into a quagmire. Clark and other officers hoped the Apache would send a clear signal to Belgrade that the Allies were not relying solely on a surgical, high-altitude war, but were prepared to use a weapon capable of taking out individual Serb units carrying out ethnic cleansing in Kosovo. In fact, Clark was in a standoff with Pentagon officials over use of the 24 Apaches because of fears in Washington that the helicopters would be too vulnerable to antiaircraft fire.

But while Task Force Hawk began as a simple proposition—a small, nimble helicopter strike force—it grew and became unmanageable. At one point, in a move that apparently overruled his combat commander, Defense Secretary William Cohen directed the deployment of 615 additional soldiers to provide "force protection" (current Pentagon jargon for security) for the task force. Once intended to make up a few hundred soldiers and 24 helicopters, Task Force Hawk grew to 3,100 soldiers and still 24 helicopters. Incredibly, that was still not enough. Within weeks, the task force grew to over 5,000, with no increase in the number of Apaches.

Given too many conflicting requirements to provide security, logistics, and support for the task force, Clark watched it become larger than anyone had ever imagined. While NATO jets were bombing Belgrade, Army helicopters were bogged down in the mud and cold at Tirana. The task force lost two Apaches in noncombat mishaps, with two soldiers killed and two injured. They were the only Army casualties in Allied Force, but they were painful to a community of soldiers who were itching to fight and, as it turned out, never got into action.

Operation Allied Force was a grim reminder of how much the armed forces had been downsized in two consecutive administrations under presidents from both parties. U.S. military doctrine still called for the Pentagon to be prepared to fight two regional wars at the same time, but the armed forces had been trimmed to 2.4 million active duty and reserve troops in 1997, compared with 3.8 million a decade earlier.

Recently the Army introduced a new "flak jacket" that weighs 35 percent less than current models.

Personal armor is nothing new. When President William McKinley fell to an assassin's bullet in 1901, Congress looked into body armor to protect public officials but balked at the tab. During the early years of the twentieth century, the Army seemed in no hurry to develop a protective garment: The "bullet-proof vests" advertised during the 1930s (and far from bullet-proof) were meant for lawmen.

During World War II, for bomber crews, the Air Corps developed "flak suits," named for the German antiaircraft gun *Fliegerabwehrkanonen,* abbreviated as "flak."

Korea was the first war in which Americans were routinely issued personal armor. One Korea veteran called the flak jacket "the infantryman's most important piece of equipment, next to his rifle." Troops initially received the M1951 flak jacket, later the two-piece M12 model, and finally the lighter (at 7 pounds, 15 ounces) nylon M1952, which became the standard until Vietnam.

In the 1960s, ceramic armor provided a technical breakthrough by giving the soldier a more lightweight protective garment. A new ceramic material, Kevlar, developed by Dupont, came in 1965 and was used in the Vietnam-era M69 flak vest, which weighed 8 pounds, 8 ounces and was a bargain for the taxpayer, at around $50 in today's dollars.

The Army introduced second-generation Kevlar 129 in its improved flak jacket known as the Personnel Armor System, Ground Troop (PASGT) in 1982.

But since the 1980s, advances in lightweight composite technology meant that reporters covering the Persian Gulf War of 1991 wore lighter (but more expensive) flak jackets than American soldiers. To catch up, the Army Soldier Systems Center is introducing the Interceptor Body Armor, which weighs 16 pounds, 4 ounces.

SEPTEMBER 11

On September 11, 2001, terrorism hit home in America. Two airliners crashed into the towers of the World Trade Center in New York City, and another jumbo jet slammed into the Pentagon building in Washington, D.C.

The United States immediately targeted the international terrorism groups in Afghanistan. By November 8, more than 50,000 American soldiers were deployed in the area, roughly half of them aboard Navy vessels. When the operation began, 80 percent of the nation was Taliban-controlled. Approximately 78 days later, the ruling government had been toppled, Qandahar airport and several major cities had been secured by U.S. forces, and an interim government had been established.

All through 2002, joint operation forces continued working against the remains of al Qaeda and Taliban networks in and around Afghanistan. A Navy carrier group remains offshore, ready to provide support and mobile bases when and where necessary.

In the last quarter-century, America carried out the mission it had started after World War II, policing the world and fighting the enemies of freedom wherever they struck.

When this volume went to press, the Army was gearing up for an expected invasion of Iraq. Chief of Staff Gen. Eric Shinseki's plans for "transformation" of the Army were proceeding apace. A great many officers and soldiers were busy focusing on what would happen the next day or the day after. But a few were looking farther ahead. A few were pondering what the future might hold.

TOMORROW'S ARMY

The soldier of the future may look something like the "Starship Troopers" of science fiction, not so much those of Robert Heinlein's 1959 novel, but more like the interplanetary warriors of the 1997 movie directed by Paul Verhoeven. In the novel, a single infantryman has atomic weapons and can leap giant steps, using technology to leap a mile or more in one bound. In the film, the soldier of tomorrow simply has futuristic gear and weapons with great destructive power. To their credit, both versions of tomorrow feature a starship named for Rodger Young, the World War II soldier in the South Pacific who gave his life for his buddies and inspired a 1945 song by Frank Loesser. Heinlein used a famous line from the song as the recall signal in the novel, linking the past to the future: "Shines the name, shines the name of Rodger Young …."

On July 31, 1943, infantrymen of the Army's 37th Infantry Division, the "Ohio Buckeyes," were pinned down by Japanese gunfire on the Pacific island of New Georgia. Pvt. Rodger W. Young, 25, from Green Springs, Ohio, scrambled forward beneath a hail of bullets to engage the foe. Young was spindly and bespectacled, resembling a bookworm more than a warrior.

Playing baseball in high school, Young sustained a concussion that damaged his hearing and eyesight. He probably could have avoided military service. Instead, in 1939, he joined the Ohio Army National Guard unit that became the 37th Infantry Division.

When U.S. soldiers came ashore on steamy Guadalcanal in 1942, Young was a sergeant. Perhaps to compensate for his diminutive size and library-clerk demeanor, he seemed a natural leader. He drilled troops on jungle maneuvering and night fighting.

But Young's hearing was getting worse. Had the Army known it, he surely would have gotten a medical discharge. He felt the handicap eroded his ability to lead, and he took the initiative to request a reduction in rank to private—but he refused to quit.

Young's final action came when he crawled toward a spitting Japanese machine gun near New Georgia's Munda airstrip. Young was drawing closer when a bullet struck his shoulder and sent him rolling over.

Others yelled at him not to continue, but with his hearing defect, Young may have been unaware. More likely, Young simply understood that the Japanese gun had pinned his buddies down.

Young crawled relentlessly toward the barking Japanese weapon. When he got within about 40 feet, a volley of rounds hit Young again. The other Americans saw his body tremble as he took the hits. But Young somehow got a grenade into his hand, pulled the pin, and lobbed it. He threw a second grenade and then a third.

The explosions ripped the Japanese position and the enemy soldiers apart. Young's buddies were able to rise and advance. But it was too late to save Young, who had been mortally wounded.

Pvt. Rodger Young was posthumously awarded the Medal of Honor on January 17, 1944.

The Army's own magazine, *Soldiers*, frequently publishes pictures of future infantrymen who look like Heinlein's interplanetary bug-killers. The Army's Natick Soldier Center is looking today at innovations to help the soldier fight and survive:

- A new kind of battle dress uniform that changes color, chameleon-like, when its background changes
- Medical body sensors that keep tabs on the soldier's health, monitor wounds, and get information to battlefield medics in real time
- A lightweight infantry weapon with advanced fire control, possibly linked to intelligence sensors
- A new helmet with a see-through, heads-up display that can show video and thermal imaging and integrated sensory enhancements, networked with information from manned and unmanned ground and aerial vehicles for collaborative situational awareness

This is heavy stuff. It reflects the American decision to rely on a relatively small all-volunteer professional Army to handle challenges around the world rather than return to a draft and a citizen-soldier Army with greater numbers. "The Army has to be small and smart," said Gen. Eric Shinseki, the service's chief of staff in 2002. The decision actually goes way above Shinseki's pay grade: The American people are more willing to wage war when somebody else's sons and daughters have to do it. The Pentagon's generals have been told that, even in the midst of a new worldwide war with terrorism, there will be no vast increases in funding. A return to conscription is unthinkable. So the Army must rely on scientific advances, digital technology, and original thinking to win the battles of tomorrow.

FUTURE FIGHTER

The short-term future will, as always, be shaped by decisions about equipment. The Army's near-future prospects don't include enough funds and a sufficient size to accommodate the Crusader self-propelled artillery howitzer, RAH-66 Comanche battlefield scout helicopter, and Objective Individual Combat Weapon (OICW). In the old Army, size mattered, a big artillery piece was a good thing, munitions were only somewhat accurate, and new weapons were designed and developed in serial fashion, each replacing its predecessor. In the new Army of the twenty-first century, small is good, mobile is even better, robust tanks and artillery guns are not necessarily wanted, munitions can be satellite-guided with extreme precision, and a coordinated grid of weapons, tactics, and training may be developed simultaneously, with the external appearance of an item of military equipment being far less important than the software inside it. The old Army used round dials, clunky weapons, and techniques that were often not well integrated with goals. The new Army is digital, and its weapons will be lighter and more agile.

Taking cover and digging in won't help enemy soldiers if American soldiers begin lugging the new Objective Individual Combat Weapon (OICW).

Supporters of the OICW say it's the Army's next-generation rifle. It looks more like a clunky science-fiction prop from one of the *Alien* movies. In reality, the OICW is a combination rifle and grenade launcher—among other things, capable of lobbing a 20-mm grenade into an enemy foxhole.

Critics say the OICW is too bulky, too heavy, and likely to exhaust the typical soldier before it even reaches the battlefield. The OICW weighs about 18 pounds, or about twice the heft of an M16.

When not functioning as a rifle, the OICW is a grenade launcher. The weapon's own mini-computer has the ability to measure the precise range of a target and communicate this to the 20-mm high-explosive bursting ammunition. The soldier aims using a laser and fires. The weapon also has the capability to track a moving target and to choose among nearby threats, identifying the closest and most immediate.

Even its strongest supporters acknowledge that the OICW has a firing recoil level greater than that of the M16 rifle.

Will the OICW become part of the soldier's arsenal in 2009, as the Army was planning when the weapon finished preliminary tests in 1999? Supporters point out that the OICW's microchips can eliminate aiming errors caused by "wobble" and reliance on Kentucky windage, or guessing at the distance to a target. Some, however, want the weapon's two functions—rifle and grenade launcher—to be separated.

The new weapons for tomorrow's wars may not resemble anything that's familiar to today's veterans. Some that are just around the corner include these:

- The Precision Guided Mortar Munition (PGMM). This is a 120-mm laser-guided mortar with extended range, expected to be lighter, more survivable, and far more accurate than current mortars, making it possible to zero in on a foe's military forces with less collateral damage.
- The XM-29 integrated airburst weapon. Equipped with two barrels, one that will fire 20-mm air-bursting munitions and the other that uses a standard 5.56-mm (.223-caliber) rifle cartridge, the XM-29 will be able to reach out a thousand yards, about three times the range of today's M4 and M16 infantry rifles.
- A weapon yet to be designed for the future Multirole Armament and Ammunition System (MRAAS). This lightweight system will fire direct and indirect munitions out to a distance of about 40 miles. It will include a multipurpose, extended-range projectile and a multi-purpose smart warhead.
- The .50-caliber XM-107 sniper rifle, designed to replace the 20-year-old M-82A3 now being used by snipers in the Army and other service branches. According to *Soldiers* magazine, the XM-107 will be able to hit targets more than a mile away.

The Army is also introducing Stryker, alias the Infantry Carrier Vehicle, a mini-tank with tires that has the capability to operate for 72 hours independently. It can carry a nine-man squad and a two-man crew, supporting them with food, water, and ammunition. One Stryker can be carried (just barely) by a C-130 Hercules tactical transport; three can be carried by a C-17 Globemaster II strategic airlifter.

The new vehicles will be placed in a Stryker Interim Brigade Combat Team. The Army wants 2,131 Stryker vehicles, equipping 6 of these special brigade teams by 2008.

The vehicle is named for two Army heroes (unrelated) who shared a surname. Pfc. Stuart Stryker served with the 513th Parachute Infantry and posthumously received the Medal of Honor for leading a December 1945 attack near Wesel, Germany. Specialist Robert Stryker served with the

1st Infantry Division and was posthumously awarded the Medal of Honor for saving the life of fellow soldiers in a November 1967 action near Loc Ninh, Vietnam.

Replacing "Be all you can be" with "An Army of one" isn't the only way the Army is changing its recruiting in the all-volunteer era of the twenty-first century. A private company is handling Army recruiting in 10 nationwide locations as part of an experiment to see if civilians can make effective recruiters.

The Stryker will come in 10 variants that include the Infantry Carrier vehicle, Mobile Gun System, Anti-Tank Missile Guided Vehicle, Reconnaissance Vehicle, Fire Support Vehicle, Engineer Squad Vehicle, Mortar Carrier Vehicle, Commander's Vehicle, Medical Evacuation Vehicle, and a Nuclear Biological and Chemical Reconnaissance Vehicle.

Army chief of staff Gen. Eric K. Shinseki accepted the first U.S.–built Stryker in a ceremony at Anniston Army Depot, Alabama, on April 12, 2002. Among units scheduled to transform into Interim Brigade Combat Teams and receive Strykers are the 172nd Infantry Brigade in Alaska; the 2nd Armored Cavalry Regiment at Fort Polk, Louisiana; the 2nd Brigade, 25th Infantry Division at Schofield Barracks, Hawaii; and the Pennsylvania Army National Guard's 56th Brigade, 28th Infantry Division.

OBJECTIVE WARRIOR

The Army is working on something called Objective Force Warrior (OFW), a package of technological improvements for the American soldier that are supposed to be put into the field for demonstration purposes under the title Land Warrior Block 3.0 in 2010. The first Land Warrior demonstrator package, called Block 1.0, is slated for 2004. The purpose of OFW is to demonstrate a carefully coordinated set of equipment and improvements for the individual soldier, ranging from protective gear to small arms to networked communications equipment.

At the core of the OFW concept is a single combat uniform that protects soldiers from chemical and biological agents, ballistic threats, and wet weather. According to *Soldiers* magazine, the OFW is also supposed to include body sensors that can keep track of an infantryman's physical status, such as heart rate and body temperature, and permit medics to provide preventive care and perform remote triage on the battlefield.

The futuristic soldier of the OFW program will look different from head to toe, with an entirely different helmet, more durable boots, and plenty of changes in between. This program to re-equip the American soldier, at least for demonstration purposes, is modular, meaning that incremental improvements can be made after 2010 when new technologies become available. The program is focusing on ways to reduce the weight soldiers carry—a goal in every army since the beginning of time. For example, why carry heavy batteries when lightweight, longer-lasting fuel cells are being developed? Why carry equipment at all when robotic "mules" can do the carrying and perform double duty as platforms for unmanned aerial vehicles that give soldiers a bird's-eye view of the battlefield? Today's infantryman lugs between 80 and 100 pounds, and the OFW would like to get this figure down to 50 pounds.

Today's emphasis on transforming and slimming down the Army may inhibit the future of the Objective Individual Combat Weapon (OICW), which looks like an infantry rifle on steroids and weighs twice as much as an M16. In August 2000, the Army began a 48-month "program definition and risk reduction" effort to evaluate the features and performance of the OICW. This phase is supposed to pave the way for engineering and manufacturing development of the OICW, to begin in 2004, and full-scale production, to start in 2008. But since the September 11, 2001, terror attacks, the Army has been rethinking the program.

Short of native speakers of the Arabic language, the Army is considering signing up noncitizen Middle Easterners for duty in Special Forces. It would not be the first time. Under the Lodge Act of 1952, aimed at raising a cadre of exiles to fight in the Soviet Union, some 230 Eastern Europeans were brought into the 10th Special Forces Group. Under the new arrangements, citizens of friendly Arab countries like Egypt and Jordan will be recruited.

THE ARMY ALWAYS

The American soldier has experienced "ups and downs" over the years since 1775, savoring victory and suffering defeat, winning the scorn of the public in one era and its admiration in another, but ultimately winning in every test of mettle or merit—winning on the embattled green at Lexington, winning on bullet-raked Omaha Beach, and winning in the famous "Left Hook" against Iraq. Looking back, the defeats were few (though Gen. George Custer might say they were important) and the moments of public scorn were isolated (except for Vietnam, mostly in times of peace), and most Americans have supported their Army and their soldiers most of the time. At the start of the twenty-first century, the Army was held in higher regard than the Congress that funds it, trusted by the public more than the corporations that supply it, and, yes, respected more by Americans than the journalists who write about it.

It would be nice if the world could look ahead to nothing but peace. That's not likely. There will always be debates about the size and shape of the Army, about the weapons and equipment to purchase for soldiers, and about the job of the soldiers themselves. But the nation will continue to need the United States Army. We have needed it since 1775, and we always will.

APPENDIX A

BIBLIOGRAPHY

The Army Almanac: A Book of Facts Concerning the Army of the United States. U.S. Government Printing Office, 1950.

Bill, Alfred Hoyt. *Rehearsal for Conflict: The War with Mexico 1846–1848*. New York: History Book Club, 1947.

Eisenhower, John S. D. *Yanks: The Epic Story of the American Army in World War I*. New York: The Free Press, 2001.

Keegan, John. *Fields of Battle: The Wars for North America*. New York: Vintage Books, 1997.

Kreidberg, Col. Marvin A., and Merton G. Henry. "Raising the Armies." *The Lesson and the Legacy, The Official Army Information Digest, U.S. Army Magazine* (August 1961): 52–59.

Parrish, Thomas. *Roosevelt and Marshall: Partners in Politics and War*. New York: William Morrow & Co., 1989.

War Planning and Training Division, Office of the Quartermaster General. *The Evolution of the Uniform*. Published in the public domain in *The Quartermaster Review*, March–April 1928.

Wright, Robert K. *The Continental Army*. The Army Lineage Series by the Center for Military History. United States Army: Washington, D.C., 1983.

WEBSITES

Army War College:
http://carlisle-www.army.mil/usawc/Parameters/98autumn/aut-rev.htm

National Alliance of Families:
www.nationalalliance.org/ovrvw01.htm

U.S. Army Center of Military History:
http://www.army.mil/cmh-pg/

U.S. Park Service's Heritage Preservation Services:
http://www2.cr.nps.gov/

The White House:
http://www.whitehouse.gov/history/presidents/ww28.html

APPENDIX B

ARMY LEADERSHIP

Reprinted from the U.S. Army Center of Military History.

THE SECRETARY OF THE ARMY: THE HONORABLE THOMAS E. WHITE

Thomas E. White became the eighteenth Secretary of the Army on May 31, 2001, after nomination to that post by President Bush and confirmation by the U.S. Senate.

As Secretary of the Army, Secretary White has statutory responsibility for all matters relating to Army manpower, personnel, reserve affairs, installations, environmental issues, weapons systems and equipment acquisition, communications, and financial management. Secretary White is responsible for the department's annual budget of nearly $82 billion. The Secretary leads a team of just over one million active duty, National Guard and Army Reserve soldiers and 220,000 civilian employees, and has stewardship over 15 million acres of land.

Secretary White is committed to the three components of the Army Vision—achieving a high quality of life for people, strengthening the Army's readiness to prevail in every mission, and making the transformation of the Army a reality. He is also dedicated to managing the Army more efficiently.

Secretary White began his public service career as an Army officer. After graduating from the U.S. Military Academy at West Point, he was commissioned in the U.S. Army in 1967, rising to the rank of Brigadier General in 1990. His distinguished military career included two tours in Vietnam and service as Commander, 1st Squadron, 11th Armored Cavalry Regiment; Commander, 11th Armored Cavalry Regiment, V Corps; and Executive Assistant to the Chairman, Joint Chiefs of Staff.

Mr. White attended the Naval Postgraduate School, Monterey, California, and graduated in 1974 with a degree in Operations Research. In 1984, he attended the U.S. Army War College, Carlisle, Pennsylvania. Secretary White retired from the Army in July 1990.

From 1990 to 2001, Mr. White was employed by Enron Corporation and held various senior executive positions.

CHIEF OF STAFF, U.S. ARMY: GENERAL ERIC K. SHINSEKI

General Shinseki assumed duties as the thirty-fourth Chief of Staff, United States Army, on June 22, 1999.

General Shinseki graduated from the U.S. Military Academy in 1965 with a Bachelor of Science degree. He also holds a Master of Arts degree in English literature from Duke University. General Shinseki's military education includes the Armor Officer Advanced Course, the U.S. Army Command and General Staff College, and the National War College.

Since his commissioning, General Shinseki has served in a variety of command and staff assignments both in the Continental United States and overseas, to include two combat tours with the 9th and 25th Infantry Divisions in the Republic of Vietnam as an Artillery Forward Observer and as Commander of Troop A, 3rd Squadron, 5th Cavalry. He has served in Hawaii at Schofield Barracks with Headquarters, U.S. Army Hawaii, and Fort Shafter with Headquarters, U.S. Army Pacific. He has taught at the U.S. Military Academy's Department of English. During duty with the 3rd Armored Cavalry Regiment at Fort Bliss, Texas, he served as Regimental Adjutant and as Executive Officer of its 1st Squadron.

General Shinseki's 10-plus years of service in Europe included assignments as Commander, 3rd Squadron, 7th Cavalry (Schweinfurt); Commander, 2nd Brigade, (Kitzingen); Assistant Chief of Staff G3

(Operations, Plans and Training) (Wuerzburg); and Assistant Division Commander for Maneuver (Schweinfurt), all with the 3rd Infantry Division (Mechanized). He served as Assistant Chief of Staff, G3 (Operations, Plans and Training), VII Corps (Stuttgart). General Shinseki served as Deputy Chief of Staff for Support, Allied Land Forces Southern Europe (Verona, Italy), an element of the Allied Command Europe. From March 1994 to July 1995, General Shinseki commanded the 1st Cavalry Division at Fort Hood, Texas. In July 1996, he was promoted to lieutenant general and became Deputy Chief of Staff for Operations and Plans, United States Army. In June 1997, General Shinseki was appointed to the rank of general before assuming duties as Commanding General, United States Army Europe; Commander, Allied Land Forces Central Europe; and Commander, NATO Stabilization Force in Bosnia-Herzegovina. General Shinseki assumed duties as the 28th Vice Chief of Staff, United States Army on November 24, 1998.

General Shinseki has been awarded the Defense Distinguished Service Medal, Distinguished Service Medal, Legion of Merit (with Oak Leaf Clusters), Bronze Star Medal with "V" Device (with 2 Oak Leaf Clusters), Purple Heart (with Oak Leaf Cluster), Meritorious Service Medal (with 2 Oak Leaf Clusters), Air Medal, Army Commendation Medal (with Oak Leaf Cluster), Army Achievement Medal, Parachutist Badge, Ranger Tab, Office of the Secretary of Defense Identification Badge, Joint Chiefs of Staff Identification Badge, and the Army Staff Identification Badge.

UNDER SECRETARY, U.S. ARMY: HONORABLE LES BROWNLEE

Mr. Les Brownlee became the twenty-seventh Under Secretary of the Army on November 14, 2001, following his nomination by President George W. Bush and confirmation by the U.S. Senate. As Under Secretary, Mr. Brownlee assists the Secretary in fulfilling statutory responsibilities for recruiting, organizing, supplying, equipping, training, and mobilizing the Army and managing its $80 billion annual budget and more than 1.3 million active duty, National Guard, Army Reserve, and civilian personnel.

Mr. Brownlee served on the Republican staff of the Senate Armed Services Committee beginning in January 1987, under both Sen. Strom

Thurmond and Sen. John Warner. From 1987 to 1996, he was the Principal Senate Armed Services Committee Professional Staff Member responsible for Army and Marine Corps programs, special operations forces, and drug interdiction policy and support. In addition, as Deputy Staff Director, he was deeply involved in policies and programs relating to ballistic missile defense, strategic deterrence and naval strategy, shipbuilding, and weapons programs.

In March 1996, Mr. Brownlee was designated Staff Director of the Senate Committee on Armed Services by then Chairman Sen. Thurmond. In January 1999, he was designated Staff Director for then Chairman Sen. Warner, serving through the recent change in control of the Senate.

Mr. Brownlee is a retired Army colonel. He was commissioned in 1962 as a lieutenant in the infantry through the ROTC program at the University of Wyoming. He is a distinguished honor graduate of the U.S. Army Ranger Course, an honor graduate of both the Infantry Officer Advanced Course and the Command and General Staff College, and a graduate of the Army's airborne course as well as the U.S. Army War College. Mr. Brownlee served two tours in Vietnam. During the last two and a half years of a four and a half year tour in the Pentagon, before retiring in 1984, he was Military Executive to Under Secretary of the Army James Ambrose.

His military decorations include the Silver Star with Oak Leaf Cluster, the Bronze Star with two Oak Leaf Clusters, and the Purple Heart. He holds a Master's degree in business administration from the University of Alabama.

VICE CHIEF OF STAFF, U.S. ARMY: GENERAL JOHN M. KEANE

General Keane assumed duties as the twenty-ninth Vice Chief of Staff of the Army on June 22, 1999.

General Keane is an infantry officer who has commanded at every level, from company to corps, and has experience in all types of infantry—airborne, air assault, light, and mechanized. Prior to his current duties, he spent the last 20 years in command and staff assignments in support of operational and joint forces.

His commands include: the XVIII Airborne Corps, the Army's largest war-fighting organization, consisting of 4 divisions and 13 separate brigades; the 101st Airborne Division (Air Assault); the Joint Readiness Training Center; the 1st Brigade, 10th Mountain Division (Light); and the 3/39th and 4/23rd Infantry (Redesignated), 9th Infantry Division. He served as Chief of Staff, 10th Mountain Division (Light); Chief of Staff, 101st Airborne Division (Air Assault); Assistant Division Commander, 101st Airborne Division (Air Assault); Chief of Staff, XVIII Airborne Corps; and most recently, as Deputy Commander-in-Chief, United States Atlantic Command.

In his early years, General Keane was a platoon leader with the 82nd Airborne Division; a platoon leader and company commander in Vietnam with the 101st Airborne Division (Air Assault); a company commander and battalion S3 in Alaska with the 172nd Infantry Brigade; Military Assistant to the Assistant Secretary of the Army (Manpower and Reserve Affairs); and a battalion and brigade executive officer in the 9th Infantry Division.

General Keane graduated from Fordham University in 1966 with a Bachelor of Science degree. He also holds a Master of Arts degree from Western Kentucky University. General Keane's military education includes the Infantry Officer Basic and Advanced Courses, the U.S. Army Command and General Staff College, and the U.S. Army War College.

General Keane's awards and decorations include the Defense Distinguished Service Medal, the Distinguished Service Medal, the Silver Star, five Legions of Merit, the Bronze Star Medal, three Meritorious Service Medals, the Army Commendation Medal, the Humanitarian Service Medal, the Ranger Tab, the Combat Infantryman's Badge, the Master Parachutist Badge, the Air Assault Badge, and the Army Staff Identification Badge.

SERGEANT MAJOR, U.S. ARMY: JACK L. TILLEY

Jack L. Tilley was sworn in as the twelfth Sergeant Major of the Army on June 23, 2000. A career soldier, SMA Tilley has held many leadership positions within the Department of the Army and Unified Command environments.

As Sergeant Major of the Army, Tilley serves as the Army Chief of Staff's personal advisor on all enlisted-related matters, particularly in areas affecting soldier training and quality of life. The SMA devotes the majority of his time to traveling throughout the Army observing training, and talking to soldiers and their families. He sits on a wide variety of councils and boards that make decisions affecting enlisted soldiers and their families and is routinely invited to testify before Congress.

SMA Tilley was born in Vancouver, Washington, on December 3, 1948. He entered the Army in November 1966 and attended basic training at Fort Lewis, Washington, and advanced individual training at Fort Knox, Kentucky. Following tours in Vietnam and Fort Benning, Georgia, SMA Tilley left the Army for two years before enlisting again in September 1971.

SMA Tilley has demonstrated his personal commitment to the Army and his soldiers as he advanced to positions of higher responsibility. He has held a variety of important positions culminating in his current assignment as the Sergeant Major of the Army. He previously held the senior enlisted position as Command Sergeant Major of the U.S. Central Command, MacDill Air Force Base, Florida. Other assignments he held as Command Sergeant Major were 1st Battalion, 10th Cavalry, Fort Knox, Kentucky; 194th Armor Brigade, 1st Armored Division, Bad Kreuznach, Germany; and U.S. Army Space and Missile Defense Command, Arlington, Virginia.

Throughout his 34-year career, SMA Tilley has held every key leadership position, including tank commander, section leader, drill sergeant, platoon sergeant, senior instructor, operations sergeant, and first sergeant. His military education includes the First Sergeants Course and the Sergeants Major Academy. He is also a graduate of the basic airborne course, drill sergeant school, and master gunner's course.

His awards and decorations include the Defense Superior Service Medal, Legion of Merit with two oak leaf clusters, Bronze Star with V Device, Meritorious Service Medal with one oak leaf cluster, Vietnam Service Medal and Campaign Medal, Presidential Unit Citation, Overseas Service Ribbon (2), NCO Professional Development Ribbon (4), Drill Sergeant's Badge, Parachutist's Badge, and the Army Staff Identification Badge.

APPENDIX C

RANK STRUCTURE OF THE ARMY

Reprinted from the U.S. Army Center of Military History.

ENLISTED

E1 Private
E2 Private
E3 Private First Class
E4 Corporal or Specialist
E5 Sergeant
E6 Staff Sergeant
E7 Sergeant First Class
E8 Master Sergeant
E8 First Sergeant
E9 Sergeant Major or Command Sergeant Major
E9 Sergeant Major of the Army

WARRANT OFFICER

WO1 Warrant Officer One
CW2 Chief Warrant Officer Two
CW3 Chief Warrant Officer Three

CW4 Chief Warrant Officer Four
CW5 Chief Warrant Officer Five

COMMISSIONED OFFICER

O1 2nd Lieutenant
O2 1st Lieutenant
O3 Captain
O4 Major
O5 Lieutenant Colonel
O6 Colonel
O7 Brigadier General (1 Star)
O8 Major General (2 Star)
O9 Lieutenant General (3 Star)
O10 General (4 Star)
General of the Army (5 Star)

APPENDIX D

HISTORY OF THE 82ND AIRBORNE DIVISION

Reprinted from the U.S. Army Center of Military History.

The 82nd Airborne Division has had its share of famous soldiers, from Sergeant Alvin C. York to General James M. Gavin. But that's not what the 82nd is really about. The real story of the 82nd is the thousands of unnamed paratroopers in jump boots, baggy pants, and maroon berets, who have always been ready and willing to jump into danger and then drive on until the mission was accomplished.

The 82nd has become so well known for its airborne accomplishments, that its proud World War I heritage is almost forgotten.

The 82nd Infantry Division was formed August 25, 1917, at Camp Gordon, Georgia. Because members of the Division came from all 48 states, the unit was given the nickname "All-Americans"; hence its famed "AA" shoulder patch.

In the spring of 1918, the Division deployed to France. In nearly five months of combat, the 82nd fought in three major campaigns and helped to break the fighting spirit of the German Imperial Army.

The 82nd was demobilized after World War I. For more than 20 years the "All-American Division" would live only in the memories of men who served in its ranks during the Great War.

With the outbreak of World War II, the 82nd was reactivated on March 25, 1942, at Camp Claiborne, Louisiana, under the command of Maj. Gen. Omar N. Bradley.

On August 15, 1942, the 82nd Infantry Division became the first airborne division in the U.S. Army. On that date, the All-American Division was redesignated the 82nd Airborne Division.

In April 1943, paratroopers of the 82nd Airborne Division set sail for North Africa under the command of Maj. Gen. Matthew B. Ridgway to participate in the campaign to puncture the soft underbelly of the Third Reich.

The Division's first two combat operations were parachute and glider assaults into Sicily and Salerno, Italy, on July 9 and September 13, 1943.

In January 1944, the 504th Parachute Infantry Regiment, which was temporarily detached from the Division to fight at Anzio, earned the nickname "Devils in Baggy Pants." The nickname was taken from an entry made in a German officer's diary.

While the 504th was detached, the remainder of the 82nd was pulled out of Italy in November 1943 and moved to the United Kingdom to prepare for the liberation of Europe.

With two combat jumps under its belt, the 82nd Airborne Division was now ready for the most ambitious airborne operation of the war, Operation Neptune—the airborne invasion of Normandy. The operation was part of Operation Overlord, the amphibious assault on the northern coast of Nazi-occupied France.

In preparation for the operation, the Division was reorganized. Two new parachute infantry regiments, the 507th and the 508th, joined the Division, Due to its depleted state following the fighting in Italy, the 504th Parachute Infantry Regiment did not take part in the invasion.

On June 5–6, 1944, the paratroopers of the 82nd's three parachute infantry regiments and reinforced glider infantry regiment boarded hundreds of transport planes and gliders and began the largest airborne assault in history. They were among the first soldiers to fight in Normandy, France.

By the time the All-American Division was pulled back to England, it had seen 33 days of bloody combat and suffered 5,245 paratroopers killed, wounded, or missing. The Division's post-battle report read, "... 33 days of action without relief, without replacements. Every mission accomplished. No ground gained was ever relinquished."

Following the Normandy invasion, the 82nd became part of the newly organized XVIII Airborne Corps, which consisted of the U.S. 17th, 82nd, and 101st Airborne Divisions.

In September, the 82nd began planning for Operation Market Garden in Holland. The operation called for three-plus airborne divisions to seize and hold key bridges and roads deep behind German lines. The 504th, now back at full strength, rejoined the 82nd, while the 507th went to the 17th Airborne Division.

On September 17, the 82nd Airborne Division conducted its fourth combat jump of World War II into Holland. Fighting off ferocious German counterattacks, the 82nd captured its objectives between Grave and Nijmegen. Its success, however, was short-lived because of the defeat of other Allied units at Arnhem.

The gateway to Germany would not open in September 1944, and the 82nd was ordered back to France.

Suddenly, on December 16, 1944, the Germans launched a surprise offensive through the Ardennes Forest which caught the Allies completely by surprise. Two days later, the 82nd joined the fighting and blunted General Von Runstedt's northern penetration into the American lines.

Following the surrender of Germany, the 82nd was ordered to Berlin for occupation duty. In Berlin, Gen. George Patton was so impressed with the 82nd's honor guard he said, "In all my years in the Army and all the honor guards I have ever seen, the 82nd's honor guard is undoubtedly the best." Hence the "All-Americans" became known as "America's Guard of Honor."

The 82nd returned to the United States on January 3, 1946. Instead of being demobilized, the 82nd made its permanent home at Fort Bragg, North Carolina, and was designated a regular Army division on November 15, 1948.

Life in the 82nd during the 1950s and 1960s consisted of intensive training exercises in all environments and locations to include Alaska, Panama, the Far East, and the continental United States.

In April 1965, the "All-Americans" were alerted for action in response to the civil war raging in the Dominican Republic. Spearheaded by the 3rd Brigade, the 82nd deployed to the Caribbean in Operation Power Pack. Peace and stability was restored by June 17, when the rebel guns were silenced.

But three years later, the 82nd Airborne Division was again called to action. During the Tet Offensive, which swept across the Republic of Vietnam in January 1968, the 3rd Brigade was alerted and within 24 hours the brigade was en route to Chu Lai. The 3rd Brigade performed combat duties in the Hue-Phu Bai area of the I Corps sector. Later the brigade was moved south to Saigon, and fought battles in the Mekong Delta, the Iron Triangle, and along the Cambodian border. After serving nearly 22 months in Vietnam, the 3rd Brigade troopers returned to Fort Bragg on December 12, 1969.

During the 1970s, Division units deployed to the Republic of Korea, Turkey, and Greece for exercises in potential future battlegrounds.

The Division was also alerted three times. War in the Middle East in the fall of 1973 brought the 82nd to full alert. Then, in May 1978, the Division was alerted for a possible drop into Zaire; and again, in November 1979, the Division was alerted for a possible operation to rescue the American hostages in Iran.

On October 25, 1983, elements of the 82nd were called back to the Caribbean to the tiny island of Grenada. The first 82nd unit to deploy in Operation Urgent Fury was a task force of the 2nd Battalion, 325th Airborne Infantry Regiment.

On October 26 and 27, the 1st Battalion, 505th Infantry, and the 1st Battalion, 508th Infantry, with support units, deployed to Grenada. Military operations in Grenada ended in early November.

Operation Urgent Fury tested the Division's ability as a rapid deployment force. The first aircraft carrying Division troopers touched down at Point Salinas 17 hours after notification.

In March 1988, a brigade task force made up of two battalions from the 504th Parachute Infantry Regiment conducted a parachute insertion and airland operation into Honduras as part of Operation Golden Pheasant. The deployment was billed a joint training exercise, but the paratroopers were ready to fight. The deployment of armed and willing paratroopers to the Honduran countryside caused the Sandinistas to withdraw back to Nicaragua. Operation Golden Pheasant prepared the paratroopers for future combat in the increasingly unstable world.

On December 20, 1989, the "All-Americans," as part of Operation Just Cause, conducted their first combat jump since World War II onto Torrijos International Airport, Panama. The paratroopers' goal was to oust a ruthless dictator and restore the duly-elected government to power in Panama. The 1st Brigade task force made up of the 1st and 2nd Battalions, 504th Parachute Infantry Regiment, parachuted into combat for the first time since World War II. In Panama, the paratroopers were joined on the ground by 3rd Battalion, 504th Parachute Infantry Regiment, which was already in Panama. After the night combat jump and seizure of the airport, the 82nd conducted follow-on combat air assault missions in Panama City and the surrounding areas.

The victorious paratroopers returned to Fort Bragg on January 12, 1990.

But seven months later the paratroopers were again called to war. Six days after the Iraqi invasion of Kuwait on August 2, 1990, the 82nd became the vanguard of the largest deployment of American troops since Vietnam.

The first unit to deploy to Saudi Arabia was a task force comprising the Division's 2nd Brigade. Soon after, the rest of the Division followed. There, intensive training began in anticipation of fighting in the desert with the heavily armored Iraqi Army.

The battle cry picked up by the paratroopers was, "The road home … is through Baghdad."

On January 16, 1991, Operation Desert Storm began when an armada of Allied war planes pounded Iraqi targets. The ground war began almost six weeks later. On February 23, the vehicle-mounted 82nd Airborne Division paratroopers protected the XVIII Airborne Corps flank as fast-moving armor and mechanized units moved deep inside Iraq. A 2nd Brigade task force was attached to the 6th French Light Armored Division, becoming the far-left flank of the Corps.

In the short 100-hour ground war, the vehicle-mounted 82nd drove deep into Iraq and captured thousands of Iraqi soldiers and tons of equipment, weapons, and ammunition.

After the liberation of Kuwait, the 82nd began its redeployment back to Fort Bragg with most of the Division returning by the end of April.

Following the Division's return and subsequent victory parades, the troopers began to re-establish some of the systems that had become dormant during their eight months in the desert. On top of the list was the regaining of individual and unit airborne proficiency and the continuation of tough and realistic training.

In August 1992, the Division was alerted to deploy a task force to the hurricane-ravaged area of South Florida and provide humanitarian assistance following Hurricane Andrew. For more than 30 days, Division troopers provided food, shelter, and medical attention to a grateful Florida population, instilling a sense of hope and renewed confidence in the military.

On the 50th anniversary of Operation Market Garden, the 82nd again answered the nation's call and prepared to conduct a parachute assault in the Caribbean nation of Haiti to help restore democracy. With the troopers aboard aircraft heading towards the island, the de facto regime capitulated, and the Division was turned back to Fort Bragg.

82nd Airborne Division paratroopers were among the first ground troops sent into the war-torn Kosovo region of the Balkans in the summer of 1999, when the 2nd Battalion, 505th Parachute Infantry Regiment, moved in from neighboring Macedonia. They were followed shortly by the 3rd Battalion, 504th Parachute Infantry Regiment, who themselves would be followed by the 1st Battalion, 325th Airborne Infantry Regiment, in January 2001 as part of regular peacekeeping operation rotations.

When America was attacked on September 11, 2001, President George W. Bush called upon the American military to fight global terrorism. The 82nd's 49th Public Affairs Detachment and several individual 82nd soldiers deployed to Afghanistan and the Central Command Area of Responsibility to support combat operations. Although not called upon as of this writing, the entire 82nd Airborne Division stands ready now to respond.

Today, as they have for 60 years, the troopers who wear the red, white, and blue patch of the 82nd Airborne Division continue to form the cutting edge of the United States' strategic combat force.

APPENDIX E

HISTORY OF THE XVIII AIRBORNE CORPS

Reprinted from the U.S. Army Center of Military History.

The XVIII Airborne Corps, with Headquarters at Fort Bragg, was originally activated as the II Armored Corps at Camp Polk, Louisiana, January 17, 1942. It was redesignated XVIII Corps on October 9, 1943, at the Presidio of Monterey, California.

The Corps celebrates its birthday August 25, 1944, when the blue airborne tab was added at Orbourne, St. George, England. On this same day, the XVIII Airborne Corps assumed command of the 82nd and 101st Airborne Divisions. Within a month, Maj. Gen. Matthew B. Ridgway, the first Corps Commander, sent his men into action in Operation Market Garden, the allied invasion of the Netherlands during World War II.

The Corps returned to the United States in late June 1945 and was deactivated October 15, 1945, at Camp Campbell, Kentucky. The XVIII Airborne Corps was reactivated at Fort Bragg on May 21, 1951.

Today, the XVIII Airborne Corps—the Army's largest war-fighting organization—is the only airborne corps in the defense establishment of the United States and exercises control over approximately 88,000 thousand soldiers assigned to the 3rd Infantry Division (Mechanized), Fort Stewart, Georgia; 10th

Mountain (Light), Fort Drum, New York; 82nd Airborne Division, Fort Bragg; 101st Airborne Division (Air Assault), Fort Campbell, Kentucky; XVIII Airborne Corps Artillery; 2nd Armored Cavalry Regiment, Fort Polk, Louisiana; 108th Air Defense Artillery, Fort Bliss, Texas; 18th Aviation Brigade; 229th Aviation Regiment; 20th Engineer Brigade; 525th Military Intelligence Brigade; 16th Military Police Brigade; 35th Signal Brigade; 1st Corps Support Command; 44th Medical Brigade; 18th Finance Group; 18th Personnel Group; and Dragon Brigade, all located at Fort Bragg.

The Corps capability for rapid deployment and reputation as the premier power projection force continues to be tested. Its operational tempo remains the highest in the Army, and its resolve as a quick reaction force has been the key to success in numerous crises.

OPERATION POWER PACK, DOMINICAN REPUBLIC, APRIL 30, 1965

The Corps served as the headquarters for U.S. forces personnel sent to restore law and order, prevent a communist takeover of the country, and protect American lives.

OPERATION URGENT FURY, GRENADA, OCTOBER 25, 1983

At the request of President Reagan, the Corps provided the bulk of land forces sent to rescue medical students and other stranded Americans and participated with our Caribbean neighbors in an international peacekeeping effort.

OPERATION GOLDEN PHEASANT, HONDURAS, 1988

When the borders of Honduras were threatened, elements of two Corps divisions exercised a show of force to ensure sovereignty of Honduran territory would be respected.

OPERATION NIMROD DANCER, PANAMA, 1989

A security reinforcement was sent to protect American citizens, facilities, and treaty rights following the elections.

OPERATION HAWKEYE, U.S. VIRGIN ISLANDS, SEPTEMBER 1989

Following Hurricane Hugo, the Corps was on the ground in St. Croix within 13 hours, with the first elements of a Joint Task Force, to restore law and order, and to provide emergency relief and rebuilding efforts for the devastated island.

OPERATION JUST CAUSE, PANAMA, DECEMBER 20, 1989

The XVIII Airborne Corps in operational command of Joint Task Force South struck 27 targets simultaneously and conducted two night parachute assaults to seize critical terrain and set the stage for a freely elected government to be established in the country.

OPERATION DESERT SHIELD, SAUDI ARABIA, AUGUST 9, 1990

Rapidly deployed as the first ground force in theater to spearhead efforts to deter aggression and assist in the defense of friendly nations, the largest American military deployment since WWII.

OPERATION DESERT STORM, SAUDI ARABIA, FEBRUARY 1991

XVIII Airborne Corps launched the first ground assault into Iraq with the 82nd Airborne Division and the attached French 6th Light Armored Division; the largest air assault in history by the 101st Airborne Division (Air Assault); and an airborne thrust by the 24th Infantry Division (Mechanized) and the 3rd Armored Cavalry Regiment. In less than 100 hours, the Corps had effectively sealed off the occupying Iraqi Army and destroyed major elements of the elite Republican Guard.

OPERATION GTMO, CUBA, NOVEMBER 1991

The Corps established a humanitarian support center at Guantanamo Naval Base to receive, transport, detain, control, and process Haitian migrants. The Corps quickly began the massive task of building and supporting a humanitarian center for more than 12,000 Haitians. By early December, the Corps had deployed over 2,000 soldiers to the Guantanamo Naval Base. The operation officially ended in June 1993.

OPERATION HURRICANE ANDREW, FLORIDA, AUGUST 27, 1992

On August 27, 1992, major units throughout the XVIII Airborne Corps began their deployment to Dade County, Florida, to assist in disaster relief operations in the aftermath of the storm. At peak strength, the Corps had 16,000 soldiers deployed to South Florida. The mission of the Corps was to provide immediate emergency relief including food, water, shelter, and medical aid. During subsequent phases the Corps conducted debris removal operations, repaired schools, established relief supply distribution centers, and assisted the local government in establishing sustained recovery operations. All disaster relief functions were eventually turned over to civilian contractors, and Corps units returned to Fort Bragg by October 21, 1992.

OPERATION RESTORE HOPE, SOMALIA, DECEMBER 13, 1992

In support of Joint Task Force Somalia, Army forces secured an airfield and key installations, and provided security to ensure safe passage of food and humanitarian supplies throughout the country.

OPERATION UPHOLD/MAINTAIN DEMOCRACY, HAITI, SEPTEMBER 1994

To ensure the Haitian Armed Forces' compliance with Carter-Cedras accords, protect U.S. citizens, restore civil order, assist in the reorganization of Haitian Armed Forces, and assist in the transition to and maintenance of a democratic government.

VIGILANT WARRIOR, KUWAIT, OCTOBER 1994

Nearly four years after Desert Storm, the 24th Infantry Division returned to Kuwait to deter further Iraqi aggression, when Iraqi forces moved south to the border. They withdrew shortly after the arrival of the Division.

Today, the Corps has more than 10,000 soldiers deployed with more than 5,000 in Kuwait to deter a possible Iraqi invasion and over 3,000 in Bosnia, constituting over 47 percent of their total force.

Over the past 2 years, the XVIII Airborne Corps has deployed countless Corps soldiers to more than 27 countries throughout the world, including Bosnia, Kuwait, Saudi Arabia, Egypt, and Haiti. From February 1996 to March 1998, the XVIII Airborne Corps has either conducted, participated in, or been the exercise director for more than 79 exercises, to include 25 Joint Exercises involving all of the services. The Corps recently completed Purple Dragon, one of the largest and most successful Joint Task Force exercises in XVIII Airborne Corps history, consisting of 33,000 sailors, marines, airmen, and soldiers.

The XVIII Airborne Corps is superbly trained in tactical operational and strategic levels of war and is capable of exercising the nation's ability to conduct strategic forced-entry operations anywhere in the world on 18 hours' notice. They have been widely recognized as a superbly trained force capable of peace operations to general-purpose war, and conducting large-scale joint and combined operations.

APPENDIX F

THE U.S. ARMY CHIEF OF STAFF'S PROFESSIONAL READING LIST

Reprinted from the U.S. Army Center of Military History.

"The Chief of Staff of the United States Army has designated this professional reading list as a list for leaders—and a pillar for his leadership development efforts. We can never spend too much time thinking about our profession. There is no better way to develop the sure knowledge and confidence required of our calling than a disciplined, focused commitment to a personal course of reading and study. Our profession is unique and, as General MacArthur said, predicated on 'the will to win, the sure knowledge that in war there is no substitute for victory. That if you fail, the nation will be destroyed.' We must all do our utmost to prepare for the heavy responsibilities of military leadership.

"The books included in this list are designed to provoke critical thinking concerning the profession of soldiering and the unique role of landpower. There are works here that address issues and challenges relevant to each of us, from private to general. This list includes books that examine the past and those that consider the future. These readings deepen our understanding of the timeless constants of the Army's values and traditions, the enduring dynamics of the human face of battle, and the future's potential to transform the profession of arms in the twenty-first century.

"The Chief of Staff challenges all leaders to make reading an important part of their professional development."

ARMY HERITAGE AND MILITARY HISTORY (FOR CADETS, SOLDIERS, AND JUNIOR NCOS)

Stephen E. Ambrose, *Band of Brothers: E Company, 506th Regiment, 101st Airborne from Normandy to Hitler's Eagle's Nest*. New York: Simon & Schuster, 1992. (335 pages)

Rick Atkinson. *The Long Gray Line*. New York: Owl Books, 1999. (589 pages)

Tom Brokaw. *The Greatest Generation*. New York: Random House, 1998. (412 pages)

T. R. Fehrenbach. *This Kind of War: A Study in Unpreparedness*. Brassey's Inc., 1994. (483 pages)

Charles E. Heller and William A. Stoft, eds. *America's First Battles: 1776–1965*. Lawrence, Kan.: University Press of Kansas, 1986. (416 pages)

David W. Hogan Jr. *225 Years of Service, The U.S. Army 1775–2000*. Washington, D.C.: CMH, 2000. (36 pages)

John Keegan. *The Face of Battle*. New York: Vintage Books, 1977. (354 pages)

Lt. Gen. Harold G. Moore (ret.) and Joseph L. Galloway. *We Were Soldiers Once … and Young*. New York: Random House, 1992. (412 pages)

Myrer, Anton, *Once An Eagle*. New York: Holt, Rinehart, and Winston, 1968. USAWC Foundation Press, 1995. (817 pages) (paperback and hardcover)

Michael Shaara. *The Killer Angels*. New York: Ballantine Books, 1974. (355 pages)

ARMY HERITAGE AND MILITARY HISTORY (FOR COMPANY GRADE OFFICERS, WO1-CW3, AND COMPANY CADRE NCOS)

Steven Ambrose. *Citizen Soldiers*. New York: Simon & Schuster, 1997. (480 pages)

Edward M. Coffman. *The War To End All Wars: The American Military Experience in World War I*. New York: Oxford University Press, 1968. (412 pages)

Samuel P. Huntington. *Soldier and the State*. Cambridge, Massachusetts: Belknap Press of Harvard University Press, 1957. (534 pages)

Gerald F. Linderman. *Embattled Courage: The Experience of Combat in the American Civil War*. New York: The Free Press, A Division of Macmillan, Inc., 1987. (357 pages)

Charles B. MacDonald. *Company Commander*. Springfield, N.J.: Burford Books, 1999. Original edition, 1947. (278 pages)

S. L. A. Marshall. *Men Against Fire: The Problem of Battle Command in Future War*. Reprint, Gloucester, Massachusetts: Peter Smith, 1978. Originally published by Infantry Journal Press, 1947. (215 pages)

Alan R. Millett and Peter Maslowski. *For the Common Defense, A Military History of the United States of America*. New York: The Free Press, 1984. (621 pages)

Robert H. Scales Jr. *Certain Victory*. Reprint, Fort Leavenworth, Kansas: U.S. Army Command and General Staff College Press, 1994. (434 pages)

Mark A. Stoler. *George C. Marshall: Soldier-Statesman of the American Century*. Boston: Twayne Publishers, 1989. (252 pages)

Tom Willard. *Buffalo Soldiers (Black Saber Chronicles)*. Forge Press, 1996.

ARMY HERITAGE AND MILITARY HISTORY (FOR FIELD GRADE OFFICERS, CW4–CW5, AND SENIOR NCOS)

Roy E. Appleman. *East of Chosin: Entrapment and Breakout in Korea, 1950.* College Station, Texas: Texas A&M University Press, 1987. (399 pages)

Graham A. Cosmas. *An Army for Empire: The United States Army in the Spanish-American War.* 2nd edition. Shippensburg, Pennsylvania: White Mane, 1994. (349 pages)

Robert A. Doughty. *The Evolution of U.S. Army Tactical Doctrine, 1946–1976.* Fort Leavenworth, Kansas: Combat Studies Institute, 1979. (57 pages)

Antoine Henri Jomini. *Jomini and His Summary of the Art of War*. Reprint, Harrisburg, Pennsylvania: Stackpole Books, 1965. (161 pages) (paperback)

Charles B. MacDonald and Sidney T. Mathews. *Three Battles: Arnaville, Altuzzo, and Schmidt.* Washington, D.C.: Center of Military History, U.S. Army. (443 pages)

James M. McPherson. *Battle Cry of Freedom: The Civil War Era*. New York: Oxford University Press, 1988. (904 pages)

Roger H. Nye. *The Challenge of Command.* Wayne, New Jersey: Avery Publishing Group, 1986. (187 pages)

Dave R. Palmer. *Summons of the Trumpet: U.S.-Vietnam in Perspective.* San Rafael, CA: Presidio Press, 1978. (277 pages)

Martin Van Creveld. *Supplying War: Logistics from Wallenstein to Patton*. New York: Cambridge University Press, 1977. (284 pages)

Russell F. Weigley. *The American Way of War: A History of United States Military Strategy and Policy.* Bloomington: Indiana University Press, 1977. Original edition, 1973. (477 pages)

ARMY HERITAGE AND MILITARY HISTORY (FOR SENIOR LEADERS ABOVE BRIGADE)

Carl von Clausewitz. *On War*. Ed. and trans. Peter Paret and Michael Howard. Princeton, New Jersey: Princeton University Press, 1984. (732 pages)

Kent Roberts Greenfield, ed. *Command Decisions.* Washington, D.C.: Office of the Chief of Military History, 1960. (565 pages)

Michael Howard. *War in European History*. Oxford: Oxford University Press, 1976. (165 pages)

Paul Kennedy. *The Rise and Fall of the Great Powers.* New York: Random House, 1987. (677 pages)

Henry Kissinger. *Diplomacy*. New York: Simon & Schuster, 1994. (912 pages)

Williamson Murray and Alan R. Millett, eds. *Military Innovation in the Interwar Period.* New York: Cambridge University Press, 1996. (428 pages)

Richard E. Neustadt and Ernest R. May. *Thinking in Time*. New York: Free Press, 1986. (321 pages)

Peter Paret, ed. *Makers of Modern Strategy from Machiavelli to the Nuclear Age.* Princeton: Princeton University Press, 1986. (941 pages)

William B. Skelton. *An American Profession of Arms: The Army Officer Corps, 1784–1861*. Lawrence, Kansas: University Press of Kansas, 1992. (481 pages)

Harry Summers. *On Strategy*. Novato, California: Presidio Press, 1982. (225 pages)

Thucydides. *The Peloponnesian War.* Trans. Rex Warner. Baltimore, MD: Penguin Books, 1972. (648 pages)

INDEX

B

C

D

G

H

I

J

K

L

M

Q–R

S

T

U

V

W

X

Y

Z